Land in America

Land in America

Commodity or Natural Resource?

Edited by
Richard N.L. Andrews
The University of Michigan

Lexington Books
D.C. Heath and Company
Lexington, Massachusetts
Toronto

Library of Congress Cataloging in Publication Data

Main entry under title:
    Land in America.

    Bibliography: p.
    1. Land use—United States—Addresses, essays, lectures. I. Andrews,
Richard N.L.
HD205 1978.L36   333.7'0973   77-14735
ISBN 0-669-01989-5

Published simultaneously in Canada

Printed in the United States of America

International Standard Book Number: 0-669-01989-5

Library of Congress Catalog Card Number: 77-14735

Contents

Foreword

Catawba Indians to Ask Congress to Settle Land Claims in Carolina.
Billions Are at Stake in California as Land-Water Fight Nears End.
Suburbs Wall Out Low-income Housing.
Metropolitan Detroit: Community or Cul-de-sac?
Is it Curtains for the [Radio City] Music Hall?
Foreigners Grab Up American Farm Land.
Every Month an Average of 4,400 Ads of Vacation and Leisure Homes Ap-
    pear in the New York Times *Classified Pages.*
Subcommittee Schedules Hearings on Mining Law Reform.
Indictments Shock Florida Town . . .
San Diego Limits Building to Avoid Sprawl.
14 Million Acres a Year Vanishing as Deserts Spread around Globe.
Lack of Planning, Not Heavy Rain, Held Accountable for Italy's Floods.
Wetlands Are Too Valuable Not to Protect.
California Tax Rollback Initiative Passes Overwhelmingly.

Each headline reflects an aspect of the multiple roles played by land today,
land subject to rules, customs, and myths of ancient origin inappropriate
for twentieth century realities. Each also suggests the critical dichotomy
that stubbornly impedes modernization of the rules: land's dual status as an
essential basis of life-support—a natural and community resource—and as
property and commodity, both public and private.

The dual status of land may help to explain the recent failure of major
political efforts to rationalize its use. Despite widespread support in the early 1970s for comprehensive land use planning, all federal bills that would
have aided the states in implementing such programs failed of passage in
Congress. The political impasse alone would justify critical reevaluation of
the reasons for difficulties with land regulation in the United States; the
continuing and fundamental importance of the underlying issues, too,
demands a more thorough airing of the subject. To that end the Citizens
Council for Land Use Research and Education (CLURE), a voluntary
organization based in southeastern Michigan, sponsored a three-day symposium at the University of Michigan in May 1977. The issues addressed
during that conference comprise the content of this book. The intent of the
symposium—entitled "The Face of America: This Land in the Year
2000"—was to provide an open forum for discussion of the dilemmas of
land in America.

CLURE's interest in the rules governing the use of land dates to 1972
when it sponsored its first symposium,—"Do the Laws Secure Our
Land?"—at Oakland University. The goal of the first symposium was to

clarify the subject for citizens: most individuals, as landowners or renters, are unaware of their stake in the incremental land use changes occurring daily in their communities. People generally assume that local zoning, planning, and other laws protect both their personal property in land and the interests of the community as well. CLURE involved lawyers, professors, developers, and public officials in a day long exposition of how the law actually works and why. By the end, the consensus of most participants was that the laws do not adequately secure either public or private interests in land, although there was acknowledgment of some emerging interpretations and statutes that recognize community interests as well as property rights in land. Most of these laws are limited to protection from identifiable physical hazards such as the misuse of wetlands and coastal zones.

CLURE has also initiated two demonstration projects designed to evaluate the effects of citizen involvement in the land use decision-making process in West Bloomfield Township, which is a suburb in the Detroit metropolitan area. The first related to the local and regional consequences of a mammoth shopping center to be located in a remote, environmentally rich corner of the township; the second concerned a long-planned superhighway that was to provide access to the shopping center. The inquiries were ultimately conducted by cooperating civic and environmental groups, local and regional, and contributed to government decisions rejecting both. CLURE is presently engaged in its third demonstration project: establishing a communitywide educational project on the geography of West Bloomfield. An understanding of local geography is an essential first step in valuing land as a resource; and as Fred Bosselman suggests later in this book, a sense of place is essential for development to be appropriate to its environment. In cooperation with both civic and public agencies, CLURE is undertaking this study of the natural heritage of West Bloomfield, whose purpose is to generate a sense of place as well as a constituency that can insist on its creation and preservation.

CLURE is deeply grateful to the distinguished individuals who generously contributed original papers to the symposium and also to those who have prepared papers or allowed earlier work to be used in this book. We hope that these essays will provide the reader with a stimulating introduction to an important set of issues in our society today.

Janet D. Lynn
Executive Vice-President
Citizens' Council for Land Use
Research and Education

Preface

Land is many things to many people. The same acre may be an area, a wetland, a swamp, a vacant lot, a site, a waterfront property, a tax ratable, an ecosystem, and so on, depending upon one's perspective. These conflicting perspectives are constantly present in people's images of their world, coexisting for the most part as parallel realities in different people's minds. They emerge in forceful political conflict, however, when someone proposes to change the status of a particular piece of land, for every such proposal raises two fundamental reality tests: what is the appropriate status of that piece of land, and who has the right to decide it?

The status of land in America historically has been dominated by a conjunction of two powerful attitudes about land: the right of the individual to own real property, free from the governmental intrusions and feudal encumbrances that bound both man and land in other nations, and the right to use that land and its resources for material gain. These rights have often been popularly believed to be absolute: many people would claim that they have the right to do "anything they want" with their land, whether to harvest its crops and forests or to extract its minerals or to pave it over or to maintain it unchanged, and they would acknowledge no obligation or responsibility to society for their treatment of it.

In fact, however, the ownership of land has always been limited at least by the government's police power and by the rights of adjacent owners. In recent years, moreover, increasing numbers of land's characteristics have been argued to be "affected with a public interest" and therefore subject to governmental review and controls. These characteristics include not only ecological functions (such as wetlands) and scenic beauty but also regional development potential (such as airport or power plant sites). Every such assertion of public interests in land raises issues not only of the physical status but also of the legal and economic status of land. A government land use plan, for instance, is not just an allocation of land uses, but an assertion by government of a right—in effect, a property right—to decide those uses; and the allocation almost invariably restructures the economic opportunities and constraints on the land as well.

Beneath all the particular issues of land use conflict, in short, there is a fundamental dualism between its status as a natural resource base and its status as a commodity. On the one hand, every piece of land is a unique physical and biological entity, a basis of living ecological systems that can provide life- and community-supporting services to humans as well as other populations. Many of these functions cannot be replicated or reconstructed by human activities if they are disrupted. Every piece of land is also unique in its location, a consideration that has both ecological and economic implications for its use, and in its structure, which includes topography and physical characteristics as well as aesthetic appearance. On the other hand, land in America is also a marketable commodity, a property subject to ownership and taxation, and a necessary platform for every human activity.

No single solution can resolve this dichotomy, but the issues that it raises deserve thoughtful discussion and debate. Ultimately, the issues of how land should be used depend upon who has the power to choose and the extent to which they are accountable to a broader community for their choices: that is, they depend on the issue of property ownership, whether that ownership is individual or in some way shared. If one asserts that the power and the right to act on land do lie primarily with the landowner, then so does the responsibility to treat the land with care, with respect for it as a special place having socio-ecological significance. There will always be problems in deciding to whom the landowner should be accountable, and even more in defining the balance between the extent to which he is expected to exercise restraint and the point at which someone else should be paying him for benefits they are drawing from his decisions; but the inevitability of difficult issues should encourage rather than discourage serious discussion. The purpose of this book is to contribute some of the basic elements of such a discussion.

This book is not a traditional text on land use planning, nor does it presume that the best solutions to land issues necessarily lie in the realm of government. It is, rather, a book about land: about the history of land in America, about people's perceptions and images of land, about ownership, and about government and land. The genesis of the book was a symposium in May 1977 on "The Face of America: This Land in the Year 2000" sponsored by the Citizen's Council for Land Use Research and Education (CLURE) in cooperation with two schools of the University of Michigan, The School of Natural Resources and the College of Architecture and Urban Planning. Many of the papers were prepared initially for that symposium, while several others were contributed or reprinted with permission from other sources.

I should like to offer special thanks to all the contributors who participated in the symposium and to all the others who have allowed their work to add to this collection of papers on the status of land. No single book could exhaust the issues on this subject, but these papers collectively raise many of the questions that deserve discussion. If they stimulate the reader to extend the debate, they will have served their purpose well.

Richard N.L. Andrews

Part I
Introduction

1 Some Thoughts on Concepts of Land

Stewart D. Marquis, Jr.

What is the "status of land"?

What concept of land or attitude toward land prevails or is valued the most highly? What concepts or attitudes are held by the people who are arguing about the development or use of land? Many different concepts and attitudes are evident, and these may either be held by individuals or may be part of the imagery of groups.

Some people conceive of land as *private property*, with specific rights of ownership and use that can be transferred to other people. This concept of land may also lead to the related concept of land as a *commodity* that can be sold in the market or given away to the owner's heirs. This commodity concept has also led to the concept of land as tracts, parcels, or lots that can be clearly described and identified for easy transferral of ownership rights, as well as for "clear title" to provide a basis for loans backed by the land as collateral. The concept of breaking up large tracts into parcels and lots for easy transfer of ownership rights is closely related to the more fundamental concepts of land as private property and as a commodity.

Other people conceive of land as common property or *public good*. This concept implies that the rights of access and use belong to everyone in the group or community and not to anyone outside it (except by invitation). Such land may be primarily that obtained by the community (by public action) to provide space for community facilities and activities, such as schools, recreation, or cemeteries. This concept of land as common or public good is becoming more acceptable as a basis for preserving natural areas from the disturbances of development and use for other human purposes.

Many people also conceive of land as common property of smaller groups such as the family, viewing it as the *homeplace* or homestead, as the territory that provides the group with its sources of sustenance, subsistence, survival. This concept of land also incorporates the idea of a territory for privacy, for protection and defense, and for relief from pressures of the outside world. This concept obviously is closely related to a "sense of place," to "roots," and to the idea of "homeland" for the larger community. It seems likely that much of the strength of the concept of land as private property and commodity is based on this much more basic concept of land as *homeplace*.

Today many people speak of the concept of land as *natural resource*. This concept can be confusing, since some people mean to think of land as a source of the separate resource materials that can be removed from the land and others think of the land itself as a source of continuous flow of renewable resources for human use, materials that can be used or consumed or that can be bartered, sold, or given away. This interpretation links closely with the concepts of land as private property and commodity, since the removal of materials is one of the separable ownership rights that can be transferred as a commodity. In this sense, land is thought of as an area that can be made productive or useful by human development actions.

Some people mean something quite different when they speak of the concept of land as natural resource. They think of land as a symbol for the *natural world* in which they live, in contrast to the social and man-built world. They view land as the unitary and holistic natural systems that are continually functioning to produce, store, transport, and transform materials and energy. They speak of land as shorthand for the natural life-support systems on which people depend. They sometimes refer to land as a natural asset or natural endowment, including nonrenewable resources and irreplaceable or difficult-to-replace natural ecological systems. This view of land as a natural resource tends to view such natural systems as reaching far beyond the boundaries of separately-owned land parcels, tracts, or lots. Land is viewed as interacting *natural systems* whose integrity is to be protected and whose primary qualities are to be preserved either in some natural state, or at the present level reflecting some degree of prior disturbances, or at some future level of human development and use. Maintaining the integrity of existing natural systems may also imply some continuing human management to keep them in their present forms, including harvesting of plants and animals.

Largely as a result of the development of cities, where the natural characteristics of land are no longer dominant or sometimes not even visible, many people have developed a concept of land completely separated from its natural systems and qualities. They conceive of land as *space* in which human activities take place, as a platform or stage on which to build, an arena in which people will act, a location in space relative to other human activity areas. This concept of land is fostered by those viewing land as a commodity and as private property, since it deals most abstractly with land as rights to be bought and sold. It also includes the leasing or renting of land as space, with little connection to the concept of land as homeplace.

In our commercial society, land as private property, with ownership rights that can be transferred—and with those rights and the contractual relations involved protected by laws, constitutions, administrative rules, and court decisions—is the prevalent concept for many people. This concept is espoused by large corporations, acting as legal individual-property-rights owners, and it also forms a large part of the conceptual basis for governmental management of public lands and for regulation of the development and use of privately owned lands. Many landowners, both individual and corporate, fight hard to maintain the predominance in our legal and political and economic system of the concept of land as private property, which the owner can alter, develop, use, misuse, abuse, and do with as he wants, subject only to direct and provable impacts on owners of other lands.

These are some of the most widely held concepts of land. The status of land can be viewed in terms of the relative status of these concepts: which is dominant or valued most highly by most people, or by the most powerful people? Where people disagree about the development or use of land, we may surmise that the status of land is uncertain or that some mixture of the conflicting concepts may come to prevail by compromise among conflicting individuals and groups. Perhaps this interpretation also provides an explanation for the difficulty of determining the status of land in any given place and time where there is obvious conflict among the actively held concepts of land.

To most people "private property" means a small city lot or large suburban tract. These are usually small areas that do not include all the interacting natural systems. If they have experienced a farmstead or larger farm fields or a campground, they may come closer to being able to visualize full functioning natural systems as being "privately owned." Not many are apt to think in terms of the large corporate land areas in agriculture, rangeland, or forest land.

For those of us who live in cities and suburbs, with many relatively small private lots and public areas that are mainly in streets, school grounds, parks, and such, we are not used to thinking of public rights in private lands. Rights of other residents are little involved in the private lots of homeowners, storeowners, or factory firms. We are used to thinking of those private lands as being exclusively for their owners' use, with no rights for us to have access and use unless we are invited.

We are not used to thinking that natural environmental systems operate over and under all these privately owned pieces, and that all of us, owners and renters and workers and businessmen alike, depend on the continuing functional integrity of all these natural environmental systems (air, water, landforms, soils, vegetation). That we all "own" some rights in the overall systems is a new concept to most of us. We are better able to visualize our joint ownership of the various publicly owned areas such as parks, school grounds, streets. Similarly, we can imagine our joint ownership rights in state and national parks and forests, but not so clearly our joint rights to lakes, streams, oceans.

As we grow up, it is more obvious to us that we depend on other people and on man-built houses, streets, and water pipes than that we also depend on the natural systems of air, water, landforms, soils, animals, plants. We have developed our human social and architectural engineering and manufacturing systems to separate us from direct relations with those natural systems. In this disparity of our perceptions lie many of today's difficult conflicts over the appropriate management of the land's resources.

2

Land Use and the States: A Variety of Discontents

Robert G. Healy

If we look at the whole range of ills that arise from the way we use our nation's land, we find problems that are created by growth—and problems only growth can solve. We find urbanization that devastates the natural environment and reduces the quality of human life—and urbanization that is not only functional but uplifting. We find some problems that demand sweeping solutions and new institutions, others that will submit to single-purpose legislation, and still others that merely require the conscientious enforcement of laws already on the books.

For example, suburban objection to new subdivisions may be primarily fiscal in origin and easily reduced by new school-financing methods or new boundaries for taxing jurisdictions. On the other hand, the objection of some Maine and Colorado residents to industrial development stems from deeply held social values, and at times flies in the face of their own economic self-interest. Thus a careful examination of land use problems, perceived and "real," is necessary both for policy prescription and for identifying the level of government most appropriate for solving them.

The Problems We See

The story of the simultaneous metropolitanization and suburbanization of America's population in the last twenty-five years is a familiar one.[1] Even as the majority of Americans were raising their incomes, dramatically improving the quality of their housing, and adopting new leisure and recreational activities, there was a recognition of what the pursuit of these good things was doing to the land—and by implication to the natural and human environments.

Urban Sprawl—And Urban Splatter

For most of our metropolitan areas, urban growth has meant urban sprawl. Encouraged by rising automobile ownership, improved highway nets, and the suburbanization of employment, sprawl is found on the edge of the new cities of the South and West and the old cities of the Northeast and Middle West. Harvey and Clark have distinguished three distinct types.[2] First is the spread of subdivisions of homes on large individual lots. A common phenomenon of the 1950s, this practice reflects the tendency for the amount of land consumed by a family to rise with income and, perhaps, a desire by urbanites for a "return to the soil." By the 1960s, the rising price of raw land and increased attention to the advantages of cluster development had made large-lot sprawl much less common than before.

A second form of sprawl involves development along transportation arteries, with the space between them left undeveloped. Not only does this involve higher costs for the extension of utilities and other public services, but it makes the extent of urbanization seem much larger to the motorist than it actually is. Often this "ribbon sprawl" consists of commercial or industrial rather than residential uses.

A final kind of sprawl is the "leapfrog development," in which tracts of land are left vacant, while subdivision continues farther out from the center.[3] At its extreme, leapfrog sprawl becomes what Pickard calls "urban splatter," as small pockets of urban use, functionally linked to the larger metropolis, begin to dot the exurban landscape.[4]

Sprawl has many critics, who often begin with its esthetics. Whyte comments that "It takes remarkably little blight to color a whole area; let the reader travel along a stretch of road he is fond of, and he will notice how a small portion of open land has given amenity to the area. But it takes only a few badly designed developments or billboards or hot dog stands to ruin it, and though only a little bit of land is used, the place will *look* filled up."[5] Sprawl also raises public service costs, interferes with fringe-area agriculture, encourages energy-using (and pollution-generating) automobile travel, and, it is alleged, leads to a loss of a sense of community.[6]

Urban sprawl reflects the divergence of interests between individuals, who wish to maximize private space and accessibility, and society as a whole, which seeks larger, contiguous blocks of open space. Often local land controls alone cannot internalize this conflict, for growth stopped at the edge of one jurisdiction will easily leapfrog out to the next.[7] The individual jurisdiction cannot convert sprawl on its periphery to density in its center—a more likely outcome will be that the growth (and its accompanying tax base) will be lost to some other municipality.

On the other hand, local policies can do much to reduce the visual impact of strip development, to speed traffic flows, and to assess charges for public services that more accurately reflect the costs of providing them.

Loss of Farmland

Another common land use worry is over the conversion of prime agricultural land to other uses.[8] Land that is level, well drained, and accessible to transportation lends itself to efficient crop production—but these very characteristics make it equally well suited to urban development. One U.S. Department of Agriculture study found that about three-fourths of the land recently urbanized in a sample of fast-growing western counties had been previously devoted to crop production, usually of high-valued, irrigated crops.[9] Unfortunately, we do not have data for the nation as a whole as to the potential productivity of land that has already been urbanized or of vacant land within urban areas. We do know, however, that there is still considerable agricultural production within the rural portions of existing metropolitan areas. In 1969 farms within metropolitan areas accounted for 14 percent of all U.S. cropland harvested.[10]

The fear that urbanization of prime agricultural lands will interfere with the country's ability to feed itself is almost certainly an exaggerated one. Even a doubling of the area in cities would cause them to occupy less than 4 percent of the country's surface area. Currently some 25 percent of U.S. land is in farms, with the potential for considerable expansion of this figure if needed. On the other hand, recent sharp jumps in world feed grain demands have underlined the possibilities for vastly increased U.S. agricultural exports. Applications of additional factors, such as fertilizers and pesticides, to less productive lands should easily make up for the loss of whatever proportion of the better lands is taken out of production, but these new factors tend to impose environmental costs of their own.

Even with food demands and prices far higher than any we have known before, however, agriculture will find it difficult to compete with urban uses. The difference in value between surburban land in agriculture and the same land in residential use is often 500 percent or more.[11]

Framing the issue in terms of the relative *fertility* of the land misses an important point. Agriculture on the urban fringe not only produces crops, but provides valuable open space. In many cases a landscape of well-tended farms is more attractive visually than even a completely natural scene. For reasons deep in the American psyche, farming, particularly farming on a small scale, is considered a virtuous kind of enterprise. Thus the loss of farmlands on the urban fringe might be considered a social loss, even aside from the loss of the fruits of the land. The vineyards outside San Jose or the orange groves near Orlando might be moved elsewhere with little aggregate loss of production. For residents of these places, however, there would be a loss of amenity.

Here again, impacts spill over both individual property lines and municipal boundaries. The suburb can hardly be expected to forego development simply to provide pleasant vistas to the city dweller. In the absence of some mechanism for reallocating costs and benefits over the appropriate region, development will take place in ways that will leave many area residents dissatisfied.

Fiscal Effects of Land Use Changes

Until recently, most communities looked upon new construction and the new residents it accommodated as attractive additions to the local tax base. True, some types of development, such as trailer parks and apartment buildings, were looked on with suspicion, but the general feeling was that if growth was good for the local private economy, it would swell municipal coffers as well. Now the pendulum has shifted, and citizens and their elected representatives emphasize the public service burden that new developments will impose.

Former Oregon Governor Tom McCall cites a study of a Florida county which, he claims, showed that an influx of 1000 new residents would include 270 new families, with 200 school children, 19 blind persons, 68 aged persons, 11 juvenile delinquents, 16 alcoholics, and 30 mentally retarded children. "Consider," he says, "that by no stretch of the imagination will these new residents pay their own way, not for years and possibly not forever."[12]

The concern is particularly acute in suburbs, where families with school-age children make up a high proportion of new residents, and in rural areas where second-home developments are springing up. In the latter case, the new residents are demanding levels of public services far higher than those which rural townships have traditionally provided. Added police protection, garbage collection, better roads, and even such urban amenities as traffic signals seem to accompany this kind of growth. A town father in one Vermont community claims that newcomers even insist that roads be cleared of fresh snow immediately, night or day. "People don't go to sleep like they used to," he says.[13]

Mitigating growth's impact on the demand for local services are the declining number of children per family and increased state and federal sharing of education and welfare costs. On the other hand, two decades of inflation and interest rates that have reached levels far higher than in the past have made the marginal costs of building and financing new capital facilities far higher than the average costs of what is already in place. Under the most common municipal practice, new residents pay the same amount for streets, schools, and utilities as do long-time residents, even though the cost of the new infrastructure greatly exceeds that of the facilities that had been built in the past.

Empirical evidence on the fiscal effects of growth is mixed.[14] Often the results of the analysis seem to depend on whether the study is produced by the developer, by the municipality, or by some citizen group wishing to exclude growth. Methodological and measurement problems include estimating the characteristics of new residents, their incomes, and their tastes for public services; measuring the excess capacity of existing public facilities; guessing at future construction costs and municipal bond interest rates; and predicting long-term and secondary effects of growth. For example, highways are generally not widened incrementally as individual new developments are built, but as a result of congestion due to cumulative growth. Allocating the appropriate proportion of the cost of highway improvement to a single new subdivision is difficult indeed.

Despite the problems with these studies, interest in measuring the fiscal effects of growth is high. Muller, who surveyed the field, estimates that during 1973, the volume of fiscal impact studies was higher than the total of those he identified during the previous five years.[15]

In a sense, the new skepticism about the fiscal impact of growth is merely a more sophisticated version of what has long been called "fiscal feudalism." Communities compete for the shopping center, with its high property and sales tax generation, and shun the trailer park, which requires services but contributes much less in taxes. They court the builder of expensive homes and discourage the builder of low-cost housing. Perhaps the only change that has occurred is an enlargement of the types of development that are considered fiscal drains. Now, even the expensive single-family home is suspect.

The competition of local governments for ratables has reached ludicrous heights in places where functional economic units are broken up into a multitude of jurisdictions. In northern New Jersey, for example, the tiny borough of Teterboro has virtually zoned out people, while zoning in an airport and industries. As a result, the town has about two dozen residents, a single public school student backed by some $75 million in assessed valuation, and the second lowest tax rate in the county.[16]

If, as we have suggested, the number of types of development considered fiscally desirable has diminished, we can expect localities to intensify their efforts to obtain these "acceptable" projects and to exclude the rest. The result, of course, is not only an inequitable distribution of the tax burden, but a tendency to bend environmental and other standards when necessary to entice a coveted project.

Degradation of the Natural Environment

The litany of environmental damage caused by poor land use is a long and familiar one. The destruction of wetlands on Long Island, the eutrophication of lakes in Florida, and the scarring of hillsides by strip mining are common fare to the reader of environmental magazines and the daily newspapers alike. One might suggest that the real problem lies not in the cases of obvious devastation, which are often overstated, but in the steadiness and irreversibility of the seemingly more minor damage. For example, for every river that is grossly and unattractively polluted by man's use of the shoreline, there are dozens that are attractive to look at but manifestly unsafe to drink. Where the worst cases are often due to some easily identified public or corporate excess (the strip mine or the paper mill), the damage caused by piecemeal and individually innocuous development may be both equally bad and far harder to repair or remedy.

When we make irreversible changes in the natural environment, we implicitly ignore the possibility that public tastes and needs will change over time. The draining and filling of wetlands is a good example. Long considered useless, unattractive, and even dangerous, swamps and tidal marshes are now widely appreciated for their fascinating ecosystems and for their significant contribution to the productivity of lakes and oceans. Similarly, there is a growing appreciation for the rough beauty of the desert landscapes of the West, once considered by most people as bothersome impediments to cross-country travel.

Many environmental problems concern the interrelation of air, water, and the land. Urban sprawl and splatter not only waste land and energy, they also can contribute to air pollution.[17] Unwise agricultural practices and careless construction and logging lead to the erosion of billions of tons of topsoil yearly. Excessive withdrawals of water from underground aquifers has caused saltwater intrusion and threatened the water supplies of cities. Building seaward of the duneline has caused beach erosion in many coastal areas, as well as needless risk to life and property. In all of these cases, the pollution or environmental damage we observe can be traced back to prior, sometimes subtle, changes in land use.

Destruction of wildlife habitat frequently accompanies land use changes. Even though bear, bison, turkey, and other formerly plentiful species now enjoy at least some protection from hunting, there is no chance they will even approach their former ranges or numbers.

Dramatic conflicts between land use changes and environmental forces occur when areas with natural hazards are developed. Despite considerable federal investment over the years in flood-protection measures, the continuing urbanization of floodplains has caused flood losses to climb.[18] Large portions of the heavily developed Florida coast lie within the one hundred-year flood zone. And, in California, building has taken place directly astride the San Andreas earthquake fault. Development in hazard areas has been implicitly subsidized by federal insurance and disaster relief programs, which have reimbursed much of the monetary loss suffered by those who have built even where the hazard was obvious or predictable.[19]

Degradation of the Visual Environment

Much of the damage to natural environments that has occurred is unseen except to the expert. Obvious to all, however, is the decline of visual amenity, particularly in those urban and suburban places where most people spend the majority of their time. Indeed, it is quite possible that the public's objection to development is not based so much on calculation of fiscal costs and benefits, ideal conceptions of urban form, or even on its effects on natural systems, but simply on how such developments look.

Billboards, gas stations, shopping centers, fast-food outlets compete for the customer's eye in city and suburb. New, less-expensive building materials have freed the designers of commercial buildings from the constraints of brick, wood, and stone and have spawned a generation of structures in which the building itself becomes part of the advertising message. This message is to be read not at the leisurely walking pace of the downtown window-shopper, but at the pace of traffic moving along a commercial boulevard or even an expressway.

Their angles as yet unsoftened by trees and other vegetation, new residential developments are often quite unattractive compared with long-settled neighborhoods. Similarly, modern expressways, despite considerable efforts by some of their designers, continue to be more functional than esthetic. Undergrounding of new utility distribution lines is increasingly popular, despite the considerable added costs, but it has been estimated that replacing those overhead lines already in place would cost perhaps $150 billion.[20] Undergrounding of high-voltage lines in rural areas is exceedingly expensive and is done only occasionally.

Local regulations have long been used to improve the visual environment, even to the extent, in some communities, of requiring approval by an art jury of new residential building designs. A ride along any long metropolitan artery, say, Los Angeles' Wilshire Boulevard or Miami's Highway A1A, is convincing evidence of the unevenness of these restrictions from community to community. The mobile city dweller finds that, even though his own municipality may be one of the fortunate ones, the habitual tracks of his daily experience take him through a variety of visual environments, many of them distasteful.

Closely allied to the decline of visual quality has been growth's near total disregard for the unique or the historic. Over one-third of the 16,000 structures listed in the 1933 Historic American Buildings Survey have already been destroyed.[21] The unique character of whole cities such as San Francisco and New Orleans has been eroded by the ubiquitous office tower, which is functional, profitable, and lifeless. Distinctive nonurban environments also face the homogenization that development brings. Resort condominiums might be shuffled from Vermont to Colorado to the northern California coast and many would not notice the change. Their designs show little appreciation of the environments that have evolved in these places over the years. In some places, such as Martha's Vineyard, heated opposition to new development has arisen, not because of the quality of the development itself, but because it would erode the uniqueness of the place.

Limitation of Housing Opportunity

Despite considerable progress in removing the most blatant forms of racial and ethnic discrimination in housing markets, residential segregation by race, by income—or by both—persists. Soaring prices for new housing and local efforts at fiscal zoning have raised the price of entry in many suburban housing markets beyond the reach not just of the poor, but of many members of the working class as well. It is a rueful joke in many affluent suburbs that most of the employees of local government cannot afford to make their homes there.

Federally funded housing programs, meager as they have been, might have made it possible for some low-income people to reside among more affluent neighbors, were it not for the enormous difficulty of getting communities to accept the subsidized families. The newspapers of the late 1960s and early 1970s have been full of stories of neighborhood efforts to prevent the construction of low- and moderate-income housing, even of the "scattered-site" variety. Frequently the rhetoric of the environmental movement is used to mask more fundamental issues of class and race.

Gainers, Losers, and Speculators

The public is both horrified and fascinated by the workings of the land market. Land speculators are almost universally condemned, while at the same time, the public praises homeownership as an investment and eagerly snaps up pieces of the New Mexico desert. Still, speculation in land might be considered as socially neutral as speculation in rare paintings or in stamp collections, were it not for three important side effects.

First, the potential for public action, particularly with respect to permitted land uses, to produce enormous changes in land values has frequently perverted the public decision process. Nearly every fast-growing metropolitan area has had its zoning scandals, and nearly every state has built roads that led principally to some favored individual's property.

Second, land speculation has caused large amounts of land to be held idle, reducing the total output of society. Landowners who suspect that their land may be urbanized in the future are reluctant to make investments that would raise its productivity as farm or forest. Often they maximize their flexibility by withholding it from *any* use. Because the form of future patterns of urban growth is uncertain, the land subject to this speculative influence usually amounts to many times the area that actual urban uses could ever absorb.

Finally, speculation has been blamed for helping raise the price of land for housing, farming, and other uses to historic highs.[22] By the usual yardsticks relating housing expenditure to income, new housing is beyond the reach of the majority, and perhaps as much as 80 percent, of the American people. Certainly not all of the recent sharp increase in housing prices has been due to land costs, but the proportion of the price of the average new home attributable to land costs has been rising steadily. Similarly, farmland prices that have little relationship to the current productivity of the land have made it difficult for aspiring young farmers to enter the business. A county extension agent in Vermont claims, "You can't make a profit by buying land at one or two thousand per acre, even if you plan to grow gold."[23]

Municipalities have considerable scope for affecting land values, but this is mainly in the form of windfalls and losses caused by zoning and investment decisions. They have neither the power to tax those who gain by their actions nor the funds to compensate those who lose.[24]

Increasing Size of Development Projects

The sheer size of many of the projects proposed or built in the last few years has made their impacts on their surroundings more obvious, has widened the zone of their impact, and has frequently caused sharp controversy. In Florida's Broward (Fort Lauderdale) County, for example, the twenty-five largest planned or ongoing residential developments would add 800,000 persons to the population—doubling its current size. Two individual projects would each contain more than 50,000 dwelling units and the smallest of the projects more than 2,000.[25]

In the New Mexico desert, a consortium of gas companies plans seven huge coal-gasification plants, each costing $400 million.[26] The Arizona strip mine that feeds them, already the largest in the nation, will be enlarged from its present 2,500 acres to nearly 30,000 acres.

Elsewhere in the country, sports stadiums, new communities (a recent survey counted more than 150), rural factories, thermal and nuclear power plants, regional jetports, amusement parks, universities, and other very large facilities have had significant economic and environmental effects extending over large land areas and, often, across several political jurisdictions.

It is unlikely that size itself is bad. In fact, large projects lend themselves to careful design, cautious review, and the planning flexibility made possible by single ownership. They bring land use issues to the public attention in a dramatic way that slow marginal changes do not. Ideally, they might be seen as opportunities for the public to improve and to redirect growth.

Unfortunately, it is this very size that has caused so many of these opportunities to be lost. The costs and benefits of large projects are spread over great areas and among several political jurisdictions, but it is only by chance that the spatial distribution of benefits coincides with the distribution of costs. To date, the general practice in this country has been to give the power to regulate land uses to the jurisdiction containing the project, not to all those affected by it. Thus, we find some large projects approved even though they impose substantial costs on other jurisdictions, while other projects are rejected even though they would confer substantial regional benefits. Moreover, many of these projects are so large and so complex in their effects that their evaluation is far beyond the analytical capability of the local governments that now bear the responsibility for regulating them.

Resistance to Change

The large projects we encounter are a symptom of the rate at which our society is changing. As the economy grows at a geometric rate, successive increments of growth become larger and larger. We are beginning to see many examples of public resistance not merely to the products of change but to change itself. This resistance extends to land use changes. In fact, people faced with disturbing political and social changes may find in their physical environment some last vestige of stability and may resist land use changes with special vigor.

Joseph Bodovitz, director of California's Coastal Zone Conservation Commission, maintains, "If I were asked to suggest two books as indispensable reading for coastal zone planners, one of them would be Alvin Toffler's *Future Shock*. . . . Obviously I do not know what was in the minds of the 4.3 million Californians who voted for our State's coastal zone law, but I suspect that one major factor was the rapidity of change."[27]

Thus a final problem we face is the problem of change itself. Sometimes the change is physical—who has not lamented the loss of the vacant lot where he played as a child? Sometimes, the change is social—land use changes bring in newcomers with different customs, different incomes, sometimes different skin colors.

Perhaps the fervor with which people try to preserve the integrity of their environment is due to their having consciously chosen that environment. Developers are often mystified when projects embodying high standards of environmental protection and architectural quality are strenuously opposed by citizens. Areas once composed of single-family dwellings may be no less appealing to an outside observer than the same neighborhood converted to high-rise apartments. The new residents of the high rises may be more than satisfied with their environment. But the old residents, who originally chose the single-family neighborhood, are likely to resist the change. . . . Do people have an inherent right to determine the way in which land around them is used? And, if they do, how much of this right resides in the present residents of a local jurisdiction and how much in society as a whole?

We have seen that the public desire to do something about land use has roots in the many problems we see around us. We might now speculate about the land use pressures we will feel in the future, the roots of our future land use dilemmas.

Problems to Come

Predicting the future is a dangerous game. In some cases, social and economic forces have had such continuing momentum that trends first noticed many years ago are still with us today. The metropolitanization of the population was well underway in the 1940s; urban sprawl was decried in the early 1950s; the movement of the population toward amenity-rich places has continued for two generations. On the other hand, other trends have been obscure—the course of the birthrate; the mix of single- versus multiple-family dwellings.

We can say with near certainty that the rate of new household formation in the next two decades will be the highest in history. The people who will form new families and who will, most probably, demand additional units in which to house these families, have already been born. Between 1960 and 1970, some 10.1 million new households were formed. The 1970s will see an additional 14.4 million; the 1980s some 12.7 million. After 1990, this source of demand for land will again depend principally on the vagaries of the birthrate.

In all likelihood, the vast majority of these families will locate in metropolitan areas. Whether they choose the central city or a suburb is less certain. Forces leading to a resurgence of the central city include smaller families, improved public transportation, greater racial tolerance, falling urban crime rates, high energy costs, and the spread of some of the old big-city problems to the suburbs. Factors leading toward continued dispersion within the metropolis are the relatively lower costs of land assembly on the periphery, the fact that a good (highway) transportation system is already in place, the continuing dispersion of employment, and the rising level of average incomes.

To some extent the mix of concentration and dispersion will depend on the land use policies that the suburbs and exurbs follow. Growth limits, development charges, and slow investment in infrastructure will raise the cost of building new housing in the suburbs, leading to infilling in the city and the renovation of existing structures.

Amenity-rich locations are likely to continue to grow much faster than the average. Better educated and more widely traveled, the population has both the desire to move to locations with pleasant environments and, increasingly, the income to express this desire. In particular, the number of retired persons is expected to grow sharply. Weakened family ties and more liberal pensions should make older people a major factor in the housing market in popular retirement areas. Unlike job-oriented migrants, pensioners are free to gravitate toward places where the climate is moderate and the living costs low. This should add to the growth both of traditional retirement destinations, such as Florida and the Southwest, and of less fashionable but moderately priced havens, such as the North Carolina and Arkansas mountains.

It is possible that the identity of places considered amenity-rich will change over time. Already, California has lost some of its appeal, and small migration streams are redirected to places like Oregon, Vermont, Colorado, and North Carolina. Major land use conflicts are likely to be associated with a huge prospective increase in second homes. Although the number of families having second homes jumped from 1.6 million in 1967 to 2.9 million only three years later, the proportion of households owning a second home is still only about 5 percent.[28] Even increases of a few percentage points in this figure would translate into enormous numbers of new units, concentrated in the limited number of areas of high amenity.

Some observers think that the United States will be drawn into a world food crisis within a decade, forced by moral as well as economic pressure to use its unmatched agricultural potential to export to starving third world nations. Similar scenarios may be foreseen for timber and for certain mineral resources. This could lead to some expansion of the land area devoted to these uses.

Another coming "crisis" may involve the housing market. Drastic increases in housing prices may lead to new mixes of housing types, great consumer unrest, and, perhaps, a reorganization of the way in which new housing is built and financed. It is not unlikely that this will involve direct public sector participation in a fashion as yet unknown in this country.

In any case, the average size of residential and commercial developments should continue to rise, and with it the size of the firms initiating such projects. Developers have become increasingly aware of the possibilities of capturing increases in land values created by their projects.[29] They can be expected to build more planned-unit developments (PUDs) and new communities, where residences, commercial properties, and industries each help increase the demand for the other. Firms should also find economies of scale in planning, particularly when sophisticated (and expensive) environmental preplanning is required.

Demands for land for industry and for power production and distribution may be high, but the outlook is uncertain. Before the recent rise in energy prices, it was estimated that in the next two decades new high-voltage transmission lines would consume 3 million acres of new rights-of-way, while at least 225 new major generating stations would require hundreds of thousands of acres of prime industrial sites.[30] Depending on the price elasticity of demand for electricity, this estimate may well be too high. New energy sources, however, may involve significant new commitments of land—for strip mines, oil shale mines and processing plants, deepwater ports, oil refineries, geothermal and atomic power plants, and coal-gasification works—engendering new kinds of land use conflicts.

Variations in pollution standards may become an important factor in the location of some industrial facilities. Much depends on whether standards are promulgated in terms of the purity of the effluent alone (treatment standards) or in terms of the effect of the effluent on the quality of the receiving medium (ambient standards).

Under a treatment standard, a potentially polluting industry would spend about the same amount on treating its effluent regardless of where it locates. Ambient standards, on the other hand, cause treatment costs to vary with location. The picture is further complicated by the possible introduction of nondegradation requirements, which would preserve environmental quality in places now considered pristine.

Demands for recreational land will probably continue to increase, although at some point today's extremely high percentage rates of growth will undoubtedly moderate. There is likely to be considerable conflict between different types of recreational uses, for outdoor recreation includes such varied, and sometimes incompatible, activities as family camping, snowmobiling, boating, hunting, operation of all-terrain vehicles, nature study, and wilderness hiking.

In general, we can expect that there will be even more conflicts among land use preferences in the future than we have already experienced. These conflicts will not be among land use aggregates—the following projection of future land requirements shows that, despite significant growth in population and economic activity and great changes in the composition of industrial output, the demand for land in broad categories of uses may not be remarkably different at the end of the century from what it was at its midpoint.[31]

Table 2-1
Long-term Demand for U.S. Land
(millions of acres)

	1950	1960	1970	1980	1990
Open farmland, including pasture	884	888	909	842	789
Other grassland and range	193	168	130	112	89
"Commercial" forest	457	502	523	499	551
Recreation, etc. land	42	62	81	103	126
Urban and transportation land	51	63	66	74	82
Public installations and facilities	26	32	34	32	39
Total land requirements	1653	1715	1743	1661	1676
Total land availability	1904	2271	2265	2264	2263
Surplus (+) or deficit (−)	+251	+556	+522	+603	+587

In the aggregate, land required for urban or recreational use can simply be shifted from other uses or from our rather large supply of unused land.[32] The conflicts, however, will occur over individual parcels of land. The wilderness advocate will not willingly accept a tract of land in Idaho when land suitable for this use can be found in North Carolina. The fact that family campers or all-terrain vehicle enthusiasts also covet the North Carolina land will not necessarily persuade the wilderness lover to settle for a far-off substitute. Similarly, the New Jersey farmer will doubtless be unimpressed by the argument that land taken out of cultivation by urbanization in his state can easily be replaced by the produce of new lands in Alabama or Delaware.

As a result of these conflicting demands for the services of the same pieces of land, we can expect that rights connected with land will be increasingly exercised, privatized, and priced. When a parcel is devoted to one use, say, farming, other uses such as forestry, recreation or urbanization often must be excluded. But even when there is no inherent conflict among uses, owners will probably increasingly exclude unregulated use by others, partly for fear of vandalism and overuse, and partly because public use may create "prescriptive" rights.[33]

Notes

1. See Marion Clawson, *Suburban Land Conversion in the United States* (Baltimore: Johns Hopkins University Press for Resources for the Future, 1971); and Irene Taeuber, "The Changing Distribution of the Population of the United States in the Twentieth Century," in U.S. Commission on Population Growth and the American Future, Research Report, vol. V, *Population, Distribution, and Policy* (Washington, D.C.: GPO, 1972), pp. 31-107.

2. R.O. Harvey and W.A.V. Clark, "The Nature and Economics of Urban Sprawl," *Land Economics*, vol. 41, no. 1 (February 1965), pp. 1-9.

3. Even within the boundaries of large cities urbanized for many years there is a surprising amount of vacant or undeveloped land. Marion Clawson, *America's Land and Its Uses* (Baltimore: Johns Hopkins University Press for Resources for the Future, 1972), p. 39.

4. Jerome Pickard, "U.S. Metropolitan Growth and Expansion, 1970-2000," in U.S. Commission on Population Growth and the American Future, *Population, Distribution, and Policy*, pp. 127-82.

5. William H. Whyte, Jr., "Urban Sprawl," *Fortune*, vol. 57, no. 1 (January 1958).

6. For a quantitative assessment of some of these impacts, see U.S. Council on Environmental Quality, *The Costs of Sprawl* (Washington, D.C.: GPO, 1974).

7. As public policy has made growth on the rural edges of suburban Fairfax County, Virginia, more difficult, building has increased markedly in the next county farther out. The commuter traffic generated there, of course, continues to pour through Fairfax County on its way to the city of Washington.

8. For example:

"If there is to be a national land use plan, I believe that the conservation of farmland should be one of its major objectives." Sen. George Aiken, in debate over the National Land Use Policy Act, *Congressional Record*, daily ed., June 19, 1973, p. 11448.

"For these reasons, consideration should be given to the preservation of all areas of prime agricultural land, particularly where these areas are adjacent to or in close proximity to existing urban areas. In addition, those areas, which because of unique soil-climate combinations support the growth of specialty crops such as wine grapes, brussel sprouts, avocados and artichokes should also be protected because of their rarity." California Legislature, Joint Committee on Open Space Lands, *State Open Space and Resource Conservation Program for California* (1972), p. 26.

"It is of absolutely critical concern that conversions of agricultural crop lands stop immediately. . . . Michigan must not further reduce land available for intensive production in the state." *Agricultural Land Requirements: A Projection to 2000 A.D.* (Lansing: Michigan Department of Agriculture, February 1973), pp. 10-11.

9. Henry W. Dill and Robert C. Otte, *Urbanization of Land in the Western States*, U.S. Department of Agriculture, Economic Research Service, ERS-428 (Washington, D.C.: GPO, 1970).

10. U.S. Department of Agriculture, Office of the Secretary, *Research and Data Needs for Land Use Planning* (Washington: USDA, 1974), p. 8.

11. See A. Allan Schmid, *Converting Land from Rural to Urban Uses* (Baltimore: Johns Hopkins University Press for Resources for the Future, 1968).

12. Address to the annual meeting of the American Society of Planning Officials, Los Angeles, April 1973. Actually, these figures are probably too high—but they typify the fears of a large number of public officials.

13. "Vermont's Loveliness Causes a Developing Storm," *National Observer*, April 1973.

14. For representative studies, see Thomas Muller and Grace Dawson, *The Fiscal Impact of Residential and Commercial Development: A Case Study*, Urban Institute Paper No. 712-7-1 (Washington, D.C.: The Urban Institute, 1972); Boulder (Colo.) Area Growth Study Commission, *Exploring Options for the Future—A Study of Growth in Boulder County*, vol. V (1973); and George Sternlieb, *Housing Development and Municipal Costs* (New Brunswick, N.J.: Center for Urban Policy Research, Rutgers University, 1973).

15. Thomas Muller, *Fiscal Impacts of Land Development: A Critique of Methods and a Review of Issues* (Washington, D.C.: The Urban Institute, 1975).

16. "Danger—Zoning," supplement to the Hackensack (N.J.) *Record*, Aug. 3, 1970.

17. The relationship is not a simple one. Dispersed patterns of development encourage greater automobile use, thus adding to the amount of emissions discharged to the atmosphere. On the other hand, because the emissions are released over a larger area, *ambient* air quality may actually be improved relative to more concentrated development. See Frank P. Grad et al. *The Automobile and the Regulation of Its Impact on the Environment* (Norman: University of Oklahoma Press, 1975), pp. 191-95.

18. A recent report showed continuing urbanization of floodplains in Denver and Kansas City, despite considerable recent flood damage. Earth Satellite Corporation, "Land Use Change and Environmental Quality in Urban Areas," report to the U.S. Council on Environmental Quality (April 1973).

19. The 1973 Federal Flood Insurance Act is a sharp break with this policy, requiring local floodplain zoning as a condition for insurance coverage and denying both insurance and disaster relief to new structures built in flood-prone areas.

20. U.S. Federal Power Commission, *National Power Survey*, 1970 (Washington, D.C.: GPO, 1971), vol. I, p. 14-7.

21. John J. Costonis, *Space Adrift: Saving Urban Landmarks Through the Chicago Plan* (Urbana: University of Illinois Press, 1974), p. 4.

22. That there has been a considerable, and rather lengthy, boom in land prices is undeniable. See, for example, Max Ways, "Land: The Boom that Really Hurts," *Fortune*, vol. 88, no. 1 (July 1973), pp. 104-9, 168-70; and "Up on the Farm," *Wall Street Journal*, Feb. 12, 1973. The role of speculators in fueling that boom and, indeed, the precise role that speculation plays in the land market, is a subject of some dispute.

23. Rutland (Vt.) *Daily Herald*, Oct. 22, 1973.

24. The use of so-called subdivision exactions, in which developers make a payment to the city for permission to develop, is becoming more common, but it is unlikely that the courts would permit them if they exceeded the direct costs of providing the property with public services.

25. "Broward: From Boom to What?" supplement to the *Miami Herald*, May 1974.

26. Los Angeles *Times*, Oct. 21, 1973.

27. Bodovitz, "The Coastal Zone: Problems, Priorities and People," address to the Conference on Organizing and Managing the Coastal Zone, Annapolis, Maryland, June 13-14, 1973, p. 5.

28. U.S. Bureau of the Census, *Census of Housing*, 1970, vol. I, pt. 1 (Washington, D.C.: GPO, 1972).

29. Compare, for example, the recent development of Florida's Disney World with that of the earlier (1955) Disneyland in California. In the California case, the success of the amusement park caused huge increases in the value of nearby land, which was not owned by Disney. In planning the Florida park, Disney purchased some 27,000 acres of land surrounding the amusement area.

30. Statement of Sen. Henry Jackson, *Congressional Record*, daily ed., Jan. 9, 1973.

31. Leonard Fischman, for Resources for the Future, 1972, alternative based on Series E population projection. The large increase in land availability in the 1950-60 decade reflects the admission of Alaska and Hawaii to the Union.

32. In particular, there seem to be opportunities for raising forest productivity through more intensive management. This could free large amounts of land for other uses, notably recreation.

33. A "prescriptive" right or easement is one which is acquired by open and continuous exercise over an extended period of time. This concept or the related doctrine of "customary" use has been successfully used in California to ensure public access to beaches (*Gion v. City of Santa Cruz*, 465, P.2d 50, 1970) and in Oregon to enjoin private construction in the areas of dry sand between the vegetation line and the water's edge (State ex rel. *Thornton* v. *Hay*, 254 Or. 584, 595-99, 462 P.2d 671, 676-78, 1969). Even if opening up private land to public use does not create a legally enforceable right, owners may fear that it will create public expectations that may be expressed through future land use controls.

Part II
Land in America

3 Land in America: A Brief History

Richard N.L. Andrews

It is widely acknowledged that there exist major conflicts among uses of land in the United States today. Many of these conflicts are characterized as between the values of land as a commodity and as a natural resource, the former based upon its market value in dollars and the latter based upon its ecological functions and physical use potentials (though there may be conflicts *among* commodity or physical values as well). Examples include the values of wetlands for waterfront development and for fish production, of urban open space for office buildings and for parks, of farmland for food production and for urbanization, and of the northern Great Plains for coal mining and for soil and water conservation. The recognition of such conflicts frequently becomes the basis for advocacy of government action to resolve them, such as by federal or state land use controls, differential taxation, or regulation of the uses of particularly "critical" areas.

But the recognition of such conflicts does not necessarily justify particular policy prescriptions for their rectification. What are their origins? Are they new or long standing? What role do government policies play in causing as well as solving them? Is the problem unique to the United States, or have other societies experienced it as well and perhaps found other approaches to solving it?

The resolution of land use conflicts requires some understanding of the history of land in America, and particularly of the origins and reasons for present conflicts. This chapter briefly reviews the history of land in America, therefore, in order to shed light on the origins of current land use conflicts and on the implications of these origins for policy prescriptions. First, however, it is necessary to note several characteristics of land itself.

Land as a Resource

The status of any resource is constrained by its physical characteristics. In the case of land, several of these characteristics are important to our discussion. First, land is a resource *base*, not merely a single resource, and its amount is more or less fixed. It is the platform for the activities of all terrestrial species, including man; its soils provide the nutrients for vegetative growth, and thereby for animal food; its vegetation and minerals in turn provide all the materials used by human beings. Small amounts of land can be added here and there by drainage or filling, or subtracted by flooding and erosion; but in general it is a finite resource *base*, not merely a discrete resource, and it has no obvious substitutes.

Second, land is more or less fixed in its location. One must say "more or less" since erosion may carry away large amounts of topsoil and, especially in coastal or riparian areas, the actions of water may dramatically alter the configuration of land. With these changes may come equally important changes in land's value both as a commodity and as a natural resource. With these exceptions, however, land is fixed in its location, unlike other commodities such as money and material goods and unlike other natural resources such as wildlife and water. This immobility leads to different principles of ownership and governance for land than for mobile resources, as well as to the importance of location as a component of its value to human societies.

Third, land differs in its physical characteristics from one location to another. One area may have an unusual concentration of fuel minerals, another of productive agricultural soils, still another of mature forests, and another yet of mountains and valleys. This is an obvious point, but important to mention since it differentiates land once again from many other commodities and resources. It is just these differences among locations that have motivated many of the most important explorations, migration and settlement patterns, transportation and trade systems, and wars in human history.

Fourth, the value of an area of land to human societies depends not on its physical characteristics alone, but on several other crucial factors as well. In the absence of a monetary economy, the simplest case, the value of land depends on its productivity for the necessities of life, such as food and fuel and fiber, and on its symbolic value in the culture and religion of its users. In the presence of a monetary economy, the land takes on additional values, based on the materials that can be mined or harvested from it (or the characteristics of it that people will pay to experience), on the demand for those products (which is itself a function of human wants and ability to pay for them), on the technologies that can convert those products into the goods wanted, and on the location of the land relative to the technology and the people who want the goods.

Finally, in the presence of an urban settlement the land takes on two more kinds of values, one based on its support of functions in a human social system or community, the other on its location irrespective of its other physical characteristics. In an urban economic context, location alone may—in market terms—justify radical modification of its physical characteristics in order to perform different economic functions.

The point of these distinctions is that the value of land has many components, not just a simplistic dichotomy between commodity and natural resource. Any land area may have *many* values, some of which can be realized in concert and some of which are mutually exclusive. These values in turn are not created by the land's ecological functions alone, nor by a single market for it as a commodity, but by a complex mixture of physical, economic, and cultural influences. This mixture changes over time and differs from one society to another.

The essential questions for our purposes, therefore, are who has the power to decide which values of land are realized; and which values do they choose to realize? In short, who owns the land and how do they use it?

The European Heritage

Since the initial European settlements, land in America has always been both property and natural resource, though it has not always been a marketable commodity nor privately owned. The origins of American patterns of land tenure owe much to their European antecedents.

In the socioeconomic system of feudal Europe, the manor was a self-sufficient economic entity, a tiny agrarian state ruled by its lord. The lord received the land from his superior in the social hierarchy, in return for his loyalty and military service; he in turn granted land to those beneath him on similar terms. Its residents received the use of land and food from the lord, and in return owed him measures of grain or days of labor. Until the enclosure movement of the sixteenth and seventeenth centuries, most of these lands were worked in common; and the land was the basis not only of subsistence but also of social and political organization. Since money and commerce were relatively limited, land was the primary form of wealth; and both the status of land and the social hierarchy were kept stable by restrictions on the transferability of land, such as primogeniture—the transfer of the estate in toto to the oldest son, rather than dividing it among heirs—and quitrents, annual payments owed to the person from whom the land was granted or chartered. Most important, land was always owned conditionally, by grant or charter from higher authority and ultimately from the king.

Beginning in about the thirteenth century, major changes began to reshape this system. New agricultural technologies increased agricultural surpluses, permitting the growth of trade centers and cities. Once begun, the commercial economy fed on itself as well as on the land: gold and silver discoveries monetized the economy, new trade routes brought luxury goods to purchase, and the kings taxed commerce and granted special privileges to merchants and entrepreneurs in order to support national armies for wars against one another. The resulting inflation ruined small feudal landowners living on fixed rents, forcing them either to consolidate and enclose their lands for cash crop production or to sell their land to merchants who would produce crops for profit rather than subsistence. The outcome was to turn both land and labor into market commodities: land by shifting from local subsistence to commercial tenant farming and labor by separating peasant communities from land-based subsistence farming, forcing the peasants either into tenancy or into employment in the cities and towns. From the peasants' perspective, this may have been either preferable or painful, depending on the circumstances, but the outcome was a major social change from agrarian subsistence to commercial market economy, including changes in the status, use, and ownership of land.

As America was discovered and colonized by Europeans, its immigrants brought with them both the legacy of feudal land institutions and their own varied attitudes toward the changes in those institutions that were then occurring in Europe. All saw land as a primary form of wealth, and saw in the seemingly limitless land of North America the opportunity for each individual to enjoy the property privileges reserved for the elite in Europe. Many saw land as a source of commercial wealth as well, particularly the entrepreneurs who first organized the colonies on the authority of feudal charters and grants from their kings. The merchants of Europe, of course, viewed the colonies as production platforms and markets, much as multinational corporations view the less developed nations of today: populations that could provide them with cheap raw materials, buy their manufactured goods, stimulate their shipping industry, and employ their population surplus in a region where land was plentiful but labor scarce. And the vast majority of people who went to the colonies to live were, of course, those surplus people themselves—some criminals, some debtors, some religious dissidents, but many farmers who had had to leave the land in Europe and wage laborers seeking better wages and land ownership. These colonists were people willing to take the necessary risks in order to build materially better and more independent lives for themselves. They were people, in short, who almost inevitably viewed America's land not as a fragile ecosystem or a scarce valued resource but as a virtually free, abundant commodity and opportunity for the production of economic benefits.

Colonial Land Tenure

The European nations did not recognize America's Indian tribes as sovereign nations, but claimed title to American lands on the grounds of discovery and settlement. The original English settlements were thus established on lands claimed by the king of England and granted by him to charter companies and colonial governors. The companies in turn consummated these claims by physical possession of them, in the persons of both settlers and soldiers. Initially, the companies sought to retain strong central control over the lands, but within a few years all began to distribute it to individuals as an incentive to both immigration and productivity. Usually the only duty of the individual was to pay a nominal annual quitrent, a legacy of the feudal system of obligations that took the form of an acreage tax. By 1700, most of the British America was populated by small independent farmers holding freehold possession of their farms: the only major exceptions were the slaves and tenants on the plantations of the coastal South and the leasehold system of upstate New York. By 1750, most colonial Americans other than slaves did own land or other productive property.

As early as the seventeenth century, therefore, the widespread availability of freehold land ownership was one of the most important differences between America and Europe; and the legacy of this difference is still manifest in the legal and socioeconomic status of land in America. In both societies, land was a primary basis not only of economic wealth but also of social and political status. Scott (1977) reports that the young John Adams, for instance, later to be president, could neither vote nor hold office nor even marry until he inherited his father's land at the age of 26. But land in Europe was scarce, while in America it was plentiful. Land in Europe was virtually all owned and encumbered by centuries of feudal restrictions and obligations linking it to a social and political elite; while in America it need only be claimed and used to be appropriated, and the nominal ownership of the king had little practical effect. The abundance of land in America thus brought both the economic benefits and the social and political advantages of freehold ownership within the reach of vast numbers of people, and in fact provided a principal motivation for immigration. The resulting diversity of land ownership in turn provided a principal foundation for the egalitarian institutions of American society. "If the multitude is possessed of real estate," wrote John Adams, "the multitude will take care of the liberty, virtue, and interest of the multitude in all acts of government." American land ownership never developed the full trappings of the British landed aristocracy: instead it developed an extraordinary commitment to the autonomy of the individual landowner, with virtually none of the reciprocal obligations of his European counterpart.

From the perspective of the colonists, the right of freehold land ownership was justified on three grounds. First, it was theirs by grant from the companies chartered by the king, consistent with traditional European law. Second, in many cases the land was theirs by purchase from the Indian tribes—although many of the Indians may have thought that these payments conferred only the right of common use, not exclusive ownership or freehold. Third, the land was theirs by natural right, under the so-called "labor theory of value." In this view, the Bible directed man to "increase, multiply, replenish, and subdue the earth"; therefore all unimproved and unworked land remained the possession of no one and could be claimed by anyone who invested it with his work. It became private property through cultivation and enclosure. Since Indian lands were thus in an "unclaimed state of nature," at least from the point of view of an agrarian rather than a hunting and gathering society, and since the colonists viewed themselves as having the natural right of Englishmen to own private property, they considered themselves justified in appropriating as much land as they were able to cultivate.

Despite popular beliefs even today, however, freehold ownership never meant absolute right to do whatever one wished with one's land. It was, rather, a *bundle* of rights in which the individual normally controlled the preponderant number. The feudal lord was bound by the restrictions of his king and patron, all-powerful though he might be to his own peasants. In colonial America, land ownership was also subject to government controls, many of which have modern counterparts. Wildlife, for instance, were an essential food supply, especially deer; and even though they might cross private lands, they were protected by closed seasons and deer wardens in all colonies but one by 1776. Gold and silver discoveries were subject to 20 percent royalties to the crown. Timber was a strategic resource, for ship timber and naval stores as well as fuel and construction, and forest resources were therefore regulated by both British and colonial authorities: Britain reserved the best trees for mast timbers for the royal Navy, Massachusetts prohibited the destruction of young tar and pitch pines, and Pennsylvania required the reservation of one acre of forest for every five acres cleared.

Land was also subject to taxation, from the earliest settlements onward. The real property tax has antecedents extending at least to the Greeks of 4 B.C. and continuing through the British "Danegeld" of the twelfth century and feudal quitrents. Despite its implied treatment of land as a commodity, it has three powerful justifications. First, in any agrarian society land is the most tangible indicator both of wealth and of income and is thus the single best measure of ability to pay. Second, since a principal function of government is to protect property rights, it is appropriate that the possessors of those rights should pay a major share of the costs of government. Finally, the taxation of real estate might provide some protection against the development of a European-style landed aristocracy, which the northern colonies particularly sought to prevent. Massachusetts levied a property tax as early as 1646; Pennsylvania levied a progressive land tax during the French and Indian Wars (1758-63), aimed particularly at the absentee landlords of the Penn family. After the American Revolution, property taxes became additionally important as a source of revenue for state and local governments, since the Constitution transferred to the federal government the authority to tax imports and exports, which had been their other principal means of support.

The freehold did not, then, imply absolute autonomy of the individual to decide the use of his land. He was never free to use his property in such a way as to interfere with the rights of others; he must pay taxes on it; and he must abide by various legal restrictions on the use of the resources found on his land, such as forests, wildlife, minerals, and water. What the freehold did mean, however, was a *presumption* favoring the individual's autonomous preferences within the constraints of the laws, including the right to change the ownership, access, or use of the land without government permission. In short, he was free to develop or sell or mine or clear his land, unless explicitly prohibited by law, for whatever price the market would pay him. The actual extent to which laws constrain the use of land has varied greatly over time; but whatever this might be, the essential issues to the colonists were the principle of freehold itself, the presumption in favor of the individual that it implied, and the republican form of government that followed from that presumption.

The commitment to freehold was complemented, of course, by recognition of the critical role of land resources in colonial America's agrarian economy. Restrictions on wildlife were accepted because they were essential to survival, and on timber because it was a strategic material: whatever the abundance of timber in America as a whole, timber that was accessible to the colonies by the transportation technologies of the day—almost exclusively waterborne—was nevertheless scarce and essential. Many first-generation settlers also brought with them European attitudes toward resource husbandry, bred in the land-scarce conditions of their native countries. Land itself was often overworked and then abandoned, but its market value was nevertheless usually commensurate with its value as a natural resource. These values did not begin to diverge significantly until the major urban, industrial, and transportation developments of the nineteenth century.

The divergence began to appear, however, with the American Revolution; for with this rejection of British rule, Americans also sought to reject all vestiges of British bureaucratic "paternalism," including governmental regulation of land and natural resources. They thus ended a period in which the natural resources of land were more actively recognized and managed than at any time in the following century.

Public Revenue and Private Enterprise

The American Revolution marks a second major watershed in the status of land in America. If colonial America saw the transition from feudal tenure to freehold, the United States from 1776 to 1876 saw the disposal, on a vast scale, of public domain lands into private ownership. British rule was evicted, and its policies rejected. Authority was vested in the thirteen states and, by them, in a new federal government. A new Constitution was ratified; the status of land was wrenched to reflect both the norms and the necessities of the new nation.

The Constitution itself said little on the subject of land: the most directly applicable principles were the property clause, which authorized the
federal government to manage public property, and the Fifth Amendment,
which prohibited taking of private property for public purposes without due
process and just compensation.[1] The actions of the new government,
however, established an early and continuing policy of using land as a commodity, as an instrument of economic and social purposes, not as a capital
stock to be managed or a natural resource to be conserved.

Virtually all of America west of the Alleghenies was at one time owned
by the federal government. A condition of the initial Articles of Confedera-
tion, in fact, was the insistence of the enclosed colonies of the east—such as
Maryland and Rhode Island—that the others cede their trans-Allegheny
land claims to the new national government, to be used for the benefit of
all. Other areas were acquired later: the Louisiana Purchase in 1803,
Florida in 1819, Texas in 1845, the Northwest in 1846, the Southwest in
1848 and 1853, and Alaska in 1867. In principle, these areas could have
been retained and managed by the federal government for their natural
resource values, and in fact many of these lands that remained in federal
ownership by 1890 have been so retained. But in the century before 1890
Americans had different priorities, and land was the primary instrument for
achieving them.

Land could hardly be viewed as scarce in early nineteenth century
America: more likely it was about the only thing that was not scarce. The
frontier was expanding continously westward, and a century of expedition
reports and settlers' letters commented on the vastness of the continent's ex-
panse, the seemingly infinite abundance of the nation's natural resources.

But the nation's economy was a shambles after the Revolution. British
export markets were cut off, soldiers had to be paid, a self-standing
economy had to be not merely restored but created. Virtually the only asset
available for the purpose was the government's land; and land therefore
became, and remained for most of a century, the primary instrument of
U.S. economic development. It was used to pay soldiers: land bounties were
given to veterans of the Revolution and later wars, including both American
soldiers and Hessian defectors from the British. It was used to pay debts:
land was sold wholesale to investment companies to raise revenues, then
retailed by them to individual settlers at higher prices. It was used to finance
state and local government: private lands went onto the tax rolls and financed
the growth of public services. It was used to generate working capital: vast
land grants were given, first for canals and later for railroads, to companies
who then sold off or mortgaged prime sections of frontage to eastern and
European investors in order to raise the funds they needed for construction.
Moreover, the alternate sections were retained by the government as an investment for later sale, once transportation improvements had increased

their market value manyfold. It was used to endow schools: the land grant colleges were financed in this way. Finally, it was used to satisfy the land hunger and aspirations of generations of immigrants and speculators, refugees from the famines and depressions of Europe as well as canny traders making quick fortunes in the speculative boom of land prices that accompanied westward migration in America.

From the earliest land ordinances on, U.S. government policy was to promote the rapid transfer of public lands into private lands, to provide both short-term revenues and long-term economic development. The Land Ordinance of 1785, for instance, and the Northwest Ordinance of 1787, established the uniform rectilinear survey of land for sale and guaranteed an absolute title to the purchaser clear of Indian rights and feudal dues; they also guaranteed noninterference by the federal government in private sale and use of land. Thence a series of hundreds of land laws offered the public lands for sale at auction, for minimum prices per acre, in variously sized lots (initially 640 acres). These prices were related only to the land's values for agrarian settlement and had no relationship to variations in natural resource endowment among land areas; the only recognition of such varia- tion was a policy of reserving certain mineral lands (such as salt and lead) in government ownership and, much later, a series of cheap disposals of "refuse" lands, such as wetlands, by price reductions and outright grants. Other laws disposed of more valuable land by grants, both to states and to private companies, for such purposes as transportation and education and economic development generally.

As the trade in land boomed, the basis of the property tax was also shifted from an acreage rate based on use value to market value. To many in the 1970s, the market value criterion now appears as a villain forcing the poor out of their homes and farmland into suburbanization. At the time, however, it was probably viewed as a reform: it based taxation on the single most tangible indicator of value, rather than on a more subjective judgment of use value that could be manipulated by owners or assessors, and it would fall most heavily upon speculative profits in the land market. The property tax did not cause the divergence of commodity from natural resource values of land, but it did adjust to this divergence and attempt to capture in- crements of the difference. The justifications for the adjustment typically combined arguments against windfall profits resulting from speculation with arguments for the interdependence of revenues with infrastructure in- vestments benefiting property ("internal improvements," such as canals and railroads and; later, sewers) and with support of the public school system. By 1890, the property tax provided 72 percent of all state and 92 percent of all local tax revenues; and at least three-fourths of these amounts were drawn from taxes on realty.

It is easy to criticize these commodity-based policies in retrospect, for most Americans today neither have the same opportunities to own productive land nor face the same hardships if they do not. Relatively stable alternatives have since been developed to provide many of the functions that were then provided mainly by land: industry and commerce as a source of employment, insurance and retirement and welfare programs to stabilize subsistence during economic adjustments, the income tax to pay for many government services. At the same time, land is no longer superabundant and free for the claiming; it is now subject to intensified use conflicts where once the competing uses could simply go elsewhere. Since the latter years of the nineteenth century, therefore, a third period in the status of land law has been unfolding, one in which the natural resource values of land have become ever more subject to government regulation in the name of a "public interest" even as the private market in land continued to operate on prices more and more influenced by urban economic functions rather than by natural resource endowments. In a sense, land has become more and more a commodity in this period, as locational advantage and inflation and speculation bid up its price; but at the same time its intrinsic endowments are more and more recognized both in its price and in governmental regulation of its use. This process progressed first and fastest on the remaining public lands of the federal government, but in recent years it has invariably affected private freehold lands as well.

Private Rights and Public Interest

Large-scale disposal of public lands continued unabated until the 1890s, though the emphasis of this policy changed over time from revenue and economic development to agrarian homesteading.[2] This shift is itself one of the dominant forces in the history of American land, but for the purposes of this discussion both were policies of land disposal as a commodity rather than land management as a natural resource.

The General Revision Act of 1891 symbolized the final victory of the agrarian land reformers over the speculators, repealing or restricting many of the earlier laws that had permitted widespread land speculation. It also, however, opened a new era in the history of land in America, by permitting the president to set aside land reserves for their natural resource values, for possible long-term public management. The reasons then were essentially the same as those given now: the perception of scarcity, the objections of the landless to lack of access, the desire to preserve the aesthetic beauty and ecological functions of the open lands, and the belief that public administration was preferable to private economic control. The status of public lands typically changed in three distinct steps: first it was *classified*, based on an inventory to identify its various natural resource endowments and potentials, such as timber, minerals, and wildlife habitat; second, it was *reserved* from private appropriation to protect those potentials from destruction or loss; and third, it was *managed* so as to promote the achievement of a chosen mixture of public purposes. The public lands of the United States today reflect basically this pattern: some areas have progressed farther than others, and major conflicts continue concerning what mixture of purposes should be promoted on each, but the basic management framework and legal status of the public domain lands is more or less clear.

The history of private land regulation, in contrast, has always centered primarily on urban lands, for it is in urban areas that greater densities bring more frequent use conflicts and that market prices most quickly diverge from both the natural and the community functions of a piece of land. Zoning, still the most widespread form of land use control, was initiated by New York City in 1916 to prevent the spread of the Garment District into fashionable shopping areas; its purpose was to maintain the market values of commercial properties, not to protect the natural resource values of the land. Zoning spread to many other cities in the 1920s and was accompanied or followed by the classified property tax corresponding roughly to the market value of the uses permitted in each zone. Regulations on the subdivision of land also have been aimed primarily at market values of land and the provision of urban services rather than at natural resource protection. The other bodies of land use regulation pertain mainly to health and safety issues, such as drainage of septic fields and construction and design standards. These were urban solutions to urban problems; until recently there were virtually no attempts to link such controls to the natural resource values of land.

There has always remained a latent tension, however, between the right of the individual to use his land and the authority of government to regulate that use. In recent years the balance between these has tipped more heavily in the direction of regulatory authority. The status of land, in short, has come to be seen as more affected with a variety of public interests than in the past; both laws and judicial decisions have intervened to protect and enforce these interests. At one extreme, few would dispute the authority of government to prevent an obvious public nuisance such as someone operating a garbage dump in a residential area; nor would many dispute the opposite extreme, that if government physically appropriates a piece of land—for a highway, for instance—it must compensate the owner. Between these two extremes, however, the status of land has shifted. Owners may now be directly prohibited, in some states, from building in flood-prone areas (as defined by government); from draining or filling wetlands; or from developing historic sites or other "unique" or "critical" areas such as steep slopes and groundwater conservation areas. They may be prohibited from other uses by air and water pollution control standards, building codes, or zoning restrictions that now may include coastal, agricultural, or conservation zones as well as traditional urban land use zones. Finally, they may be further restricted by conditions attached to government grants or permits: for example, requiring soil conservation practices as a condition of watershed protection grants, requiring flood insurance as a condition of federal mortage insurance in flood-prone areas, and requiring erosion control and dedication of open space as conditions of subdivision or site plan approval. In each of these cases, the status of land now includes a mixture of private rights and public interests that must be "reasonably balanced" if put to a legal test. The government may not act capriciously, nor may it regulate away all economic potential from the land without compensating the owner, but it can regulate in the name of an increasingly broad range of public interests—many of them based on the natural resource values of the land—as long as it shows a rational basis for the regulation and leaves some economic uses open.

Land in America Today

The legal status of land in America has thus swung from predominantly government ownership to predominantly private freehold and back to a middle position in which both private rights and public interests are recognized and balanced. The socioeconomic status of land, however, has changed dramatically. The nation's principal economic base is no longer land but industry, and employment has now shifted overwhelmingly from agriculture to industry and commerce and government. Productive land is owned by a relatively small number of individuals and corporations. Land ownership is still a major cultural and economic value in America, but now as a consumption good rather than an economic production unit: the most widespread form of land ownership is probably the single-family home and urban or suburban lot, and more and more now the vacation home as well.

Moreover, the natural resource values of land have become far more recognized and reintegrated with its commodity value: by government fiat; by consumer tastes for natural lands and rising disposable income to act on these tastes; by increased automotive mobility, which has made location a less limiting influence on many land uses than in the past; and by speculation fueled by all the above.

It is important to recognize, therefore, that even as land is more appreciated as a natural resource, it is still—and perhaps more than ever—a profitable commodity and object of speculative investment. For the householder it is usually his first and often his only major investment, a modest tax shelter as well as a physical shelter and a gradually appreciating asset. For the more wealthy investor it is both a tax shelter—in depreciable or tax-loss deductible uses such as mining and agriculture—and an investment at least as safe and profitable as the stock market.

The current result is a major wave of investment in land, bidding up prices across the country often at rates far in excess of the general rate of inflation. The implications of this wave pose important questions for land status in the future. In the country, land purchased for vacation homes is unlikely to be managed for natural resource production, except in some cases rental farming of existing agricultural lands, and over time it may instead be subdivided for more intensive residential development; farming meanwhile is squeezed by economic forces into larger units controlled by fewer owners. In favorably located small towns, especially those on coasts or water courses, land sales and new migration bring the psychological and economic benefits of rising land values and civic growth—a relief after years of gloomy predictions about rural decline. But with them they bring inflation, new public service demands, and people with Arcadian land attitudes often quite at odds with those of long-term residents. In the suburbs, skyrocketing home prices are causing dramatic increases in tax assessments, in effect helping public services to keep up with inflation. But these increases may also bring taxpayer revolts that would fundamentally threaten public services, even as the price increases themselves force some people out of the market and absorb more and more of the disposable income of those who remain.

Finally, in some large cities economic disinvestment and emigration of jobs and of mobile populations may leave increasingly heavy public service burdens on the remaining productive lands, even though the public services already exist to support a larger population and more activities. Competition by local governments for new industrial plants meanwhile exacerbates the problems of both cities and suburbs, by offering long-term tax exemptions that reduce the new locality's tax revenues; by luring industry away from another locality where it may be a taxpayer; and by stimulating migration, which increases public service demands in the new locality.

It would be deeply satisfying if we could claim that, as a result of the past decade's environmental enlightenment, land is now more carefully conserved and managed as a natural resource. In some respects and in some places it is; but more frequently the recognition of its natural resource status may simply have added new dimensions to its profitability as a commodity. Despite recent efforts at reform, such as environmentally oriented land use zoning and regulation—and in some cases even because of them—we are now in the midst of a period of accelerated migration and land speculation that has at least as much chance of simply recreating old problems of urbanization in new places, while leaving the old places burdened with the obligations of their former status as economic centers but without the economic base to fulfill them. For some, this is progress. For others, however, it is frustration or conflict or despair; and for the land, it is merely change, though the change is often irreversible in its effect on the land's economic status and resource endowment.

Notes

1. This is not surprising, however, for the purpose of the Constitution was to establish the proper relations between citizens and their government, not the status of land as a natural or economic resource.

2. For example, the Homestead Act (1862), Timber Culture Act (1873), Desert Land Act (1877), Timber and Stone Act (1878), and General Allotment Act (1887).

References

Beale, Calvin L. "The Revival of Population Growth in Nonmetropolitan America." Economic Research Service, U.S. Department of Agriculture, ERS-605, 1975.

Benson, George C.S., et al. *The American Property Tax: Its History Administration, and Economic Impact*. Claremont, Calif.: Claremont Men's College, 1965.

Clawson, Marion. "Historical Overview of Land Use Planning in the United States." In *Environment: A New Focus for Land Use Planning?* Edited by Donald McAllister for the National Science Foundation, pp. 23-54. Washington, D.C.: U.S. Government Printing Office, 1973.

Engelbert, Ernest A. "American Policy for Natural Resources: A Historical Survey to 1862." Ph.D. dissertation, Harvard University, 1950.

Hibbard, Benjamin H. *A History of the Public Land Policies*. Madison: University of Wisconsin Press, 1965 (original edition 1924).

Lynn, Arthur D., Jr. "Property Tax Development: Selected Historical Perspectives." In *Property Taxation USA*. Edited by Richard W. Lindholm, pp. 7-19. Madison: University of Wisconsin Press, 1967.

McClaughrey, John, "The New Feudalism—State Land Use Controls." *Environmental Law*, 5, pp. 675-702, 1975.

Scott, William B. *In Pursuit of Happiness: American Conceptions of Property from the Seventeenth to the Twentieth Century*. Bloomington: Indiana University Press, 1977.

4

The Quiet Revolution in Land Use Controls

Fred P. Bosselman and
David Callies

This country is in the midst of a revolution in the way we regulate the use of our land. It is a peaceful revolution, conducted entirely within the law. It is a quiet revolution, and its supporters include both conservatives and liberals. It is a disorganized revolution, with no central cadre of leaders, but it is a revolution nonetheless.

The *ancien regime* being overthrown is the feudal system under which the entire pattern of land development has been controlled by thousands of individual local governments, each seeking to maximize its tax base and minimize its social problems, and caring less what happens to all the others.

The tools of the revolution are new laws taking a wide variety of forms but each sharing a common theme—the need to provide some degree of state or regional participation in the major decisions that affect the use of our increasingly limited supply of land.

Land use controls developed very late in the history of the United States, primarily after the turn of the century. As experience in other countries has demonstrated, there is little to quicken interest in such controls if there is a super-abundance of land. During the first century of a nation in which a strong belief in the inviolability of private property rights was coupled with a largely agrarian economy, there was no impetus to control the use of land.

Land use controls in the United States have therefore logically developed against a backdrop of the emerging importance of the urban area as steadily receding western frontiers dwindled. As early as 1692, for example, a law was passed in Massachusetts Bay Colony forbidding "nuisance" industries from operating in any but certain districts designated for such uses by town officials, but even then the law was applied only to Boston, Salem, Charlestown, and other market towns and cities of the province—the urban areas of the day.

It was in the cities that it became apparent that regulations were needed to prevent one man's use of his land from depreciating the value of his neighbor's property. Those who were concerned about these issues called themselves *city* planners, and they viewed the use of land as an urban problem. Rudimentary ordinances regulating building height and land use appeared in Boston and Los Angeles around 1909. Then in the next decade

From *The Quiet Revolution in Land Use Controls*, by Fred P. Bosselman and David Callies, a report of the U.S. Council on Environmental Quality (1972).

many cities passed local ordinances dividing real estate into districts which permitted some uses and excluded others. This system of local "zoning," as it came to be known, provided planners and legislators with a process containing a wide range of political options with which to achieve a consensus of interests within the local community. After the Supreme Court gave its blessing in 1926 the issue became, what kind of restrictions and where?—rather than whether there should be restrictions at all.

From the beginning the state governments saw land use control as an urban problem. A Standard Zoning Enabling Act delegating the responsibility for zoning to the city governments was prepared by an advisory committee appointed by the then-Secretary of Commerce, Herbert Hoover, and variations of it were quickly adopted by most of the states. Through the 1940's and 1950's zoning techniques were refined. The number and kinds of zones increased; greater flexibility was introduced through open space ratios, floor plan ratios, and performance standards. Planned unit development—the uniting of compatible uses and relaxation of standard restrictions according to a development plan—was added to the arsenal of zoning devices.

The complexity of the new techniques cannot obscure the fact that local zoning remains essentially what it was from the beginning—simply a process by which the residents of a local community examine what people propose to do with their land and decide whether or not they will let them. The comprehensive planning envisioned by zoning's founders was never achieved, in part because the growing interrelatedness of our increasingly complex society makes it impossible for individual local governments to plan comprehensively, and in part because the physical consideration of land use, with which zoning was in theory designed to deal, frequently became submerged in petty local prejudices about who gets to live and work where.

The real problem is the structure of zoning itself, with its emphasis on very local control of land use by a dizzying multiplicity of local jurisdictions. While the Standard Act was a *state* enabling act, it was nonetheless an *enabling* act, directed at delegating land use control to the local level, historically at the city level where the problems which called zoning into being first arose. It has become increasingly apparent that the local zoning ordinance, virtually the sole means of land use control in the United States for over half a century, has proved woefully inadequate to combat a host of problems of statewide significance, social problems as well as problems involving environmental pollution and destruction of vital ecological systems, which threaten our very existence.

It is this realization that local zoning is inadequate to cope with problems that are statewide or regionwide in scope that has fueled the quiet revolution in land use control. A recognition of the inadequacies of local zoning must not, however, cause the values of citizen participation and local control, which local zoning so strongly emphasizes, to be submerged completely in some anonymous state bureaucracy. Although the governmental entities created by the states to deal with land use problems are statewide or regional rather than local in orientation, these innovations have never involved a total usurpation of local control, and have rarely constituted an attack on the integrity of the local zoning process. Even Hawaii's statewide system of land use controls, sometimes thought to vest exclusive authority over land use in the state, recognizes the importance of a major role for local governments.

The innovations wrought by the "quiet revolution" are not, by and large, the results of battles between local governments and states from which the states eventually emerge victorious. Rather, the innovations in most cases have resulted from a growing awareness on the part of both local communities and statewide interests that states, not local governments, are the only existing political entities capable of devising innovative techniques and governmental structures to solve problems such as pollution, destruction of fragile natural resources, the shortage of decent housing, and many other problems which are now widely recognized as simply beyond the capacity of local governments acting alone.

For example, Hawaii, Vermont, and Maine have each adopted a statewide land regulatory system, but the techniques of land use control employed by each of the three are markedly different. Other states have not adopted statewide land use controls, but have provided land use controls for "critical areas" of each state's environment. Thus Wisconsin protects shorelands around lakes and along waterways, while Massachusetts is one of the states that has adopted laws to protect its wetlands, and California has created a special agency to deal with the problems of San Francisco Bay.

Other innovative legislation focuses on key types of land development. The New England River Basin Commission, like other such commissions, attempts to control the placement of dams and similar structures that are determinative of development patterns within river basins. In Minnesota the Twin Cities Regional Council regulates development by controlling the location of sewers, airports and a variety of other key facilities. And Massachusetts has created a new state agency to ensure that housing can be located in accordance with statewide needs.

The nature of the innovations in land use regulation varies from state to state, and sometimes from one institution to another within a state. Some of the devices employed are old ones in novel juxtaposition. Others are entirely, imaginatively new in concept and design. But if there is a commonalty it is a regional and land resource orientation that attempts to preserve and protect a vital resource—land—for the use of the region as a whole.

Key Issues in State Land Use Regulation

Given the youth of this legislation, and the charged-up atmosphere in which it is administered, it is not even easy for the outside observer to sit back and view it from a broader perspective. But the following six issues seem to recur throughout most of the states that have been affected by the quiet revolution.

1. Toward a New Concept of Land

If one were to pinpoint any single predominant cause of the quiet revolution it is a subtle but significant change in our very concept of the term "land," a concept that underlies our whole philosophy of land use regulation. "Land" means something quite different to us now than it meant to our grandfather's generation. Its new meaning is hard to define with precision, but it is not hard to illustrate the direction of the change.

Basically, we are drawing away from the 19th century idea that land's only function is to enable its owner to make money. One example of this change in attitude is that wetlands, which were once characterized as "useless," are now thought of as having "value." As we increasingly understand the science of ecology and the web of connections between the use of any particular piece of land and the impact on the environment as a whole we increasingly see the need to protect wetlands and other areas that were formerly ignored.

This concern over the interrelatedness of land uses had led to a recognition of the need to deal with entire ecological systems rather than small segments of them. San Francisco Bay, Lake Tahoe, the Hackensack Meadowlands, Adirondack Park are now all seen as single entities rather than as a collection of governmental units.

The new attitude toward land can also be seen reflected in the increasing concern about its scarcity. Industries that in an earlier day seemed to have their choice of an unlimited supply of land now see land as a limiting factor. With some, such as the forest products industry, this recognition came early—with others, such as agriculture, it is just beginning in states like Hawaii and California.

The economically productive users of land are not the only ones who are increasingly recognizing its scarcity. Wilderness buffs have recognized this for some time. But now the large segment of Americans who just want to live in the country, and who once seemed to have a wide choice of location, now find their supply of land limited. The jet plane, and particularly the interstate highway network, have permitted millions of Americans to achieve their goal of "country living" on either a permanent or temporary basis, but they are finding that there isn't as much "country" to live in as there used to be. Their annoyance is reflected in the new legislation in Maine and Colorado.

The scarcity of land reflects both its increasing use and the increasing limitations put on its use by local governments. The problems of inner city dwellers seeking adequate housing seem impossible to solve unless we can overcome the scarcity of suburban land on which low and moderate-income housing can be built. The Massachusetts Zoning Appeals Act was passed in recognition of this scarcity.

Conservationists describe the changing attitude toward land by saying that land should be considered a *resource* rather than a *commodity*. But while this correctly indicates the direction of the change, it ignores the crucial importance of our constitutional right to own land and to buy and sell it freely. It is essential that land be treated as *both* a resource and a commodity. The right to move throughout the country and buy and sell land in the process is an essential element in the mobility and flexibility our society needs to adjust to the rapid changes of our times. Conservationists who view land only as a resource are ignoring the social and economic impact that would come with any massive restrictions on the free alienability of land. But land speculators who view land only as a commodity are ignoring the growing public realization that our finite supply of land can no longer be dealt with in the freewheeling ways of our frontier heritage.

The idea that land is a resource as well as a commodity may appear self-evident, but in the context of our traditions of land use regulation it is a highly novel concept. Our existing systems of land use regulation were created by dealers in real estate interested in maximizing the value of land as a commodity. Subdivision regulations which encouraged uniform lots fronting on public streets enabled land to be divided into tradable units. Traditional zoning ordinances with only a few use districts, each governed by relatively nondiscretionary regulations, attempted to give these lots some of the fungible qualities of corn futures or stock certificates, making it possible to determine in advance the specific type of use permitted on the land and providing quick shorthand labels for identifying various categories of land. Bulk and yard regulations created an envelope on each single lot which enabled the owner of that lot to build without further consideration of the relationship of his land to the land of his neighbors, thus assuring potential buyers of the land's usability. The highest goal of the system was to enable barkers to sell Florida lots in Grand Central Station.

The promoters of these land use regulations in the 1920's made no attempt to conserve land for particular purposes or to direct it into a specific use, but only sought to prevent land from being used in a manner that would depreciate the value of neighboring land. The traditional answer to the question, "Why regulate land use?" was "to maximize land values."

To achieve this purpose they sought to restrict those uses of land that adversely affected the price of neighboring land by concentrating them in specific parts of the city.

Where development would not harm property values it went unregulated. Zoning permitted residential uses to be built in the most polluted industrial districts on the theory that any development which did not reduce the value of the surrounding land should not be prohibited. Land use regulation was limited to urban areas where the close proximity of land uses made it likely that the particular use of one man's land might reduce the value of another's, but there was no regulation of land outside urban areas where such a reduction in value was not likely to take place.

In a dynamic and mobile society such as ours the ability to buy and sell land readily is an essential ingredient in the operation of the system, and the extent to which zoning and subdivision control have been adopted throughout the country testifies to the usefulness of these original concepts. The last 20 years, however, has seen increasing recognition that the purpose of land regulation should go beyond the protection of the commodity value of land. A realization is growing that important social and environmental goals require more specific controls on the use that may be made of scarce land resources.

This recognition is seen not only in the new state role in land use regulation, but in the actions of many local governments. Modern zoning ordinances typically rely less and less on pre-stated regulations and require developers to work with local administrative officials in designing a type of development that fits more closely into the specific circumstances of the surrounding neighborhood. Similarly, regulations tend to encourage larger scale development in which the various land uses are arranged and designed according to a comprehensive plan for the specific site, as opposed to the traditional lot-by-lot development under which individual lots were sold to individual purchasers who might develop each lot according to pre-established rules. More specialized use districts, which permit only those uses appropriate to a specific geographic area rather than some abstract category of uses such as M-1 or R-4, are also evidence of local governments' growing attempt to tailor land use regulations to local needs.

Most importantly, perhaps, numerous systems of local land use regulation are beginning to contain regulations that recognize land as a resource as well as a commodity. Exclusive agricultural and industrial zoning preserves land as a resource for these important uses. Regulations prohibiting topsoil removal or requiring common open space find their justification in the protection of land as a resource for recreation and beauty. Regulations which require that a specified percentage of dwelling units in each housing development be reserved for low-income groups are recognizing the importance of land as an essential resource for housing all elements of our society.

Recent years have seen a rapid increase in local zoning and subdivision regulation in relatively undeveloped areas. Here the concern is not that the use of land might injure immediate neighbors, but that it might impair the possibility of more desirable long-range land use patterns. Increasingly the question being asked is not only, "Will this use reduce the value of surrounding land?" but "Will this make the best use of our land resources?"

The clearest evidence, however, that there has been a change in the attitude toward why land should be regulated is in the legislation described in this report. The purposes sought to be achieved by the various bills are a far cry from the simple value-maximization concepts of early real estate interests. Hawaii seeks to conserve the land for agriculture and to preserve scenic beauty. In Tahoe and San Francisco the goal is to preserve the amenities of the area. Maine and Vermont are trying to protect the rural atmosphere of their states. Massachusetts wants to preserve some suburban land as a resource for low and moderate-income housing and to preserve wetlands as a resource for wildlife and other ecological values. In the Hackensack Meadows the goal of New Jersey is to utilize this centrally located land for the ideal combination of development and conservation purposes.

But the recognition of new purposes for regulating land should not and does not mean that the old concerns with land's value and salability should be ignored. On the contrary, the longer-range view expressed in the new land regulatory systems will enhance land values over the long run to a far greater degree than systems motivated primarily by a desire to increase immediate salability. The preservation of the amenities of San Francisco Bay is of tremendous economic value to all landowners in the Bay area. The preservation of the quality of Maine's lakes and coastline will be of great value to owners of property in those areas, not just today but for years to come. Today's broader view of land values recognizes that in the long run land values will reflect our ability to maintain a society in which people will want to own land, and this is the overall goal of the legislation now being enacted by the states.

2. The Role of the State

Changes in a state's pattern of land use involve thousands of individual decisions—to drill a well, to widen a street, to build a power plant, to build a garage—the new patterns that result are the sum of all of these decisions, some major, others very minor. The state's goals can be achieved if only the major decisions can be regulated. One of the important issues in each state land regulatory system is to separate the major decisions from the minor so that state officials are not bogged down with gas station applications when they should be considering power plant sites, and so that irate homeowners do not have to go to the state capital to get permission to build a garage.

To succeed in solving this dilemma it is essential to avoid the classic bureaucratic trap. *Regulation is not desirable for its own sake.* Any system of land regulation imposes substantial costs. These include not only the costs borne by the taxpayers who pay the administrators' salaries and expenses, but the costs borne by the developers and eventually passed on to the consumer. Time is a particularly important cost to most land developers because heavy front-end expenses are usually paid with money borrowed at relatively high interest rates, which makes each additional day of delay a significant factor in increasing the cost.

The costs imposed on developers by land use regulations have a peculiarly regressive nature. Developers of expensive housing, for example, can much more easily absorb the cost of regulation than developers of housing designed for lower income groups. The cost of processing an application to build a mobile home park and a luxury apartment building may be approximately the same, but when considered as a percentage of the consumers' cost per unit the costs loom much larger to the mobile home buyer.

Regulation has other inherent disadvantages. Any complex system of regulation has a natural tendency to reduce innovation. Minima become maxima. When regulators approve one design it creates a powerful incentive for other builders to use the same approach. The monotonous subdivision of the 1950's is being replaced by the monotonous planned unit development of the 1970's.

For these reasons all of the states engaging in land use regulation have used some method of concentrating their energies on a limited number of important development decisions to avoid diffusing the state regulatory power too widely. A variety of methods are used: In the Twin Cities regulation is concentrated on major capital improvements, such as airports and sewers. Both Vermont and Maine have attempted to define development subject to the state's jurisdiction in a way that excludes small-scale development and concentrates only on development of more significant size. Hawaii classifies development into four basic categories and (in theory at least) the state attempts to decide only the proper category applicable to a particular piece of land, leaving the details to be worked out by the counties.

The problem of isolating the types or areas of development that have a significant state or regional impact does not seem headed for an easy solution. Further experimentation with the various methods now in use in the states may discover increasingly better methods. But the need is apparent for some method of concentrating state efforts on major land use issues if the burdens of regulation are not to exceed its benefits. Those who cry for comprehensive regulation of all development by the state merely show that they have not thought through the problem.

3. The Role of Local Government

Local regulation of land use has been in existence for many years in at least the urbanized portions of most states. These local systems of zoning and subdivision control have proven quite adequate for controlling many types of development, particularly small-scale development in urban areas. At a time of increasing demands for citizen participation and community control, the value of encouraging local decision-making wherever possible is obvious.

A common failing of most of the new state land regulatory systems is that they do not relate in a logical manner to the continuing need for local participation. Most of them tend to by-pass the existing system of local regulation and set up completely independent and unrelated systems. This requires the developer who is subject to both systems to go through two separate and distinct administrative processes, often doubling the time required and substantially increasing the costs required to obtain approval of the development proposal.

Most states have chosen to create duplicating procedures in order to eliminate the need to make any change in existing zoning and other regulatory systems. By leaving local zoning alone the state reduces the number of potential enemies of new legislation. Moreover, in many states the motives behind the state land regulatory system were solely to *prohibit* development that would otherwise occur. To persons having this motive the duplication does not seem to be a problem because duplication can only operate to prevent and not to encourage development.

Not all of the states have accepted the idea of duplication. The Massachusetts Zoning Appeals Act explicitly rejects it; here the state system comes into play only as a means of reversing a decision of a local board. The Hawaii system also minimizes duplication; some of the major development proposals require action by both state and county agencies, but most ordinary development needs action by only one or the other.

As the states move toward more balanced systems of land use regulation that are not weighted exclusively toward the prevention of development, it will be increasingly necessary to merge both state and local regulations into a single system with specific roles for both state and local government in order to reduce the cost to the consumer and taxpayer of duplicate regulatory mechanisms.

4. Regulation and Planning

Once government recognizes that land can be a resource to achieve many different goals, some method is needed to balance these various goals to see which uses of land will provide the greatest overall benefit. The operations of the Hawaiian Land Use Commission offer a good example of this balancing process. The Commission is constantly weighing the need for more housing against the need for agricultural land—the need to protect the views of the mountains against the need to attract jobs and tourists.

"Planning" can be defined as just this kind of balancing process. The Hawaiian Land Use Commission is engaged in "planning" although most of the Commissioners do not think of themselves as planners. Similarly, many similar agencies in other states are determining the best use of land by a planning process which measures alternative uses against the overall goals and policies of the state. In some cases these policies are clearly articulated and the process is consciously perceived as "planning," while in others it is not.

In Maine, for example, the statutory direction given to the Environmental Improvement Commission would also appear to preclude much balancing of conflicting goals. The statute directs the Board to insure maximum protection of the environment and does not provide any process by which countervailing development needs can be weighed. In practice, however, the Board utilizes a balancing process in deciding how far to press its jurisdiction.

Other statutes more explicitly instruct the administrator to consider a variety of goals. The Wisconsin Shorelands Act, although primarily oriented toward protecting the environmental values of the rivers and lakes, does recognize the need for some types of development. Similarly, the Massachusetts Zoning Appeals Act, although primarily oriented toward making land available for housing needs, also recognizes that it is important to protect health and safety and preserve open space.

Other statutes involve more sophisticated planning processes. In Vermont, although the present regulatory process is oriented primarily toward protection of environmental values, the planners are directed to prepare a plan that takes into consideration both environmental and socio-economic conditions. The Twin Cities Regional Council uses a comprehensive planning approach as a basis for the decisions assigned to it. Similarly, the Tahoe Regional Planning Agency and the Hackensack Meadowlands Development Commission are taking into consideration a wide variety of factors in preparing the plans on which their regulatory systems are based.

It seems clear that as state land regulatory systems evolve they will increasingly spawn better planning processes on which to base regulatory decisions. The Massachusetts Wetlands Act, for example, does not ask its administrators to balance the pros and cons of various uses of the wetlands. The legislature has presumably done this balancing itself and concluded that the goal of preserving the wetlands outweighs all other possible goals. Consequently, the administration of the Act can be said to involve a minimum of planning. But as it increasingly becomes recognized that other values are involved, it seems reasonable to assume that the state will institute a planning process that will take all values into consideration.

To see regulation as the predecessor of planning is not wholly logical. But Americans have rarely looked kindly on the idea of planning for its own sake, and have paid attention to planning only when it immediately affects decision-making. As a political matter probably the most feasible method of moving toward a well-planned system of state land use regulation is to begin with a regulatory system that concentrates on a few goals that are generally perceived as important, and then to gradually expand the system by adding more comprehensive planning elements, as is being done in Vermont. To insist that the planning precede the regulation is probably to sacrifice feasibility on the altar of logic.

If the land regulatory systems are to be assisted by competent land use planning it will require substantial redirection of current state planning efforts in many states. The Department of Housing and Urban Development has increasingly been directing the state's attention toward the management of state government programs, with the result that many states have been drifting away from the more comprehensive approach toward land use planning that was characteristic of the states in the 1930's. There is no reason why land use planning is inconsistent with budgetary and management planning, and if the state planning agencies are to perform a meaningful role in land use regulation, they must reassert their interest in comprehensive planning for land use. Unless the state planners divert at least a share of their attention toward land use issues they may find that other more specialized agencies will have taken over, and the opportunity for a comprehensive approach will have been lost.

5. Constitutional Limits on Regulation

One of the most important issues in any land regulatory system is the extent to which the use of land may be restricted without violating constitutional rights. Almost every state and local government that is trying to implement an environmentally-oriented land regulatory system finds itself plagued with constitutional doubts. The constitution prohibits the "taking" of property without payment of just compensation. Judicial interpretations of this clause have held that the regulation of property in a manner to severely limit its use may in some cases be interpreted as such a taking. These cases pose a constant problem to land use regulators.

Most land regulatory systems find a need to prevent all "use" of at least some portion of the land within their jurisdiction. Funds are not usually available to pay the owners of this land for the loss in speculative value to which they might claim to be entitled. The administrators therefore find themselves in the difficult position of either permitting uses that would be environmentally harmful or facing court challenges that may endanger the entire regulatory program.

This dilemma posed by the "taking" issue requires a creative legal response on the part of the regulatory agencies and their attorneys. A number of approaches are promising:

First, if one really studies the cases the law on this subject has by no means been as bad as most people seem to assume. The Supreme Court of the United States has frequently upheld regulatory systems that prevent any development of a man's land if the regulation is essential to promote the public health or safety, and the preservation of a livable environment and a desirable ecological balance is in the long run clearly essential to the health of the nation. "Brandeis briefs" and expert ecological testimony, when combined with a sophisticated analysis of existing case law, can provide sound constitutional arguments for the validity of many regulatory measures that might otherwise be thought so restrictive as to require compensation.

Second, draftsmen of regulations need to make a careful analysis of the types of activities that may be allowed to take place on land without destroying environmental values. Too often regulations have taken the form of blanket prohibitions when a variety of activities could be permitted on the land without detracting from the values that the regulations are designed to protect.

Third, further exploration is needed to provide a sound legal rationale for setting off benefits created by the regulatory program against the losses caused by restrictions. A regulatory program that prohibits the filling of low-lying land in a flood plain, for example, may reduce the value of the portion of a man's land on which filling is prohibited, but it may substantially increase the value of the higher land by reducing the threat of flooding. Mechanisms by which these benefits can be set off against any losses can be very helpful in reducing the necessity of paying compensation.

Fourth, where compensation must be paid, new legal methods of relating the amount of compensation more exactly to the losses suffered should be devised. The government should not be forced to purchase the entire land if some lesser remedy provides equitable compensation. Compensation through the purchase of development rights, a year-to-year-interest or some type of easement should be considered.

This chapter is not the place to discuss in detail the many ramifications of the constitutional issue, and the many interesting approaches to it being undertaken around the country. Those who create systems of land regulation based on modern ecological knowledge should be aware of the constitutional issue, but should not be so afraid of it that they ignore the approaches that are available for working creatively within the constitutional limits.

6. Choice of State Agency

The selection of the proper agency to exercise the state's role in land use regulation has not followed any uniform pattern. Three alternatives seem to be found in the existing legislation: line agencies of state government, independent state commissions, and state-created regional commissions.

Line agencies have been used primarily for systems of regulation that focus on a single purpose or a small number of purposes. Thus, both the Massachusetts Zoning Appeals Act, the Wisconsin Shoreland Protection program, and most wetlands acts are administered by line agencies. All of these programs have relatively specific goals that fall within the purview of an existing agency.

Where more comprehensive statewide land use regulation has been tried, independent state commissions have been chosen. Hawaii, Vermont and Maine have all used this model, and public attitudes in the three states would all seem to favor continuation of independent commissions for statewide land use regulation—existing state agencies are all thought to be too biased toward the existing programs they administer to do a fair job in balancing the full range of policies that go into these decisions. But independent commissions contribute to the fragmentation of executive authority at the state level.

The ideal approach from a textbook standpoint would be a new line agency directly under the governor, but in some states centralization of power in the governor is not popular. State planning agencies might serve a regulatory function, but in many states these agencies have paid little attention to land use matters.

Where the regulation is concentrated in a specific geographical area of the state, the states have generally chosen to set up independent commissions having a regional orientation. In some cases members of the commission are appointed by the governor. In other cases the local governments in the region exercise direct or indirect control in the selection of members of the commission. Some of the regional agencies have proven quite successful, but participation by the local governments in the selection of members seems likely to produce a strong pro-development bias because of the dependence of local governments on new development to produce tax revenues.

Selection of the appropriate agency to represent state or regional interests will undoubtedly vary with the specific conditions in each state at each particular time. It is hoped that the inter-agency bickering that accompanies so many programs of an interdisciplinary nature can be minimized.

5

Next Steps in Land Policy

Daniel R. Fusfeld

The status of land in the United States today is changing from private property to community resource. The change is seen in the legal status of land, in its treatment by administrative agencies at all levels of government, and in public attitudes. It is now generally recognized by almost everyone involved in decisions concerning land use and development that the old status of land, as private property pure and simple, is long gone. No longer can the private owner be said to be the sole determinant of the uses to which his land can be put. Population growth, greater affluence, and increased mobility have changed the relationship between land and community in the United States; and as those trends continue, so will the trend toward an increased public interest in land as a community resource.

At the same time, the public interest in land is not being well served. Our legal tradition is one of private property, which stresses the rights of ownership. This legal tradition is supported by an economic theory of resource use which shows that the "best" or "most economic" use of any natural resource, land included, results from its use in response to the acquisitive self-interest of the owner. And the economic theory is supported by business and commercial interests that seek potential profits from private land development in the old tradition. Finally, public agencies involved with land use policies are often allied with private economic interests that seek profit from the use and development of land. The law, economic ideologies, economic interests, and administrative agencies have all helped to keep land in its status as a commodity and have resisted the trend toward a public interest in land as a community resource.

It is true that the law itself is changing, as is the attitude of courts that interpret the law. And economic theory is starting to stress concepts like "externalities," meaning that owners of land can often shift some of the costs of particular land uses or development to other people; or conversely, that some types of land uses add to the benefits derived by people other than the owners. Administrative agencies, too, are under growing pressure from public opinion to give greater emphasis to the community interest in land use and development. Nevertheless, there is a lag of law, ideology, and administration behind the demand for a transition to a changed status of land that would place increased emphasis on land as a community natural resource.

Several specific proposals to change the status of land have been made in recent years. Generally, they center on organizational, legal, and administrative changes that would enable the public interest in land to achieve a greater impact on decisions concerning land use and development. I will examine these proposals shortly, but before I do, I would like to note one proposal that is noticeable because of its absence.

Public ownership of land, except for areas clearly and fully dedicated to public use, is not widely considered as an alternative to the present status of land as private property. This is due in part to some widely recognized desirable aspects of land as private property: the owner who directly uses his land has an interest in protecting and preserving the land and its value. For example, the same people who litter public parks and highways keep their own lawns spotless. And much public opposition to unwise commercial development of land comes from small homeowners whose interests would be adversely affected. If land is to be well used and protected, it would be well to encourage those private interests that benefit from using and protecting their own. Any comprehensive land policy should take this aspect of private property into account.

Furthermore, federal and state government land policies leave much to be desired. There is no unified and coherent land policy among the numerous federal agencies dealing with land. Private business interests often exert strong influence over public land use policies. And public agencies dealing with land are often old-fashioned, bureaucratic, and inept. It is not surprising, then, that public ownership of land can hardly be considered a panacea.

Rather than public ownership, there is a need for methods by which the public interest in land as a community resource might be extended and developed. For example, consider the possibilities of:

1. Development of a network of citizens' organizations to express the public interest in land.
2. Use of "community impact statements" in assessing the effects of land development projects.
3. An amendment to the federal constitution to give the status of land as a natural and community resource equal standing with its status as private property.
4. A federal Department of Land (or Land and Natural Resources).

There is clearly a need for a network of community organizations concerned with land as a community resource. Citizen groups of this sort are needed at three levels—local, state, and national—to correspond to the three levels of government at which decisions about land use and development are made. CLURE, Citizens for Land Use Research and Education, is such an organization, and there are some in other parts of the country.

CLURE was organized in 1972 by a group of citizens in the area northwest of Detroit, where the spread of urbanization, growth of shopping centers, and highway construction were changing the shape of the natural environment in ways that were highly profitable to real estate developers but not always in ways that developed humane values or protected the land as a community resource. CLURE's experience has shown that local interest in good land use policies is strong, that this interest can be mobilized, and that it can be effective in making community interests felt by policymakers at local, regional, and state levels.

Local citizen groups need support, however, in the form of information, communication with similar groups in other communities, and expert assistance in such widely diverse areas as cost-benefit evaluation of development projects, land policies, community organization, and development of leadership. There is clearly a need for regional and statewide organizations to provide these services and to deal with land policies and management at the level of state governments.

A second step toward more reasonable land policies would be legislation requiring community impact statements prior to administrative approval of land development projects. This proposal is modeled after the National Environmental Policy Act of 1969, which requires that a "detailed statement of environmental impacts" be prepared for every "major federal action significantly affecting the quality of the human environment." These statements are designed to provide information on unavoidable adverse effects, possible alternative actions, any irreversible commitments of resources, and the trade-offs between short-term and long-term effects. A number of states have enacted similar laws.

Something similar is necessary for land development projects, particularly at the state and local level. Any change in land use, and any land development project, will affect the local community for both good and ill. Yet all too often projects are approved by state and local government agencies with little or no study of the long-term effects on the social and economic life of the communities affected. In particular, adverse effects are often ignored, and little attention is given to costs indirectly imposed on people or community. Environmental impact statements, for the most part, give little attention to social and economic effects. Any private or public organization that proposes a land use or development project should be required to prepare a full community impact statement that carefully itemizes and describes the full benefits to be derived, both direct and indirect, the full direct and indirect costs, and the expected changes that will occur in the community in both the short and long run. Public agencies concerned with approval of land use and development projects will then have better information on which to base a decision. The general public will also be able to assess more fully the impact of the project on the community.

A third change is needed: the law must recognize the public interest in land as a natural and community resource as equal to that of private ownership in land as private property. As the public interest in land has grown over the last hundred years, the law has increasingly recognized modifications of the concept of private property in land, such as, for example, zoning regulations, national and state environmental legislation, and historic preservation laws. Nevertheless, the federal and state constitutions contain strong provisions protecting private ownership interests, and a large body of case law based on those constitutional provisions exists. In the federal Constitution, for example, the Fifth and Fourteenth Amendments prohibit both the federal and state governments from depriving anyone of life, liberty, or property without due process of law, and the Fifth Amendment requires just compensation for private property taken for public use. The law tends to view land as a commodity. Land can be broken up into units that the owner is free to use as he wishes, and the law allows owners to buy and sell land as a privately owned commodity.

As land begins to be viewed as a natural resource—as part of an integrated environmental system—and as a community resource—as part of the continuing life of an ongoing social system—its legal status as a commodity acts as a barrier to citizen efforts to protect the land and the natural environment and community of which land is a part. There is a clear need for a new legal status for land that will express its status as natural and community resource in addition to its status as private property.

A new legal status for land does not require that the constitutional protections of land as private property be removed, but rather that they be supplemented by similar protections for land as natural and community resource. A constitutional amendment to provide that protection might be based on the wording of the judicial decision in a recent Wisconsin case [*Just* v. *Marinette County*, 56 Wis. 2d 7, 201 N.W.2d 761 (1972)]:

> An owner of land has no absolute and unlimited right to change the essential natural character of his land so as to use it for a purpose for which it was unsuited in its natural state and which injures the rights of others.

This wording may not be appropriate for a constitutional amendment and might need to be modified. But it expresses the essential idea: protection of the land, and the community interest in land, requires that private owners not be allowed to change the land or its uses in any way they wish. Put more positively: the right of private owners to use their land must be consistent with the public interest in land.

Finally, a federal Department of Land, or Land and Natural Resources, is needed to bring together all federal programs and agencies related to land under a single administrative agency whose head would have cabinet rank. The federal government is the largest landowner in the country, holding some 760 million acres. Some 71 percent of this area is administered by the Department of the Interior, including the Bureau of Land Management (474 million acres), U.S. Fish and Wildlife Service (28 million acres), National Park Service (24 million acres), Bureau of Reclamation (8 million acres), and Bureau of Indian Affairs (5 million acres). But the U.S. Forest Service (187 million acres) is in the Department of Agriculture; the Department of Defense owns 27 million acres, including the land of the Corps of Engineers (7 million acres); and the Department of Energy holds 2 million acres.

Administrative and regulatory functions are also scattered. Soil conservation is in the Department of Agriculture; planning of urban land use is in the Department of Housing and Urban Development, which is also the home of the Office of Interstate Land Sales Registration; and highways and urban mass transportation are in the Department of Transportation. Furthermore, all the federal departments concerned with land use have major responsibilities elsewhere. There is no central place in the federal government where land policies are concentrated and which deal primarily with land. The Department of the Interior is the department in which land as such is a major responsibility, but even that department has other major responsibilities. Establishment of a Department of Land, or Land and Natural Resources, could bring all or most of these scattered functions under a single agency, bringing greater coherence to the federal government's policies with respect to land.

As we look ahead to the year 2000 and beyond, we can expect greater public interest in land and its uses, if only because land is a limited resource while population is growing and economic activity is expanding. As land use becomes more intensive and land becomes scarcer relative to other resources, its status is changing. We are seeing in our lifetime a shift away from land as solely a privately owned commodity to land as a natural and community resource. As that trend develops, we can work toward other changes as well, such as those suggested above.

**Part III
Images of Land**

6

The Open City: Potentials in Urban Space

William H. Whyte

What I am going to present is an account of a six year study of how people use—or don't use—the spaces of the center city. I will try to make it sound quite sequential and logical, just as I have when applying for foundation grants to support the study. In fact, however, the study came about rather haphazardly. I thought it would be interesting to watch people on the streets, and in 1970 I had an opportunity to enlist some students as observers. We started looking at playgrounds and found, to our surprise, that the big problem was not overuse, but underuse. When we started studying people in the center, we found the same was true there.

At about this time the research committee of the National Geographic Society offered a generous grant. They thought it would be novel if the observational techniques so long and well used for the study of far-off peoples were applied to the study of people in the city. Our project, in sum, was to be an expedition. (Quite literally, too; I had to sign papers as expedition leader that all the researchers were properly prepared, inoculated, and such.) We would use a variety of techniques—including questionnaires and interviews. But our main emphasis was on direct observation.

Before getting on with our expedition, let me say a few words on observation. In the social sciences it has sunk to a very low position. Look in the index of textbooks and you are apt to see something like "observation; defects of"; "problem of participant observer bias." It is treated as the most rudimentary, unsophisticated of techniques, and it is taught very briefly—usually in freshman survey courses, preliminary to the more advanced, highly quantitative techniques. Few people have been trained in observation, and it is especially wanted in the design and planning professions. One would assume architects and planners would be eager to have a look at how their buildings and plans work out. Not so. Read the architectural journals and you will note that when new buildings are discussed, function is taken almost as axiomatic. The building may not even be up yet, but the text will discuss how well the architect has massed the inner courtyard space, how well it draws people from the periphery, and so on. Whether it will in fact do so is a question, but years can go by before anyone asks it by looking.

New York's new plazas were cases in point. Since 1961 the city had been allowing builders to add additional floors over and above zoning limits if they would provide plazas at the base. This incentive zoning was very successful in one respect: every builder took advantage of it, and a great deal of very expensive open space was provided for people.

Unfortunately, not many people used the plazas. At lunch hour, we found, the number of people sitting on plazas averaged four per thousand square feet of open space. This was an appalling underuse of space for so high density an area. We put the matter to the City Planning Commission. We would study the plazas to determine the principal denominators of the successful ones and of the unsuccessful ones and propose guidelines for future design. The Planning Commission said that if we could buttress the recommendations with solid documentation it would use them as the basis for a new zoning code.

We set to work. First we studied the social life of the spaces—in all, sixteen plazas and three small parks. In good weather and bad weather, at peak and off-peak hours, we tracked the flow of people, where they sat, how long, what they did. We interviewed people to find where they came from, where they worked, how frequently they used the plaza. On any one plaza, we found, patterns of use were very consistent. Some spots are heavily favored, others not, and though the absolute number of people using the plaza may vary considerably, the relative distribution from sector to sector remains quite uniform. Men tend to the front locations, women to the rear. The most favored spots for both are those that afford a full view of the action up front, but that are also somewhat protected—such as a slightly recessed area under a canopy of leaves. The way men stand and talk—"schmoozing" in New York parlance—is also quite regular. Not often will a group of men stay long in the middle of a large space. They gravitate to edges and objects. They are strongly attracted by pillars and flagpoles, obeying a primeval instinct, perhaps, to have something solid at their backs. Whatever the reason, they like defined places. You will see them in a straight line parallel to and just inside a portico; along the curb of a sidewalk, facing inward.

The most important space for a plaza is not on the plaza. It is the street corner alongside. Watch the activity on one closely and you will note that much of it is satellite to that of the plaza. This is particularly the case when a food vendor is to be found there. He will generate traffic between the corner and the plaza, and this traffic will in turn attract additional people. Activity begets activity.

Street corner behavior provides a fascinating documentation. In one of our early studies, we had focused our time-lapse cameras on a number of corners to test several hypotheses. One was that people who encountered each other, or paused to talk, would move out of the pedestrian traffic stream. They didn't. Quite the contrary, they stayed there or moved into it, and the longer the conversation, the more apt it was to be right in the middle. Whatever they may say, people are attracted to other people.

This shows very clearly in comparisons of plaza usage. The most heavily used plazas are the most sociable. They have a higher than average proportion of people in twos and threes. They also have a higher proportion of females, and of females in pairs. Loners favor the most heavily used places and are usually to be spotted on the most conspicuous spots on them. Not so paradoxically, the sociable plazas also attract, in absolute numbers, more singles than do other plazas. If one is going to be the amused spectator, a place with the passing parade is best.

Let me jump ahead of our story a moment. The research described in this report was done in 1972 and 1973 and was concentrated largely in New York City. Our hypothesis was that we were essentially studying human beings and that the patterns we discerned in New York would be similar to those in other locations. Since then we have made comparison studies in other cities and have found our hypothesis borne out. The principal variable is size of city. In smaller cities, densities tend to be considerably lower, pedestrians move at a slower pace, and there is less of the social activity characteristic of high traffic areas. In most other respects, pedestrian patterns are similar.

But the greatest similarities are to be found in very large metropolitan centers; the people in them tend to behave more like their counterparts in other metropolitan centers, whatever the country, than their fellow nationals in smaller cities. Tokyo, for example: a study we made in 1977 revealed that the pedestrian's proclivity for stopping and talking in the middle of department store doorways, busy corners, and the like is just as strong as in New York. Sitting patterns in parks and plazas are very much the same. Similarly, schmoozing patterns in Milan's Gallenia are remarkably like those in New York's garment center. A modest conclusion is that given the basic elements of a center city—such as high pedestrian volumes and concentration and mixture of activities—people in one place tend to act very much like people in another.

Back in 1973, however, our universe was New York City and we had to come up with some specific recommendations. What, in sum, distinguished the successful plazas from the unsuccessful? To determine the key physical variables, we measured the spaces this way and that, tracked the sun angles, pedestrian flows, nearness to mass transit, enclosure afforded by adjacent buildings. As we piled up the data, overlay by overlay, one conclusion became clearer and clearer: *People tend to sit most where there are places to sit*. This may seem an unusually obvious point to make, but it was certainly not clear at the time to many architects and planners, a number of whom believed that the aesthetics of design was what most attracted people. Some still do.

Other factors are indeed important, but the key variable is "sittability." In some cases it is inadvertent: the plaza of the Seagram Building, one of the best of all, was not intended as a sitting place. Because the architects didn't gussy up the ledges with railings or shrubbery, however, it was in fact sittable and so people found it. The element most important was choice: generous-sized benches and long ledges let people sort themselves out. In all too many cases, however, benches are short, mean little affairs placed in isolation from one another. Their function is to punctuate architectural photographs.

Obviously, a major recommendation was going to be the provision of plenty of sitting space. But this conjured up another question. How much was too much? How many people were too many? If the new zoning promised to attract many more people to a space, might not the numbers crowd out the very amenity being sought? The Planning Commission hoped our research could give some answers.

To get at the question of effective capacity, we did a series of close-up studies of the most used places on the most used plazas. From place to place peak usage was fairly similar. Per one hundred feet of linear sitting space the average number at any time during the lunch period would be about twenty-eight; the maximum, forty. This yields a rough rule of thumb for architects; to determine the effective capacity of a prime sitting area, divide the number of feet by three.

This is not physical capacity. The kind of use being studied is voluntary use. Were choice more forced—as on a bus, for example—capacity would be somewhere around sixty-six people per one hundred feet. That it is considerably less in free choice situations is due to many factors. One is supply. Many people must pass by a place to provide the fraction who will stop and sit. (In his studies of Copenhagen, Jan Gehl has found a consistent ratio between the number of people walking on the city's main pedestrian way and the number of people sitting on its benches.)

But the main determinant of capacity is human instinct. This was best demonstrated by our study of the north front ledge at Seagram's. Through time-lapse photography we recorded a typical day in the life of the ledge and charted it minute by minute from 9 a.m. until 6 p.m. On a long chart that looks very much like a piano player roll, we recorded each sitter, where he sat, and for how long. There was much turnover of people, but during the peak hours the overall number remained quite steady, running between eighteen and twenty-one people.

Good spacing, one might surmise. To a point, yes, but the amount of available space doesn't really explain the consistency. At no time were the people evenly spaced out over the ledge like starlings on a phone wire. In some spots people would be bunched closely together; in others there would be enough empty space for eight or ten more people. Some other factor seems to be at work. It is as if people had some visceral sense of what is the norm for a place and were cooperating to maintain it that way, obligingly leaving or sitting down to keep the density within range. There is no such compact, of course, but the effect is the same and the patterns are similar in other high-use places. Happenstance is at work too—the four friends who squeeze into space left by three, the chance arrival of three loners—but over the long run, happenstance is quite regular too.

Usage, in sum, tends to be self-leveling. There are exceptions—even the most delightful parks, such as Paley and Greenacre, sometimes get a bit too busy. At their most pleasant, however, they have an astonishingly high density—forty-five to sixty people per thousand square feet. The carrying capacity of a well-planned space is much greater than most assume. The prerequisites, furthermore, are a set of basics, and they do not require elaborate expense or design acrobatics.

The proposed guidelines for plazas and similar urban spaces required that they:

1. Be sittable. Minimum requirement is one linear foot of sitting space for every thirty square feet of open space. Maximize sittability of ledges and walls; make them low and, where possible, two backsides deep. Extra incentive for provision of movable chairs.
2. Maintain a close relationship to the street; be no more than three feet above or below sidewalk grade. Except for a compelling reason, no sunken plazas.
3. Provide food, e.g., open air cafés, food kiosks, pass-through windows for snack bars.
4. Provide more trees. In addition to more along the sidewalk, more should be planted within the space—where possible, in groves.
5. Provide for the needs of the handicapped; clear walkways, ramps, easy steps—which is to say, easier access and movement for all.
6. Performance bond to be posted by developer to ensure proper provision and maintenance of facilities.

It seemed like being for motherhood and the flag, and we were glad the work was done, for we had other research to do. But the proposals stirred a surprising amount of controversy, and we spent a fair amount of time presenting our findings to planning boards, officials, civic groups, and developers. The mills ground slowly, but at length, in May 1975, the zoning was finally enacted by the City's Board of Estimate.

The results have been encouraging. Two years later a companion measure was enacted for residential buildings, in effect mandating small neighborhood parks in exchange for extra floor space. A number of new office building plazas have already been designed to meet the guidelines. More important, developers have been stimulated to redo existing plazas and have been adding such previously unpermitted uses as open air cafés. Many more benches have been provided, on streets as well as on plazas. In their own way, other cities have been rediscovering the benefits of such basic amenities. We like to think our expedition to the center did find something of value—and not least, a place to sit.

In the process, I like to believe, we learned some larger lessons about the city and I will conclude by submitting a set of propositions.

1. The overcrowded city is a myth. The problem with most center cities is not that they have too many people, but that they have too little.
2. A high concentration of people in a compact space is what makes a center city work.
3. Because of, not despite, this concentration there is proportionately more social interaction in the center city than in suburban centers.
4. What draws people most is other people. They may not recognize this themselves; what people say they do, however, and what they actually do, can be quite different. As we saw in the film sequences of street corner conversations, people show a very definite tendency to seek out the places where the most people are.
5. There is a sort of critical mass that is needed to make an urban place work. Just how this can be brought off no one can say for sure, but I suspect that the margin between failure and success in downtown revitalization can be a very narrow one. When you look at some of the malls that have been tried out in medium size and smaller cities you get a feeling that they have spread over eight or ten blocks what should have been concentrated into two or three. The tendency seems to be too much toward dispersion.
6. Without a critical mass, amenities and good design can be futile. They can also make the critical difference, however.
7. One big missing element in our civic planning machinery is any systematized effort at evaluating the impact of physical changes. This requires no elaborate bureaucratic process. Essentially, what is needed is somebody whose job it is to check plans and designs out there—where the reality is.
8. Simple observation will reveal that the physical amenities people like the most are simple and basic: a place to sit, for example, some trees, water.
9. Congestion is not a result of concentration and high density. It is a result of bad planning. It is quite possible to have a very high density area that feels quite pleasant and uncrowded.
10. For people, the sense of congestion and overcrowding is caused disproportionately by particular choke points—a narrow subway stair; a sidewalk that is blocked by a cluster of poles, wastebaskets, newsstands, and what not.

11. In free choice situations—such as sitting on benches—capacity is self-leveling. People have an inherent sense of what is comfortable for a given spot and usage tends to follow a norm.
12. The best used places often seem the most uncrowded, even though the density is quite high.

There is reason for optimism. One by one, the kind of particulars we have been discussing may seem marginal; together, however, they can make a whale of a difference. Go past a plaza or city square that really works, one where people are laughing and joking, schmoozing, eating, or reading, or just snoozing in the sun or peacefully observing the human comedy. This has everything to do with the ancient function of the city, the quality of its life, and it is achievable.

If we look.

7 The World as a Park

Fred P. Bosselman

This year the Cubs opened at home, so my son and I went to the ball park. Soon thereafter I had occasion to visit a client's office in an industrial park. And then I drove alongside a national park in southern Florida.

What kind of a word is "park" that it can encompass such diverse places as Wrigley Field, Hackensack, and the Everglades? My legal education taught me to deride words so imprecise—the product of sloppy draftsmen. Yet the fact that so many places are called parks may reflect something more important than precision. It may indicate a need to think of places as somehow special, a need I cannot define with legal precision but can only suggest by inference.

The Specialness of Places

I believe that "special" places tend to be developed in ways that are more compatible with the environment than places that are thought of as just ordinary.

Most people would agree that development should be compatible with the surrounding environment. That is, the development should be undertaken in a manner that will enhance or at least maintain, rather than detract from, the qualities that make a place attractive. "Compatible development" is a goal generally agreed upon, even among people who might disagree strongly on how to define it.

In the course of my work, I have often observed that some places grow and develop in a way that is quite compatible with the existing environment, while other places get messed up.

To illustrate my point, let me offer a series of examples. In each of the following pairs the one in the first column is a place that is generally regarded as somehow special. The one in the second column is a place that is generally regarded as just another place. In my opinion, development in the places in the first column tends to be more compatible with the environment than in the places in the second column.

Reston	Sun City
Back Bay	Brookline
San Francisco	San José

Hilton Head	Myrtle Beach
The French Quarter	Downtown New Orleans
Hudson River Valley	Charles River Valley
Greenwich Village	The West Side
Key West	Grand Bahama
Santa Fé	Phoenix
Cape Cod	The Poconos
Chadron, Nebraska	Ogallala, Nebraska

I have used only North American examples in this list, but I could give similar examples from many other countries. I hasten to add that this is a list based on my personal, subjective opinions.

While recognizing that "specialness" is only one of many complex factors, I would like to offer the following proposition for further discussion: *Development tends to be more compatible with the environment in places that are generally regarded as somehow special.*

The terms of that proposition are deliberately vague because the proposition is one that does not lend itself to precision. The most vague term of all is "somehow special." A special place is perceived as having a unique combination of desirable qualities that make this place different from places in general. These qualities might be found in either the natural or the built environment and might include historical or religious associations having no outward physical manifestations. They must, however, be associated with the land or its fixtures, not with purely portable characteristics. (The encampment of the Ringling Brothers' Circus gives a place a very special quality, but the quality disappears when the circus disappears.) Also, the quality must be one that is perceived as desirable. The strip mines of central Florida have certain unique qualities but do not qualify as "somehow special."

It was in the 1950s that books such as Lynch's *The Image of the City* and Whyte's *The Organization Man* spurred new interest in studying the ways we relate to the environment that surrounds us. It is not my purpose to analyze the extensive writings that have appeared since that time. Rather, let me grossly oversimplify by saying that this research indicates that some places tend to be generally regarded as having special attributes, while other areas are not generally regarded as being places at all—that is, people do not easily identify them or connect them with any particular characteristics. It is when people identify an area as having special and desirable qualities that development tends to be more compatible with the environment than in places that are "no place."

If you will accept this hypothesis as a working tool from which this chapter begins, a second proposition then is derived from the first one: *We can get better development by emphasizing the special qualities of more places.*

An attitude of specialness is not derived from inherent qualities of a place over which we have no control. The attitude of specialness can be created in two ways: first, by learning more about the desirability of existing qualities of an area, and, second, by creating new qualities of a desirable nature.

I was thinking about the first proposition while driving across the Florida Everglades recently. These lands were, until quite recently, called "swamp and overflow lands." It was considerd socially productive to fill these lands so that they could be used for some worthwhile purpose.

Today our attitudes have changed completely. We now perceive such desirable qualities in the Everglades that we are buying large tracts of adjoining land to protect them. The qualities were there all along, but only recently did they gain public recognition.

The same thing can happen to our perception of the qualities of a neighborhood or a building. When I was growing up in Chicago, Louis Sullivan buildings were commonplace. When I first heard that the Carson, Pirie & Scott store was an architectural landmark, I, and many other people who had grown up in Chicago, found this hard to believe. To us it was just an ordinary building. As I grew older I came to understand the unique qualities that make the building important (though I may never outgrow my initial perception of the building as just another department store).

These are only two of many examples of changing attitudes that have made us realize the specialness of places that once seemed commonplace. Moreover, numerous examples could be cited of urban development that has created a uniquely desirable environment. Reston and Hilton Head were mentioned earlier, and hundreds of examples on a smaller scale could be given. The neighborhood preservation movement has concentrated much of its attention on defining the special qualities of particular neighborhoods. These trends are cause for optimism, but there is another trend—less obvious perhaps, but quite disturbing—towards *deemphasizing* the specialness of places.

"Deplacement"

When society makes a human individual seem more like a number than a person, we describe this process as "dehumanizing." I am aware of no comparable term to describe the process of deemphasizing the special qualities of a place, so please forgive my invention of a word: "deplacement."

The process of "deplacing" land is nothing new. A typical motive was to make the land a more valuable commodity by emphasizing its common qualities rather than its unique ones. Thus the Northwest Ordinance, the gridiron plan town, and the Euclidian zoning ordinance all were techniques designed to emphasize lands' common qualities, making it easier to determine an appropriate price for a piece of land by comparing its qualities with the qualities of other land.

Today, however, the pressures to "deplace" land come more frequently from the same sources that are threatening to dehumanize us: namely, the bureaucratic procedures necessary to deal with a growing population and a growing list of social goals.

Consider a few examples. The Washington bureaucracy has long advocated that the nation be divided up into "substate districts" for the purpose of collecting data and administering state and federal programs. Moreover, each such district is to have a similarly organized planning agency which would prepare plans for its region just like the plans prepared for each other region, and would exert similar powers to review and comment upon the expenditure of federal funds in the region. Existing legislation has moved us a long way toward that goal, and a bill sponsored by Congressman Thomas Ashley in 1977 would make the system even more uniform.

The emphasis on obtaining uniformity among regions pushes each region to look as much like every other region as possible. If our section 208 plan resembles every other section 208 plan it will receive approval more quickly than if it raises novel issues. Quick approval means fewer budgetary problems and a smoother running operation.[1]

But it is impossible to use uniform regions for all purposes without distorting the value of much of the work that is done. Some types of issues can only be sensibly considered in terms of, for example, a watershed. For many such issues, checkerboard squares simply are unworkable.

What percentage of the public can correctly identify the boundaries of the regional planning agency exercising jurisdiction over their home? Many of the substate districts are abstract aggregations of lands put together for statistical purposes, not a "place" with which anyone identifies.

In fact, many of the best regional planning agencies are those created under special legislation that established regional boundary lines defining a place people think of as special, rather than the arbitrary lines established by federal regulations. I think of Tahoe, the Adirondacks, San Francisco Bay, the Hackensack Meadowlands, and the California Coast. Many of these agencies have had difficulty obtaining federal funds because they were "different."

I believe the attempt to divide us into tidy substate districts has had the unfortunate consequence of deemphasizing the qualities that make places special and emphasizing the qualities that make places alike. John Betjeman summarized this nicely some years ago in a poem about British planning. "The planners will soon have us looking," he said, "as uniform and tasty as our cooking."

Another example of the deplacement process is found in a recent decision of the United States Supreme Court—*United Jewish Organizations of Williamsburgh, Inc.* v. *Carey*, 97 S. Ct. 996—decided March 1, 1977. A group of Hasidic Jews lived in a very cohesive Brooklyn neighborhood. A congressional redistricting divided the neighborhood in half so that each half became a minority in a district dominated by other ethnic majorities. The Hasidim contested the redistricting, alleging that if they had all been placed in one district they would have been able to obtain more significant political representation. The court rejected this challenge. Under the principle of one-man-one-vote, the court ruled, the legislature need not give special consideration to historic associations with particular places.

Recently, Martha's Vineyard has also attracted attention to its battle to retain representation in the Massachusetts legislature. They too are without success, at least to date.

Must the one-man-one-vote rule mean that representation is no longer given to places, only to abstract collections of people? Couldn't we select representatives based on traditional boundaries of places and then weight their votes according to the population of the place? No doubt this method creates complications, but I think it is worth more attention than it has received.

As a third example, consider the Clean Air Act. In 1970 the Congress determined that there should be national ambient air quality standards that establish a uniform level of air quality throughout the nation. The basic purpose of uniform national standards is to ensure that states which are willing to put up with lower air quality are not able to use their tolerance to lure industry away from states with higher standards.

At the time this legislation was being debated, attention was naturally focused on the idea of establishing uniformly *good* air quality throughout the nation. Only later, however, was it realized that in places where existing air quality is significantly cleaner than national standards these standards might be viewed as permitting uniformly *bad* air quality throughout the nation. This has led to the national debate over whether air quality in such "pristine" areas should be allowed to significantly deteriorate—a debate that at this writing Congress is still trying to resolve.

Perhaps we need to reexamine the basic question of whether the air should be uniform in quality throughout the country. In Vail, Colorado, I recently learned that a violation of air quality standards occurs on calm winter mornings because of the smoke from wood-burning fireplaces. Need we really deodorize our air so thoroughly that skiers can no longer relax be-

fore an open fire and rise to the pungent mixture of wood smoke and pine? I
am reminded of what Gertrude Stein once said:

> After all anybody is as their land and air is. Anybody is as the sky is low or
> high, the air heavy or clear and anybody is as there is wind or no wind
> there.[2]

I want to make it clear that I am not personally opposed to regional
planning, to the principle of one-man-one-vote, or to national ambient air
quality standards. These are important goals, and programs designed to
achieve them should be supported. I suspect, however, that little attention
has been paid to these programs' side effect in detracting from the special
sense of place that I believe is so important to a community. I think it likely
that programs to achieve these goals could be devised in ways that would
minimize this side effect.

To summarize, therefore, I believe that there is value in emphasizing the
special qualities of places, because public awareness of these special
qualities fosters compatible development. Government programs should be
encouraged to emphasize the special qualities of places rather than uniform
characteristics.

Parks as Special Places

Some government programs do emphasize the unique and special qualities
of places. In that category I would put most government programs dealing
with parks.

The word "park" has many meanings, as has been pointed out. Most
usages of the term carry the connotation of a place having specially
desirable qualities. Because of this emphasis on the special qualities of
places that qualify them to be parks, our national parks have been created
one by one rather than through the use of abstract criteria. Thus, for example, we have no national legislation declaring that any place shall be a national park if it contains more than fifty-six species of vertebrates and an
average grade of at least 20 percent, etc.

The national parks have been remarkably free from deplacement. In his
survey a decade ago, Sir Frank Fraser Darling emphasized the need for in-
dividualistic treatment of each national park. We must ask "What is *this*
national park for?" he said. The process "calls for individual consideration
of every situation where development is contemplated."[3]

If there is any volume of the code of federal regulations that might be
called refreshing to read, it is the volume dealing with the National Park
Service. It is refreshing because it is so thin—only some thirty pages of regu-

lations applicable to national parks as a whole. The unique qualities of each individual national park have largely frustrated the bureaucrats' congenital tendency to make everything "uniform and tasty."

The great city parks have also attained that status because they have special qualities—qualities that could not have been achieved if the land had been selected at random. Sometimes these qualities are inherent in the physical characteristics of the land itself. Flagstaff Mountain Park in Boulder, Colorado, comes to mind. So do Rock Creek Park and Griffith Park. Other parks attain their special qualities through the interrelationship between their natural characteristics and the characteristics of the built environment that surrounds them. Central Park, Grant Park, and Golden Gate Park might be good examples. Finally, the other urban parks attain their special qualities by serving as front yards for works of beauty created by man. The Mall in Washington and Balboa Park in San Diego come to mind.

This emphasis on the special qualities of parks has served their cause well. The public awareness of the special qualities of parks has meant that public attention is focused on decisions relating to development within parks. The public is aware that the special qualities of the park can be maintained only through a maintenance of a balance between the parks' two main functions: preservation and recreation. Almost any decision to develop (or not to develop) park land will arouse comment from groups who believe the decision properly or improperly affects the balance.

For example, the Chicago Park District has been trying for over fifteen years to find a location and design for a new bandshell in Grant Park that will meet the approval of citizen watchdog organizations, musicians, and music lovers. Or consider the extent of debate over the type of development to be permitted in the Boundary Waters Canoe Area—or how many cars should be allowed to drive on the beach at Fire Island.

Because the public is aware that these parks are special places having unique qualities, the public has taken a great interest in decisions regarding the development of these places. The result has been the achievement of a high standard of compatibility between development and the environment in parks. Of course, many people believe that an even higher standard of compatibility could be and should be maintained, and in some cases they may be correct. But when the compatibility of development with the environment in parks is compared to the compatibility of development with the land elsewhere, most would agree that the standard of compatibility in parks is much higher than in the world at large.

But parks are also sometimes affected by "deplacement." In the early days of the "parks movement," city parks were thought of as fringe benefits to the labor force. City dwellers were entitled to a week's vacation, free smallpox vaccination, and eighteen square yards of green turf. The goal was "a grand park within the reach of every citizen," and access to nature was a way of saving immigrants from temptations.[4]

Today the same tendency is found in regulations requiring developers to dedicate 5 or 10 percent of their land for parks. The law doesn't care which 5 percent is dedicated. What is called for is a statistical abstraction rather than a special place.

Parks of this type have often failed to produce the benefits sought by their promoters because they have no special qualities that make them attractive. At most they provide a welcome break in a steady pattern of urbanization.

We should be concerned about the deplacement of parks. But we should also apply the lessons of the successful parks in a broader context.

Expanding on the Park State of Mind

Because the concept of parks has been successful in achieving compatibility of development with the environment, would it be possible to expand the concept of parks so that more land could achieve the same degree of compatibility?

Of course, we could merely add to the park system by the public purchase of large quantities of additional land. Doubtless there are some places where such acquisition would be desirable, but I question whether land acquisition alone can ever achieve a high degree of compatibility for the world at large. In the first place, the amount of funds available for public land acquisition is unlikely to be enough to acquire more than a small fraction of the world's land resources, and thus this technique would be successful in dealing with only a small part of the problem.

Moreover, public land acquisition by itself does not guarantee that development of that land will be compatible with the environment. One need only observe the operations of our Bureau of Land Management to be fully aware of that proposition.[5] In fact, the difference between the national parks and the great expanses of federal domain managed by the Bureau of Land Management exemplifies the proposition with which this chapter began. The national parks, being regarded as somehow special, have been developed with much more sophistication than the leftover lands managed by the BLM, which are, almost by definition, characterized as the lands having insufficient special qualities to be put into any of the other boxes.

If land is acquired by the public merely because it is there, not because it has any special qualities, it may suffer a similar fate. The important factor, therefore, is not the acquisition of land but the creation of a public consciousness of the special qualities of land. Once such a public consciousness is created, then acquisition of the land may be desirable—but on the other hand it may not. For the public consciousness of the area's special qualities may achieve a compatibility between development and the environment without the need for acquisition of the land. This proposition can be illustrated with a number of examples.

First, consider the Adirondack Park, one of the few American examples of a large park containing a high proportion of private land. The public recognition of the uniqueness of this area stimulated the creation of the Adirondack Park Agency. That agency has used land use controls to achieve a degree of compatibility with the environment that, if not perfect, is high by standards of the state at large. Efforts are now being made to undertake similar programs in other places, such as the Santa Monica Mountains, the Catskills, and Martha's Vineyard.

Parks made up primarily of private land are common in Europe and Japan. John Dower, commonly called the father of the English National Parks argued that it would be a waste of public money to acquire land within the national parks, when the same goals could be achieved through planning and economic incentives.[6]

Places such as Adirondack Park and the Santa Monica Mountains require only a minimal stretching of the concept of park to be easily understood. The concept is capable of being stretched much further, however. As the next step, consider the various "critical areas" being designated under various state laws. For example, the Florida Keys, the Big Cypress, and the Green Swamp have been declared critical areas by the state of Florida. Planning, regulation, and incentives are being used to achieve compatible development in these areas.

Consider also the various historic and special districts created by local governments throughout the nation. If we can call the Adirondacks a park, we can call Beacon Hill a park—and Old San Diego, and German Village in Columbus, Ohio, and New Orleans' French Quarter.

Even entire communities have very special qualities and people who recognize the importance of maintaining those qualities. Sanibel, Florida, and Vail, Colorado, are places in which I have recently observed that phenomenon.

Finally, many "parks" are achieved primarily, if not completely, through the use of private means. I believe Walt Disney World, Historic Williamsburg, and Hilton Head are entitled to the status of a park under my definition.

Many other ways might be found to emphasize the special qualities of places and create the public awareness necessary to ensure that these qualities are maintained. For example, the English have designated many of their most picturesque farming areas as national parks. In the United States we have achieved little progress in saving a share of our rural heritage for future generations.

Additionally, many countries are far ahead of us in designating urban neighborhoods as conservation areas or otherwise seeking to maintain their special qualities. Nevertheless, I am optimistic that the growing tendency toward recognizing the specialness of places will to some degree counteract the equally obvious trend toward "deplacement."

Efforts to emphasize the special qualities of places should be encouraged. By citing these various examples I hope to emphasize the common thread that runs through them and to encourage others to apply similar techniques to additional areas, or to devise new techniques to deal with the special qualities of new places. But I doubt the wisdom of any new legislation devising some uniform system for recognizing the special qualities of places. Almost by definition such a program would have a "deplacing" influence.

It may be argued that emphasis on the uniqueness of particular places has undemocratic overtones. If people recognize that places have special qualities, will they conclude that the residents of those places also have special qualities and should therefore have special privileges? Does the idea that one place is special carry with it a stigma that all other places are of secondary value?

From observation, I have concluded that this is not the case. People who have become aware of the special qualities of a particular place tend to broaden their consciousness of the special qualities of land in general. Those who have recognized that their neighborhood has an individual character tend to see special qualities in other neighborhoods that they might not have perceived before. They may begin to look upon a larger community as a special place.

And people who take an interest in the special qualities of their community, in my experience, tend to take more concern in the qualities of their region and state and even of their nation.

The recognition that areas have special qualities does not encourage petty factionalism or a chauvinistic sense of superiority. Rather, it is a recognition that *land* has special qualities. Once that fact is recognized, similar qualities are seen in other areas as well.

Barbara Ward has phrased it eloquently. "We can hope to survive in all our prized diversity [only if] we can achieve an ultimate loyalty to our single, beautiful and vulnerable planet Earth," and we must achieve this "enlargement of allegiance" without wiping out our respect for the smaller places we can more easily comprehend. It is this respect, in fact, that moves us toward a broader allegiance. In this way we take the first step toward the recognition that the whole world is a park.

Notes

1. Incidentally, the uniformity of requirements is often demanded more by the regional planners who want the security of strict guidelines than by

the federal agencies who are establishing the requirements. The history of HUD's attempt to set guidelines for land use plans is a history of HUD's attempts to encourage innovation being defeated by local and regional demands for greater specificity and uniformity.

2. Gertrude Stein. *What Are Masterpieces?* Los Angeles: The Conference Press, 1940, pp. 61-62.

3. Sir Frank Fraser Darling, and Noel D. Eichhorn, *Man and Nature in the National Parks.* Washington, D.C.: The Conservation Foundation, 1967, p. 20.

4. August Heckscher, *Open Spaces.* New York: Harper and Row, 1977, p. 164.

5. In addition, the efforts of socialist countries to manage their land resources provide convincing evidence that public ownership does not necessarily produce development that is more environmentally compatible.

6. It should be noted that the British try to retain traditional agriculture and other economically productive uses within the parks. If a tract of land was required for the sole purpose of free public recreation, the British government would acquire the land, just as the American government would.

8

Preservation Policy and Personal Perception: A 200-Million-Acre Misunderstanding

Charles E. Little

In the spring of 1972, a consultant in landscape preservation was invited to a New England town undergoing extraordinary growth. The consultant was taken on a tour of the town. He was shown the village green and the Revolutionary houses. He was asked to climb to the top of a drumlin to view a lush valley sprinkled with white farmhouses and laced with stone fences. He was driven to countryroad vistas of apple trees in bloom and soft meadowlands. At the end of the day, the consultant sat on his host's deck overlooking a woodland and a dramatic ridgeline of greening hills and reflected on what a fine place this town would be to live in.

The following morning he had to get to work to earn his consulting fee. He met with conservation commissioners and with planners, and he discussed with them planned unit development, municipal costs and taxes, hydrological problems, recreational needs, and government grant programs. At length, a map was unfurled, a map being the sine qua non of discussions like these. It was an open-space preservation map said to represent one of the most ambitious plans in the whole state. The consultant took a long look at the massive areas colored in various shades of green, but he was at a loss to be very helpful. In spite of his lengthy tour the day before, only in one or two instances had he been shown the land that was proposed for preservation.

What this hardly unique experience suggested to the consultant was that there must be two sets of values: one, a mapped set of landscape-preservation values capable of being rationalized as public policy; the other, which he had been instructed in the day before, landscape-preservation values associated with actual personal perception. Only in a very minor way did they overlap. The *place* and the *plan* were essentially two different things.

Under ordinary circumstances, this gulf might not be very important, for the political processes characterized by town meetings, boards, and commissions made up of local residents, the effective political clout of civic and neighborhood organizations, might tend in time to coalesce the two sets of landscape values into one transcendent plan—a proper synthesis.

The trouble is, given the current disenchantment with local land-use control in favor of returning regulatory powers to the states, that these ordinary circumstances of local landscape dialectics may be on the way to oblivion. If, as is said, some 200 million acres of land will be urbanized in the period remaining to us in this century (Reilly, 1973), it is perhaps of more than routine importance to landscape planners and aestheticians to recognize how seriously we have been co-opted by "scientism" and the inhumane quantifications that can produce a landscape preservation plan so at variance with the realities of ordinary perception. For as the decision-making process is removed further and further from the people—as would be the case if municipal control is seriously weakened by state-level regulations—then the landscape "expert" gains power. Given the current level of ignorance of those of us who pose as experts, the results could be disastrous.

Here is some of the background. Since the emergence of environmental quality as a national goal, air and water quality have been addressed by government, industry, and public-interest organizations with a relatively high level of conceptual consistency. New quantitative measurements of pollution, based principally on public health, have provided a foundation for methodologies that can be agreed upon sufficiently to sustain rational debate. Air and water quality can be measured on the basis of purity. Total purity is the ideal, unachievable, but nonetheless the ideal, meaning a 100 percent absence of measurable pollutants. Thus, air and water quality goals can be set and depolluting technologies applied. Given quantitative systems of measurement together with a clear national understanding of the common interest, legislation can be enacted—and enforced—to see that the common interest is served.

Thus, for two of the three primary components of the biophysical environment, the road to progress, if not solution, is well marked. But for the third primary component, the land, the story is quite different and of uncertain outcome. There is no direct quantitative method to measure the quality of the land nor can there be. A standard of purity, 100 percent absence of pollution, is perhaps possible to conceive of theoretically as primeval wilderness in which man functions as a biological, nonmanipulative organism. But such a standard is of no value to a species needing to live, work, and spend leisure time in community, and who can (and therefore must) alter the biophysical environment to maintain and improve its civilization and culture.

Because environmental quality standards as they apply to the land, and would govern the use of land, cannot be achieved through quantitative measurements of pollution, the land-use decision-making process has traditionally been ad hoc, local, and without reference to secondary effects. The control mechanism was located, and has remained, at the lowest of government levels for good reason—so that decisions about the land could reflect, theoretically at least, the value judgments of those who have the most intense relationship (economic and otherwise) to the land, and have the most effective access to government processes for redress.

In an agrarian economy such a scheme had few serious drawbacks. But many believe, given the complexities of metropolitan settlement patterns in an industrial-cum-technological age, that Jeffersonian local control of land use has been found wanting. Metropolitan-scale infrastructure, inequalities of property-tax income, and the specialization and physical separation of differing land uses have so distorted local decision making that many have given up on local control as a way to express a coherent value system. Local interests, some say, cannot be responsive to the manifold needs of the larger, metropolitan community.

As a result, there is a strong effort to return the land-use apparatus to the states. But there is no corollary affirmation of landscape "values" in this changing of the guard. The principal purpose of the recent land-use policy bill introduced in Congress was to deal mainly with the question of who should make the decisions, rather than the development of a clear public policy informing the decisions to be made.

That the development of national policy is desirable is, at this point, beyond question. But given the nearly complete absence of national consensus on the matter of landscape quality goals, there is no identifiable reference point for the beginnings of reform. This is, of course, the reason why proposed federal legislation has so far failed to come to grips with any component of qualitative policy save a need for more or better planning—an essentially circular approach.

However, we are not without constructs, most of which come from the processes of rationalizing governmental action in behalf of landscape preservation. Landscape preservation based on cultural values that stand in opposition to the materialistic utilitarian values promulgated by the industrialists of the nineteenth century is a relatively new phenomenon, although the impulse—the Edenic search—spans millenia (Marx, 1964). The city garden, the pastoral landscape, and the wilderness retreat are as old as literature itself, and are based firmly on landscape aesthetics and the "spiritual values" of nature (Shepard, 1967).

But as the agrarian economy was displaced and as the industrial revolution created its upheavals of both land ownership and society, the potential for imminent loss of many highly treasured landscapes became increasingly a cause for alarm. William Wordsworth, in perhaps some of the longest letters to the editor ever published (*Morning Post*, 1844), decried the proposed railway spur from Kendal to the edge of Lake Windermere. "Is then no nook of English ground secure/From rash assault?" he complained in a sonnet accompanying one of his letters. Wordsworth, who had spent a lifetime documenting the value of a dynamic man-land relationship that could lead one into a deeper sense of God, self, and human worth, feared in the 1830s that his beloved Lake District would be trampled to death by thousands of city folk induced thither not by the natural scene but by gaming houses, boat races, and other false lures.

Meanwhile, on the other side of the Atlantic, Henry David Thoreau feared for the landscape of Concord, Massachusetts.

> That devilish Iron Horse whose ear-rending neigh is heard throughout the town, has muddied the Boiling Spring with his foot, and he it is that has browsed off all the woods on Walden shore, that Trojan horse, with a thousand men in his belly, introduced by mercenary Greeks.

Both Wordsworth and Thoreau came to approximately the same conclusion—basically a preservationist position. Thoreau complained (1862) of the potential effect of private ownership of land.

> At present, in this vicinity, the best part of the land is not private property; the landscape is not owned and the walker enjoys comparative freedom. But possibly the day will come . . . when fences shall be multiplied, and mantraps and other engines invented to confine men to the public road, and walking over the surface of God's earth shall be construed to mean trespassing on some gentleman's grounds . . . . Let us improve our opportunities, then, before the evil days come.

A few years earlier, Wordsworth, who had the ocean at his back rather than a still unbroken wilderness, set forth a practical solution that has come to be accepted and acted upon in most nations of the world—a national park. In his geography, *A Guide to the Lakes* (fifth edition, 1835), he urged that the Lake District be preserved (finally accomplished in 1949) as a "sort of national property, in which every man has a right and interest who has an eye to perceive and a heart to enjoy."

But the Romantic consciousness of a landscape aesthetic that was more profound than mere "scenery" could not, in spite of its persuasive exponents, survive the philosophical onslaught of the utilitarians and the ineluctable economics of laissez-faire capitalism. Thus, constructs for landscape preservation were invented that assiduously avoided such nonstatistical phenomena as aesthetic perception. The language of the utilitarians was pressed into service, if not its values. Preservation became conservation, dating, for all intents and purposes, from 1864 when George Perkins Marsh published *Man and Nature*. "Conservation" is straight out of the utilitarian book and antithetical to the Romantic view. As Gifford Pinchot put it at the turn of the century, in connection with the conservation of forests, "the greatest good for the greatest number for the longest time." Cost-benefit became the rationale for landscape preservation, and still is in many respects even today.

It was Aldo Leopold in the 1930s who saw how utilitarian conservation—for recreation as well as resource husbandry—was essentially seductive of landscape aesthetics and a philosophical sham to boot. But at the same time that he proposed the validity of experiencing the natural landscape on its own terms, he was constrained to base his persuasion on a new justification, which in the hands of fools and Philistines was as separable from aesthetics as was economics. That justification was, of course, ecology. And as utilitarianism was twisted out of shape, so has been ecology as a rationale for land preservation. No fault of Leopold's of course. The problem lies in the difficulty inherent in mistaking subsidiary rationales for the primary value. Aware that this might happen, Leopold warned (1949) about confusing the servant (ecology) with the master (perception). "Let no man jump to the conclusion," he wrote, "that Babbitt must take his Ph.D. in ecology before he can 'see' his country. On the contrary, the Ph.D. may become as callous as an undertaker to the mysteries at which he officiates."

Landscape planners and preservationists have not heeded his warning. Just as aesthetic perception was displaced by cost-benefit economics (and later by recreation-as-social-uplift) as the basis for public decision making, so ecological determinism tends to do the same thing. Professional environmentalists are now thoroughly hooked on ecology as a primary rationale for public action in respect to land preservation and control.

With this background in mind, let us now examine the public-policy justifications for landscape preservation.

Land is "saved" (from bulldozers, draglines, and other instruments of destruction) in one of three ways. It is bought or, preferably, bought back from private interests by the public; or private interests are required by the public not to destroy their land if there would be a dire secondary effect of such destruction. Hence, some wetlands are zoned against filling; shoreline industry and commerce are barred. Or, finally, private interests are paid not to destroy their land. This payment comes in a variety of ways, although most of it is in the form of negative income: allowing developers to build at higher densities, reducing taxes on farmland, and so forth.

Since the exercise of any of these public actions tends to remove land from the economic sector, the public decision to do so must be convincingly rationalized. Therefore, rationalizations, which are essentially post hoc, are commonly proposed as the *primary* motives for preservation. While the impulse to preservation is derived from a nonrational aesthetic sensibility, the justifications are invariably rationally nonaesthetic.

What follows is an irritatingly simplified and heavily biased analysis of the rationales commonly set forth in an effort to see where they have led. Ideally, the point will be made by this process that the confusion between the rationale and the primary impulse—aesthetics—holds great dangers.

Three rationales will be treated here: economic benefits of preservation, the social necessity for outdoor recreation, and ecological determinism in land-use planning.

Environmentalists discovered the value of cost-benefit analysis as a device to rationalize public decisions at the municipal level in 1958. This was the year that Roland Greeley published a famous letter in the Lexington, Massachusetts, *Minute Man* to the effect that if the town of Lexington would buy up 2,000 acres of vacant land it would *save* the taxpayers money. Greeley, a planner and professor, knew what he was talking about. He calculated that the cost of schools, fire and police protection, sewage, drainage, and welfare costs would add up to "far more" than the annual cost—some $75,000 per year—for retiring a $1,000,000 open-space-acquisition bond.

For landsavers all over the country this piece of news was roughly comparable to the invention of the wheel. In the suburbs of big cities, environmentalists made their own calculations to prove that the preservation of land, any land, was cheaper than the zoned alternative, which was usually single-family houses on half- or full-acre lots.

Developers, the traditional enemy of the landsaver, fought back. The Urban Land Institute, under a grant from the National Association of Home Builders, tried to prove (Mace and Wicker, 1968) that single-family homes *could* pay their way if the calculations were made differently. Moreover, the developers found a way to characterize themselves as social reformers, asking where all the poor people were going to live if the suburbs were to become one gigantic nature preserve. But it was too late. The Open Space Institute (Little, 1969), among others, took up the cry and publicized the new municipal math far and wide. In a valiant effort at compromise, Whyte (1964) and others had proposed cluster development as a way to save open space, maintain zoned densities, and reduce construction costs. But the compromise failed, by and large, since it served neither the landsavers, who were hardly interested in houses of any kind, nor the developers, who smelled a larger opportunity.

If, they reasoned, the primary rationale were economics, then they could fashion an effective petard for the landsavers. This they did and called it planned unit development. By agreeing that development should pay its own way, and by agreeing that a modicum of open space should be preserved, they backed their way into builder's heaven. They proposed uncommonly high densities, including garden apartments, some highrises, and townhouses along with a smattering of single-family homes—their old standby. Such a scheme, which could allot as much as a quarter of a large site to "open space" of one kind or another, would also pump fresh blood into the tax base, since not all tenants or owners would be of that uniform species that produce 2.4 school-aged children. Moreover, through economies of scale a planned unit development could provide many of its own municipal services.

If there have been any "Yeah, buts" recorded by landscape preservationists and putative aestheticians, they have been stomped to death in the stampede to the metropolitan countryside to build new communities that look like little chunks of city arbitrarily sprinkled about the rural scene. Possibly some would except from this negative assessment the Columbias and the Jonathans. The point is arguable. The fact remains that the countryside accessible to metropolitan centers is not the countryside the landsavers had in mind at all, in spite of the fact that cows sometimes cohabit with the condominiums. So much for the new municipal math. By capitulation to cost-benefit analysis, landscape preservationists not only failed to make a convincing case, but in fact probably encouraged land-development patterns wholly inconsistent with even the most rudimentary pastoral aesthetic.

The ecological justification does not have nearly so much direct danger attached, and, intellectually, the postulates of ecological determinism are attractive. Many have even tried to relate ecological balance with aesthetics. Fraser Darling has said (Fraser Darling and Eichhorn, 1967) that landscapes in balance are also beautiful to behold. One can believe this or not. To be sure, there is nothing wrong with ecology as a way to understand how the biosphere functions. Moreover, the ecological justification—as a rational system—is potentially helpful in the preservation of wetlands, alpine environments, deserts, and other such habitats that contain a delicate interlocking of creatures, plants, climate, and topography. Such insights are not endlessly projectable, however, to every copse or lea.

Ecology as an approach is, of course, neutral. It can be useful or not to the landscape preservationist, depending on the circumstances. But ecological *determinism* is not neutral. It tends to insist (McHarg, 1969) that all land-use policy questions can be answered by understanding the biological linkages. Moreover, in the hands of those who believe that the hydrological cycle is the prime indicator of ecological balance, the determinations made thereby are worse than incomplete. They are boring and irrelevant to real people who are trying to figure out how to maintain a humane environment.

Like the landsaver's cost-benefit analysis, ecology has been eagerly embraced by developers. In the old (pre-ecology) days, the best a developer could do was to leave as many trees standing as possible. Or, like the developer who was the president of a local Audubon Society in Westchester County, he could dig up and transplant all the wildflowers on his site on Sunday so that he wouldn't have to worry about what his bulldozers would do on Monday. These days land developers prepare maps showing unbuildable gorges, swamps, and outcrops splashed with green ink and labeled "conservation area." Nothing wrong with this, of course. Except that it may delude the landsavers into giving up a fine visual landscape, such as a meadow or even an old apple orchard, that may have absolutely no value under a system of ecological determinism.

The third justification for preservation that is often mistaken for a primary value is the need for outdoor recreation. We may define outdoor recreation as a set of leisure-time activities necessary to the underclasses and categorically different from the interests of those who plan recreational facilities for them. Where the intelligentsia of the out-of-doors treasure the slap and gurgle of a canoe moving across a wilderness lake, the masses are required to toss beer cans out of a hired aluminum outboard roaring across a reservoir. If the wilderness lake is too crowded, it is judged a failure. If the reservoir is not crowded enough, it is judged a failure.

On the banks of the Hudson River, landsavers had argued for years that a certain point of land jutting into the river, favored by many for bird watching, rock sitting, and similar activities, should be set aside. The county stepped in, set it aside, covered a meadow with a parking lot, blasted aside rocks for a boat launching ramp, installed swings, picnic tables, charcoal grills, grass, and signs that said "No —" and immediately complained that there wasn't enough money for maintenance. Some people liked that point of land once, for what it was. Now nobody does; it has been demoted to a "facility."

The story of the national parks is too dreary to dwell upon. The reader is directed to Edward Abbey's *Desert Solitaire* (1968) and the Conservation Foundation's *National Parks for the Future* (1972). The question is not *whether* many of the national parks have become tawdry, ridden with automobiles, and callously operated by that segment of the tourist industry with the largest share of market (larger even than that of Disney), which we call the National Park Service. Rather, the question is *why*.

The reason for this state of affairs is that the policy justification of national parks has been substituted for the primary values that led to their preservation in the first place. The justification was "outdoor recreation"—one of the least expensive ways a society based on the exploitation of resources and labor could pretend that it believed in the sanctity of nature and the dignity of man. Also, two weeks among the tall trees would make for a more efficient and less troublesome work force, not to mention the offsetting profits to be made by the "leisure-time" industry. Everybody could be happy, except, of course, those who were expected to find solace and renewal in natural surroundings.

The selling of outdoor recreation as a justification for landscape preservation simply has led to the destruction of landscapes rather than their salvation.

The problem is particularly acute in cities, where parks are thought to fail as landscapes unless they are so heavily used that they cannot be anything but failures as landscapes; and where recreation planners are unable to differentiate between social space—turf—and parks; and where the good social space—streets (Rudofsky, 1969)—functions as parking lots for those with money enough to own cars, but who refuse to bear the cost of parking, asking instead that poor people provide it for them on their streets and be taxed unjustly and disproportionately to pay for traffic cops, street maintenance crews, and the like.

Such is the tortured logic that derives from mistaking outdoor recreation for a landscape "value."

What we have been illustrating here, in these three examples, is philosophic deception—and it is mainly self-deception. In part, it may be because landscape preservationists and aestheticians have had no courage that the state of affairs vis-à-vis landscape quality has turned out so badly in the United States.

When one loses faith in the leadership, one must resort to the wisdom of the people: no small assignment. To that end, three experimental landscape "value sessions" were held recently in an inner-city area, a suburban area, and a rural area, all of them in or near Minneapolis, Minnesota. In all, about 36 people participated in this project, a pilot study that might lead to a full-blown program entitled, for lack of something better, "American Land Forums."

The Forums were introduced as follows:

The Conservation Foundation of Washington, D.C., in connection with its project "Expectations of the American Land," is initiating a series of citizen forums in cities, suburbs, and rural areas throughout the United States. The objective of these meetings is to get behind the rhetoric of land use planning to a basic understanding of how Americans really feel about their land and landscape.

The Foundation believes that the insights so gathered can have a significant impact on national, state, and local land use policy. And the insights will be timely, for today many basic assumptions about growth and development are being questioned. Major legislation such as the National Land Use Policy Act and state-level initiatives concerning land regulation suggest that during the next three to five years we will have to create fundamentally new policy directions concerning our use of land.

Each of the forums, made up of approximately twelve participants, will engage in an informal and candid discussion about personal values as they are associated with this emerging public consciousness that the American land has a "cultural" meaning as well as an economic one.

Cultural meanings are concerned with such expections of the land as these:
—Ecological expectations: the degree to which land should perform ecological work, mitigate the extremes of environmental forces, provide a sense of natural "balance."
—Aesthetic expectations: the degree to which the land should provide scenic beauty.
—Social expectations: the degree to which the land should provide an optimum setting for community, social diversity, and amenity.

These expectations are the terms in which noneconomic values are generally expressed, rather than discussion topics in and of themselves. The discussion should instead focus on personal experiences and beliefs in connection with the land and the basic impulses, as well as they can be expressed, that have led to the growing demand that land use policies be developed that will make our communities worth looking at and living in. What is sought in each forum is passionate statement rather than a critical analysis of planning technique. Moreover, a spontaneous interaction between forum members is of greater value than are considered responses to questions posed by the moderator.

The responses were predictable, useless, but deeply affecting. The moderator posed no question, although he feared he might have to. The discussions took off spontaneously and ran on their own fuel. And although many of the participants were concerned with environmental affairs, their responses in this kind of setting may be significant and not necessarily at variance with those of any citizen who has thought for 15 or 20 minutes about landscape quality.

No one spoke of the need for outdoor recreation facilities, although they did speak of walking in the woods. No one spoke of ecology, although they did speak of environmental hazard. No one spoke of the cost-benefits of open-space preservation, although they did speak of the real estate profits earned by others.

But is hard to write the truth about these meetings. The responses could be used to prove just about anything anyone wanted to prove. This much can be ventured: they indicated confusion, maybe even despair, on the part of virtually all participants.

So much confusion surfaced, in fact, that "values" of the kind an expert advisor of decision makers would dearly love to record, ascribe numbers to, and see decisions made by seemed almost moot. As one participant observed to the moderator at the end of a session, "What's the point of talking about 'values' when the processes of the political and economic systems are immune to such values?"

This view was unique only in its bluntness. The very first topic taken up in a meeting of farmers in a rural county on the far edge of the metropolitan area was a story that had the sense of legend about it, a circumstance that had taken place 30 years before but was felt to have a kind of universal applicability.

"Albert," began one of the farmers, "you might want to tell him about what happened when the federal government took over . . ."

"Well, I'll tell you. We seen men walking across our lands, and they must have been taking soil samples, that's all I can figure out. We were wondering what they were doing. And then, all at once, the last week in March, there comes a federal officer—big cap and stripes on his sleeves—and gives us a warrant to move in 30 days. How in the world can you move 35 sows and 25 cows and 300 chickens in 30 days? That's the kind of orders they gave us."

"When was this?" asked the moderator.

"This was on the tail end of World War II," said Albert.

"Why was the land taken?"

"Well," said Albert, "they just condemned it to put some kind of factory on it. I don't remember just quite right."

The mythic force of the legend dominated the session. Stories were told about developers that threatened to take this rural community to court unless they upzoned; there were stories about farmers who thought they had to sell out. One man recollected about his uncle who had done this. "He turned around and sold for about $1,200 and bought other land for $450, so he has a cash reserve in the bank for his old age. And he still has 160 acres. But it wasn't quite what he wanted. No, it never is."

"When we moved out of that area," said Albert, back at the myth again, "we were just like orphans. We couldn't adjust to no different area. It takes a while, because every square foot of that land you've got to know."

"I can't move out," put in another. "I'll stay here—I'll fight. I'm going to stay on my land until . . . as long as I can."

"I'm going to live and die on my farm," said a third, "I'm attached to the community, churches, friends, neighbors—all that's worth something to me. You can't buy that with money. Isn't that right?"

"Right. That's right."

"Yes," said Albert.

Later, of course, they all agreed that a man'd be a fool not to sell for $1,500 or $2,000 an acre.

In a suburban session, the forum members spoke for a while about tearing up Montana to coal-stoke the industry of Minneapolis.

"I think it's immoral to go out there and do to Montana what they did in northern Minnesota to get the iron ore out," said a lady who wrote a column for a suburban newspaper.

"That's hardly a scratch on the surface compared to what strip mining's done to the South," observed an architect.

"I've been to Kentucky; I've been in Appalachia," said a schoolteacher, shaking his head.

Then someone asked, "Okay, well, that's the position you take. All right. We're not going to take the coal out of Montana then, so the industrial plant in this city is not going to keep growing anymore; then what's going to happen to this metropolitan area if you don't take the coal out of Montana?"

The wife of a physician complained that such a discussion was not really relevant. "A lot of us are involved on scales that are much smaller than that, in problems that are a lot easier to cope with and don't cause the situation where push comes to shove, where you have major forces clashing."

"Most of us here," she went on, "are involved in issues that have to do with relatively small acreages of land—a matter of 20 feet on one side or another of a stream, whether to build on these 5 acres here or whether to move over a few hundred yards. And we can't get anywhere even with *those* kinds of land use problems."

Later they talked about an ecologist who had been appointed to a governmental commission.

"He was on our team when we were trying to clean up the creek and save it," one lady said. "Now he's on the commission and I don't even go to their meetings any more, because I have never heard them turn down any developer when he asked for anything."

"But in that position he can't be arbitrary or capricious to anybody," put in a man who wanted to be fair.

"Oh, bullshit," said the lady who wrote the newspaper column.

In the inner city, a professor at the University of Minnesota said, "I get so damn depressed, you know. I've become a radical sort of environmentalist, mau-mauing state agency meetings and things like that. I am distrustful of planners, I'm distrustful of people that come to me and say they're going to help me with my urban landscape, particularly if they are officials, because I think that the urban landscape is up for sale to the highest bidder."

Tales of civic frustration ran around the table, of freeways and highrises that were constructed despite their efforts to prevent them.

"You know," said one woman, "I'm sick of going over to the legislature and lobbying and looking eye to eye with guys making 35 thou a year to do what I do on behalf of the environment for nothing."

"All we're doing," the moderator observed, "is talking about governmental processes, not perceptions of a more humane landscape."

"I'm sorry," said the woman.

"I'm not sorry," said the professor. "No, I wouldn't be sorry because I happen to feel very strongly that the process is impeding the vision, not the lack of vision impeding the process."

And so it went. But in spite of their confusion, their despair that anything could be done, and their panic over the loss of *place*, visions of landscape quality crept in.

"I need trees," said an employee of the 3M Company in the inner-city session. "Trees are now used as economic things—all the same type, all the same heights, all harvested when they're 25 years old for economic purposes. They're not grown for my needs. My needs are for a huge tree that's tangled, jumbled, not economically worthwhile at all."

"You know," said a woman. "I heard something that was *very* interesting. St. Catherine's College is right in the city, but close to the river, and they have a little woods in back, but it's very little. And they saw a *deer* in there."

"No kidding."

"I mean, that's amazing when you consider that the deer must have come through back yards."

"That's really an exciting thought, that a deer can actually get into the city. If the city could re-create itself so that this kind of thing could actually occur . . ."

Diversity was what the city residents recommended. "As soon as you simplify the environment, you lose the safety," one said. And they were concerned with small spaces, not large parks, which they thought could just as well be natural areas. They disliked both suburbs and automobiles! Suburbs because they destroyed the countryside, which they did not want to have destroyed; cars because they destroyed the city. They discussed gardens—for flowers and vegetables in small spaces. And they thought that the bulk of the streets could be done away with; used instead for gardens and trees, as well as for "genuine urban densities."

They spoke of funny, surprising little places in the city. And decided that you don't get that kind of thing with planning. In fact, the point was made that planning is probably antithetical to true urban diversity: the jumble city, productive of a good urban lifestyle.

Safety, urban surprise, and that recurring theme—trees—came together in the remarks of a young woman who was a Vista volunteer. "There's value in ugliness. I live above a warehouse, and I can leave my door unlocked. My windows are open. I frequently lock myself out, but I can crawl up into an open window in a matter of about 5 seconds. And because my place appears to be ugly it is very safe. Nobody suspects that anybody would want to live there."

And then she revealed her secret. "In the back I've got my roof garden and I look out my window and there's an old box elder tree which fills up my window. So what if a box elder is a weedy tree? It's nice and green. I lay in bed and see it against the sky. Of course, if I lay in bed the other way I see an office building."

If in the city the perceptions were related mainly to lifestyle, in the suburbs there was a more abstracted notion of natural beauty. "I have a real love for idle land," said a high school science teacher, "land that man can just keep his cotton-picking fingers off of and just let it go its way."

The talk was of childhood summers in the out-of-doors and of the effort to re-create that spacious sense for their own children in a metropolitan milieu.

There was one exchange that seemed to express not only the suburban view of the landscape, but also the most profound kind of value in terms of preservation. It took place near the end of the session.

One participant put the question this way to an avid preservation advocate, "But why? Why do you care?"

The woman answered, "It's sort of like a sense of security. We look at the natural order of things as ongoing. To see a river continue on is life."

And a man added, "A man's sanity depends on associating with and being able to know that the river is there, and that it's going to be there. Whereas everything else we're associating with is going to be here today and gone tomorrow. Yet, you know, that river . . .''

It may be, the moderator ventured later, that the suburbs are just as dangerous as the city but in a different way. Man is undependable in the city, and that is dangerous. But in the suburbs, nature itself seems undependable, since the landscapes are so massively transformed. "Getting back to nature" may involve something other than recreation. Perhaps it is a compulsive effort to reestablish the permanence of "the natural order," an escape from the placeless suburbs to natural dependability.

"You don't have to get too far away," said the science teacher, "to be a long ways away. And I think this is an important value."

The farmers were experts on real estate economics, sensitive to environmental hazard as might be expected, and grieving over the encroaching realization that they were anachronistic.

One farmer, a bit of a poet, put it this way: "Most of those new people like to have a farmer living near them, so they can sit and look out the window and watch everything he does. And they do that. The older people and the kids especially. A lot of people say, 'Oh, we watch you all the time. We listen to you sing!' ''

The moderator of these three sessions despaired, and still does, of making some kind of useful analysis of all this. Perhaps it can be done after many more forums are held. Or perhaps not at all.

But everywhere he went he was struck by the people's sense of loss of *place*, of personal "locatability." The changes are too many, too big, too fast even for the most exuberant and adaptable of citizens. And the people sense their lives are in disarray. They believe that they are being manipulated by government and business, but they seem reluctant to admit that a humane landscape and living environment is wholly out of reach, if only they could really *organize*. And when that thought is uttered, their hopelessness returns, sometimes with a shrug and silence, sometimes with a kind of protorevolutionary stridency.

At the forums there was excessive talking and unburdening, a reluctance to end the sessions. One of them ran to 4 hours and continued past midnight in a parking lot.

There is no instruction in this chapter for the planner or the preservationist, perhaps not even for the aesthetician. One hopes that it is enough to raise a few questions. Still, there would appear to be a difference between authentic landscape values deriving from ordinary perception rooted in the necessity for a dependable *place* and the dry intellectual constructs that preservationists have developed to justify their arguments and which they then confuse with reality.

If we continue to mistake the one for the other, we may well fail; for without humanizing our planning concepts, we may be unable to create humane or particularly meaningful metropolitan landscapes. We shall fail, not because we are wrong in the narrow intellectual sense, but because we shall move no one.

And that is the problem. There has been a good deal of puzzlement on the part of many planners and preservationists about how to justify aesthetic perception. We have invented such arguments as ecological balance, outdoor recreational opportunities, and economic benefits, sensing danger in proposing public action on the basis of personal perception.

Perhaps we cannot justify a humane landscape this way. Perhaps we can, but few have had the nerve to try. Most of us, excepting people like Lady Bird Johnson, have been embarrassed to voice a flat-footed celebration of *place*, without the diversionary tactic of ringing in a brass band of ecological, sociological, and economic scientism.

Landscape perception and the impulse to the preservation of place is, perhaps, no more or less than an authentic existential act, free of deterministic rationalism, undertaken as a way to dignify a man and to make his surroundings more humane.

Camus' classic existential metaphor is Sisyphus, who is condemned to push a stone up a hill only to have it tumble down again as he nears the crest. The hero of this legend is not the rational stone, which with a regularity characteristic of its essence, obeys Newton and rolls downhill. The hero here is the man, Sisyphus, who, Camus holds, not only endures but also finds joy in his task. Sisyphus was heard in the "value" forums reported here.

In these technologically parlous times, the impulse born of aesthetic perception and the fruitless search for Eden is, surely, absurd. But it is authentically affirmative of life. What further argument for landscape preservation is needed?

References

Abbey, Edward. *Desert Solitaire*. New York: McGraw-Hill, 1968.

Conservation Foundation. *National Parks for the Future*. Washington, D.C.: The Conservation Foundation, 1972.

Darling, Sir Frank Fraser, and Noel D. Eichhorn. *Man and Nature in the National Parks*. Washington, D.C.: The Conservation Foundation, 1967.

Leopold, Aldo. *A Sand County Almanac*. New York: Oxford University Press, 1966 (original edition 1949).

Little, Charles E. *Challenge of the Land*. New York: Pergamon Press, 1969.

Mace, Ruth L. and Warren J. Wicker. *Do Single-Family Homes Pay Their Way?* Washington, D.C.: Urban Land Institute, 1968.

McHarg, Ian L. *Design With Nature.* Garden City, N.Y.: Natural History Press, 1969.

Marx, Leo. *The Machine in the Garden.* New York: Oxford University Press, 1964.

Reilly, William K. (ed.) *The Use of Land: A Citizens' Policy Guide to Urban Growth.* New York: Thomas Y. Crowell, 1973.

Rudofsky, Bernard. *Streets for People: A Primer for Americans.* Garden City, N.Y.: Doubleday, 1969.

Shepard, Paul. *Man in the Landscape: A Historic View of the Esthetics of Nature.* New York: Knopf, 1967.

Whyte, William H. *Cluster Development.* New York: American Conservation Association, 1964.

Land as a Commodity "Affected with a Public Interest"

Richard F. Babcock and
Duane A. Feurer

We abuse land because we regard it as a commodity belonging to us.[1]

Today there is a vigorous challenge to old assumptions concerning the appropriate locus and nature of government control over land use. Some of those in the vanguard of the attack on the old styles of land use policy insist it is essential to cease regarding land as a commodity to be bartered in the marketplace. The suggestion that land should no longer be treated as a commodity but rather regarded as a resource has a compelling ring which appeals to many people in these days of a heightened concern over environmental degradation.

One hazard with this approach, however, is that it suggests that if land is treated as a resource—a public trust—the perceived problems in land use policy will be alleviated. The history in the United States of the management of *public* lands, which are legally held in public trust, does not indicate that pursuit of the public trust analogue as applied to all land will lead to a result which will please the advocates of the concept. Recent controversies such as the mining in Death Valley National Monument, the Disney development at Mineral King in the Sierras, the controversies over extensive clear-cutting and over-cutting of national forests, and innumerable other examples illustrate that the government is carrying out its role as trustee of the public lands with less than due regard for the public beneficiaries. There is little to suggest that the influence of mining, lumber, grazing and other interests seeking to exploit public lands is any less damaging to implementation of beneficent land use policies when exerted at a national level than when exerted at the state or municipal level.

The more serious difficulty with such a pious sentiment as a rallying point in a "revolution" (quiet or otherwise) in public policy is that it may go further than is acceptable to most people or, indeed, than is necessary to achieve the objective of a more rational land use policy. It employs a rhetoric so sweeping as not to be taken seriously. Those who urge such a

This article is an elaboration of suggestions made in a speech by one of the authors before the American Society of Planning Officials in Vancouver, British Columbia, in April 1975. That speech appeared in the June 1975 edition of *Planning*. This expanded version appeared, with extensive citations, in the *Washington Law Review* (University of Washington) vol. 52, no. 2 (1977) under the same title. It is reprinted with permission.

99

posture rarely put forward useful methods for transforming such a cry into a program of more than parochial scale.

It is our purpose to suggest that a land use policy which is socially equitable and environmentally sensitive is not resolved simply by labelling land as a "resource" rather than a "commodity." Instead, we propose to examine the special status land has enjoyed for many centuries, and which distinguishes it from other commodities, and to suggest that land transactions and land use should at last be scrutinized in a manner not unlike the treatment extended to a multitude of other commodities no more "affected with a public interest" than is land.

For centuries government has been more reluctant to regulate transactions in land than it has transactions in personal property. Even the modern use of the police power through zoning and subdivision regulations is less a matter of *public* regulation than it is a system for granting *private* benefits or protecting *private* interests. We propose that the doctrines developed in the past century in public utility law may be worth pursuing in the attempt to construct a rational land use policy. There are at least four instances where such an analogy may correct or mitigate current abuses or inequities: (1) scrutiny over cost, profit, price and service, (2) the use of quotas and priorities, (3) the limited protection against competition when it is in the public interest, and (4) the power of condemnation by private developers upon certification by a public agency.

Finally, we acknowledge the high risks in the use of analogy and the difficulties of transferring doctrines applicable to transactions in personal property to dealings in real estate. What follows, then, is more a suggestion for a new way of viewing public regulation of transactions in private land and the use of such land than a precise framework for a new scheme of regulation. If this proposition offends environmentalists and frightens developers, they should consider the record extending over many centuries before they judge such an approach.

I.

Throughout Anglo-American history land, in contrast to other commodities, has occupied a privileged status in society. "Land was wealth, livelihood, family provision, and the principal subject-matter of the law. To begin with, moreover, land was also government and the structure of society."[2] Land was the key to the power of the feudal lord and ultimately of the sovereign. All land in England belonged to the king who granted the various tenures to lower lords and peasants. The king's absolute power over land, and his authority to levy on land and seize it for non-payment led to the confrontation among peers at Runnymede and the adoption in 1215 of the Magna Carta, which contained protections against the seizure of property without proper legal process. Although the English kings varied in the vigor with which they honored the Magna Carta, by the time of the colonization of North America, rights in land had been secured against the royal prerogative of seizure. It takes only a small stretch of the imagination to view the current contest between municipalities and land owners over land use policy as a similar confrontation.

The feudal, pre-industrial focus on land as a source of wealth might explain the special concern over the protection of that commodity, but this status goes back so far that it transcends a feudal aberration. Throughout history, chattel property has not enjoyed a similar status: "[T]he ownership of land was a much more intense and completely protected right than was the ownership of a chattel."[3] During the Middle Ages, production of goods was often controlled by the guilds, associations of producing craftsmen who controlled prices. Various elements of trade and commerce, including the wool trade and a variety of commodities such as beer, bread, wine, and timber, were subject to extensive regulation, including price regulation, as early as the thirteenth century in England. But unlike trade in personal property—a business of the rising middle-class merchants—land remained the special prerogative of the sovereign and the nobility. In short, it enjoyed a special class-oriented position.

The American Revolution arose out of a political conflict; it was not a social upheaval. The united colonies did not intend to repeal centuries of common law, including those privileges of land ownership so relished by some leaders of the revolution. Indeed, the records of the Constitutional Convention of 1787 underscore the importance attached to ownership of land: "Probably no member of the Convention believed that a government, republican in form, could be entrusted to men who were not qualified by the possession of real estate. Property was considered to be the anchor of government."[4] It is not surprising, then, that from the earliest days of the republic, American law has extended the privileges attached to the ownership of land leavened by the democratic notion that through acquisition of land a nation of wanderers could be converted to responsible citizens.

Although the long established exemption from execution and sale for payment of debts of the homestead (the family home and a limited amount of appurtenant land) has by now been extended to such items as automobiles and some jurisdictions limit the value of exempt real property as well as personal property, other states that limit the value of exempt personal property place no limitation on the value of exempt real property. In addition, some states continue to provide limited property tax exemptions with respect to occupied family residences. Mortgage moratoria were enacted to protect owners of real property but no similar deferments were granted to ease the burdens on debtors with respect to obligations on other types of property.

The Internal Revenue Code provides additional examples of the special status of land ownership. When a homeowner sells a residence at a profit and purchases a more expensive home, he can postpone recognition of any capital gain realized on the sale. Land is the only property which commonly benefits from this favorable tax treatment.

The law governing landlord-tenant relationships contains illustrations of the special treatment accorded by the law to land related matters. Courts in the past have treated covenants in leases as independent. A landlord could continue to collect rent even though he had breached covenants in a lease. Even when a landlord had agreed in a lease to make repairs to leased premises, the failure to make such repairs did not absolve the tenant from the obligation to pay rent. In contrast, a purchaser of goods or services which are not delivered in accordance with the terms of a contract can defend an action by the seller to recover the purchase price by asserting a defense of recoupment pursuant to which the purchaser's loss is off-set against the claim of the seller. The landlord's obligation to surrender quiet possession of the leased premises to the tenant in return for rent was a different obligation than the one to supply heat or hot water, and the landlord's failure to provide such necessities did not absolve the tenant occupying the premises of the obligation to pay rent.

The law of landlord-tenant relations, however, is one area of real property law where both judicial and statutory changes are presently being made to remedy many of the above inequities. Nevertheless, such changes have not been as widely or readily adopted as have comparable remedies in connection with the sale of goods.

The special status of land appears in the application of the theory of inverse condemnation. Government agencies that impose valid police power regulations on particular land are being challenged by landowners who allege inverse condemnation for the diminution in the value of their land by virtue of government regulations. Courts have found inverse condemnation even where the regulation has not involved physical invasion by the government of the property of the landowner. There is no such analogue in government regulation of commercial interests or personal property. Although inverse condemnation rationally would seem to be as applicable to personal property as to real property, we have found no instances of government being forced to pay the owner of a business or other personal property because of the exercise of valid government regulation. Government control over real property may be stricken as a deprivation of property without due process or for some other reason, but it appears that government can regulate many businesses or commodities and diminish their value substantially without payment to the owners for that loss in value.

Nothing demonstrates the chasm between the treatment of trade in land from the trade in personal property more than a comparison of the history of the regulation of the sale and trading in investment securities with the sale of land. Under federal law, as well as securities laws in many states, the sale and trading of investment securities has been subject to extensive regulation for more than forty years.

Although various states had become involved in some securities matters earlier in our history, the first general securities law was adopted in Kansas in 1911. The first comprehensive federal securities legislation was enacted in 1933 after the stock market crash of 1929. Brokers and dealers of securities are also regulated and must meet specified qualifications. Even "investment advisors" are regulated. The advertising materials used to offer securities to the public must be filed with and approved by the securities regulatory agency. The federal rules narrowly define the scope of permitted advertising of securities offerings to provide some assurance the securities will not be "puffed" without giving potential investors the necessary data to evaluate securities for themselves. Persons who control organizations that have committed violations of the the Securities Act may also be liable to the same extent as the organizations actually committing the violations unless the controlling person can establish a lack of knowledge or reasonable grounds to believe a violation had occurred. The Securities Act extends to fraudulent interstate transactions in securities even though the securities involved may be exempt from registration requirements of the Act. Furthermore, the Securities Exchange Act of 1934 specifically authorizes the Securities and Exchange Commission to promulgate such rules as it deems necessary to protect the public against the use of manipulative or deceptive devices or contrivances in the sale of securities.

There has been substantial documentation of abuses in the subdivision and sale of land but efforts to enact legislation to regulate land sales in a manner comparable to the regulation of securities have come up quite short. To a limited extent, the federal securities laws as well as some state blue sky laws have been extended to cover sales of interests in real estate, such as condominiums and subdivision lots, where the particular objects of sale take on the character of traditional securities. Such interests are often sold to individuals who do not propose to use the property for permanent residences but intend to rent the property for income and often use the seller as an agent to manage and rent the property. Where it is apparent that real estate ventures purposely have been designed for sale primarily as investments rather than as residences, the securities regulation requirements have been held applicable.

Although securities have been regulated for half a century, it was not until 1968 that Congress enacted the Interstate Land Sales Full Disclosure Act. That legislation, however, establishes a regulatory mechanism much less pervasive than the federal securities laws. When Congress finally did act, more than half the states had no legislation regulating the sale of undeveloped land. Additional states have adopted laws to regulate sale of subdivided land in recent years, but there is still little uniformity. The Federal Interstate Land Sales Full Disclosure Act, in comparison with the federal securities laws, does not contain any requirement for the registration or licensing of dealers or salesmen, or provisions for the control of advertising materials used in connection with the sale. Although a property report must be delivered to a purchaser, there is nothing to preclude the use of substantial advertising prior to the registration of a subdivision to generate interest. The Secretary of the Department of Housing and Urban Development has authority to make and issue rules and regulations as necessary to exercise the functions and powers conferred by the Act, but this grant of authority is by no means the broad grant found in the Securities Act for establishing rules to control the use of manipulative or deceptive devices in the sale of securities. There are civil and criminal penalties for violation of the Act, but the liability is not extended to "controlling persons" as in the case of the securities laws, nor does the Act extend criminal or civil liability for the fraudulent sales of property sold pursuant to an exemption from the Act's registration requirements. Many states do require licensing or registration of real estate dealers, but it is stretching the imagination to suggest that the regulation of real estate dealers is as extensive as are the regulation and supervision of securities dealers under federal securities laws.

In short, reform in the public surveillance of transactions in land has lagged far behind the public supervision of the markets in personal property.

II.

Although we have suggested that land has occupied a rather special status, enjoying special privileges and exempt from much of the kind of regulation that is imposed on other businesses and personal property, it cannot, of course, be contended that land is not subject to regulation. The host of land use and environmental controls implemented and administered by all levels of government do affect the use to which particular land may be put and how that use may be carried out.

Zoning, the traditional American legal mechanism for control of land use, is not a system of *public* regulation in the same sense as securities laws or public utility laws. Zoning policy and practice today reflect a contest between competing *private* interests in real estate: the developer versus the protesting property owners or neighbors. In zoning, the invitation to individuals to seek changes is a major feature of the law. Amendments, variances, conditional uses, planned unit developments all reflect the probability of change at the behest of some individual or group of individuals. Of the more than 10,000 reported decisions on American land use controls since *Euclid* v. *Ambler Realty Co.*,[5] substantially all of them arose because a zoning change was denied or because it was granted. Although one party to the lawsuit is often a municipality, it usually is a surrogate for the real parties of interest—property owners who propose a change or object to a proposed change. Zoning has been constructed through the balancing of private interests, either in the courts or in political forums. The landowner/developer who protests what he regards as an unconscionable public restraint on his property rights is really protesting the benefits that restraint grants to other owners of private property who resist his proposal. The often outrageous municipal practices that discourage or prevent development are essentially designed and intended to further the interests of one group of landowners, those who are aboard, against another group, those who want to sell their land to others who wish to come aboard. Indeed, the strong and generally successful opposition of local governments to efforts to establish a state-wide land use regulatory policy suggests that a zoning ordinance is frequently viewed more as the bylaws of a private club than it is as a statement of public policy.

Beyond this special characteristic of zoning which rebuts its alleged "public" regulatory feature, neither zoning nor any other system of regulation exists which provides a comprehensive oversight of transactions in land similar to that found with respect to securities as well as other commodities and services deemed to be affected with a public interest. It is, for example, the declared national policy that a goal is "a decent home and a suitable living environment for every American family,[6] but most of the regulatory mechanisms applicable to land use do not provide any assurance that people in need of land or structures on land will be able to fulfill those needs at a reasonable cost. Indeed, more often land use and environmental regulations have forced the costs of housing and land to a point where many people are priced out of the market.

The kind and intensity of land development is, of course, regulated by government through regulatory programs such as building and housing codes and environmental controls, all of which affect the kind and quality of activities or development that may take place on land and, indirectly, the profits that may be obtained. Builders may be required to put in streets, sewers, curbs, sidewalks and a variety of other publicly imposed standards relating to the use and development of land.

Although such controls are ubiquitous, they do not impose on the vendor of land the same measure of oversight as is found, for example, in public utility law. Building or housing codes come into play only when a vendor elects to build a particular structure. Minimum requirements in terms of strength of building materials, use of electrical conduit rather than open wiring, plumbing and other specifications, room size, sanitation, and a variety of other requirements will significantly limit the builder's choice of materials and manner of construction. Such codes, however, do not insure a consistency in the design, availability and quality of construction. There may be substantial variation in codes from one local jurisdiction to the next. In addition, they often contain unnecessarily high standards and are unevenly administered and enforced. Furthermore, these codes provide little assurance that a building constructed in compliance with code requirements will maintain its standards after final inspection.

In contrast, public utilities that merchandise a service or personal property are subject to continuous oversight by regulatory agencies to assure a consistently high level of service. Utilities are not permitted to provide only that type of service they elect to provide, because regulatory agencies may require them to provide particular kinds of services deemed to be in the public interest. These agencies also adopt rules and regulations concerning the quality of service provided by utilities, and utilities are subject to monitoring and surveillance to assure that service quality standards are met on a continuing basis.

Environmental regulation may significantly affect land use. When streams and lakes are polluted or sewage treatment capacity is overloaded, new industrial or residential construction may be precluded because there will be no place to dump wastes. The current controversy in the United States Congress concerning amendments to the Clean Air Act to deal with the deterioration of air quality in areas where air meets national ambient air quality standards will, if seriously enforced, influence the shape of future development throughout the country. Pollution control programs, however, are not designed for the purpose of controlling the use and development of land. Land use controls may be a means to an end in pollution control programs, but the end is clean air, clean water, or freedom from excessive noise and pesticides. Pollution control programs do not provide oversight concerning the type, quantity, and quality of land use activities unless those activities will interfere with the attainment of pollution control objectives.

Other environmental programs such as wetlands, shorelands, critical areas, and wild river programs seek to provide a more pervasive and positive set of land use controls in the name of preserving the special natural features of particular geographic areas. Development along San Francisco Bay is controlled by the San Francisco Bay Conservation and Development Commission, efforts are being made to preserve the deep blue of Lake Tahoe through a bistate compact agency, the Tahoe Regional Planning Agency, public and private land alike are subject to controls by the Adirondack Park Agency in overseeing development in a 6,000,000 acre park in upstate New York. These and other similar programs are all characterized by their limited application to particular geographic areas which have been identified as having a very special significance to citizens of a particular jurisdiction. They are also notable by their focus on everything but housing needs.

Although land is subject to regulation that may affect the quality, quantity, and costs of development on particular land, real estate by and large retains its "special status." The principal means of land use regulation are fractured municipal regulations which are imposed as a result of superior persuasion by other landowners. The sale or trading in land is relatively immune from regulation, and unlike regulation of other commodities, land use policy shows little concern for a broad social interest.

A more fruitful approach to public policy on land would begin with an appreciation of the arcane ways in which the ownership of land has been annointed; ways which no longer deserve the protection not extended to ownership of, and transactions in, personal property. If the mystique of ten centuries of the development of real property law could be put aside, land regulation might be dealt with on a more pragmatic basis reflective of and complimentary to existing economic, social, and environmental public policies. The timeliness of such a reappraisal is suggested by the current restlessness about land use policy as we have known it for half a century.

III.

The development of a land use policy is, as Professor Norman Williams has suggested, at a "Y" fork.[7] Fifty years ago the states delegated direct and overt controls over private land use to municipalities by means of zoning and subdivision regulations. More recently, less obvious but equally influential control has been exercised by state and federal agencies in such areas as the underwriting of mortgage insurance, highway programs, and environmental regulations. Which stratum of public control will emerge victorious is unknown.

In the past decade both of these levels of power have been challenged. The municipal dominance of overt controls has been subject to widespread criticism. At the other level, the FHA has been accused of initiating "redlining" and subsidizing the white ring around our central cities, the highway lobby has discovered that the little old ladies in tennis shoes are a force to be reckoned with, from Franconia Notch in New Hampshire, through Overton Park in Memphis, to the Halawa and Moanalua Valleys in Hawaii, and the environmentalists have been accused of everything from elitism to racism.

Those concerned with the economics of land transactions are also restless. They suggest it is necessary to find new methods to determine a fair level of expectation from investment in land. Land values often fluctuate substantially because of activities of government in granting favorable zoning, building highways, extending water and sewer mains, or any of a multitude of other factors. The landholder affected by such activities can reap enormous profits simply by having the good fortune to own land in the right place at the right time. Proposals have been made for ways to "recapture" some of the value added to land by public activity. The chief of the United States Department of Transportation's Urban Mass Transportation Administration and the administrator of the Federal Environmental Protection Agency have both urged development of programs to permit public agencies to realize more fully the incremental values created by public expenditures. Of course, the effect of public activity on land value is not always to produce a windfall to the landowner. The opposite may also happen.

Most of the criticism of current land use policy is directed at the American system that delegates land use control to the myriad of municipal governments which jealously seek to protect their sovereign power to control what happens to land within their own haphazard boundaries. The character of many American suburbs has been attributed, in large part, to the use of local land use controls to exclude "undesirable" types of development. Through such devices as large lot zoning, density controls, minimum floor area requirements, and other substantive controls, not to mention a Byzantine system of administrative procedures, the cost and type of housing in many suburban areas has been controlled in such a manner that only the expensive single family or multiple dwellings are feasible. Thus, many persons with low incomes, particularly racial minorities, are prevented from "polluting" the suburbs. A look at some of the cases that crowd state and federal courts provides evidence of the continuing concern, at least in the state courts, for exclusionary zoning. Some state legislatures in the early years of this decade directed the establishment of programs pursuant to which state agencies are exercising an increasing influence and even direct control over important aspects of land use planning and control.

The paradox is that while some state legislatures and some state courts are questioning municipal domination, imaginative municipal governments are implementing initiatives to control more firmly the development of land within their jurisdictions. Such plans are receiving favorable acceptance by the courts, although scrutinized to prevent racial and economic discrimination. Timed development ordinances, moratoria on building permits, controls to limit second home development, historic preservation designations, charter amendments to put a cap on total permissible dwelling units within a municipality, and other municipal control efforts going beyond traditional zoning and subdivision programs have received judicial approval.

The disquiet over the present system does not only result from the struggle between those who seek to substitute regional control for municipal power and those who would invent ingenious techniques to maintain local

control. The unrest is also apparent in the increasing demands that, in the
larger cities at least, community organizations be given a greater voice in
land use policies which affect their neighborhoods. The call for greater
citizen participation in land use policy has been implemented by the increasing use of the initiative and referendum to check local legislative decisions
on land development policy.

Perhaps the most renowned uprising was the passage of Proposition
20—the creation of the California Coastal Zone Conservation Commission—by a voter referendum in California in 1972. Voters in San Antonio,
Texas, recently forced a referendum on a regional shopping center approved by the San Antonio City Council and voted to reverse the Council's
approval. Other examples of voter referenda limiting action of local governing bodies are to be found. Many of these programs and actions have been
responses to the conviction that municipal governments have lacked a
resolve to resist the blandishments and political pressure from interests
seeking to use land for their personal gain. One can only speculate as to
what effect the United States Supreme Court decision in *City of Eastlake* v.
Forest City Engerprises, Inc.,[8] which upheld a charter provision requiring a
referendum before final approval of land use changs, is going to have in encouraging even greater resort to the polls to preclude new development.

So this is an era when the old verities on land use policy are up for
grabs. The environmentalists, after five years of persistent victories, sense a
backlash and protest that the rape goes on unabated; the developers are in-
credulous that municipalities can lawfully take away what they regard as
their inalienable rights in property; and the civil libertarians curse both their
houses, confident that the ecologists too often serve as a respectable if un-
witting cover for less legitimate purposes, yet nervous of making an entente
with the builders against a perceived common enemy. Finally, those
associated with municipal agencies are coming to realize that they are at the
end of an era of tranquility, at the close of a half century during which all
powers to regulate land use affairs were unquestionably municipal.

There may be a common ground upon which an acceptable accommodation among those divergent interests may be reached. What is
necessary is this: that a theoretical base for a land use policy be constructed
that has some prospect for achieving reform, will be acceptable to most interested parties, and is based on some established parallels in Anglo-
American law and politics.

IV.

The flaw in the current debate on land policy is that the choices offered by
the antagonists often are too extreme. Either the landowner should be

compelled by uncompensated regulation to make no economic use of his land or, indeed, to dedicate it to the public, or he should be free to do as he pleases, subject to whatever accommodation he can make with other landowners (neighbors) in any one of the multitude of jurisdictions that may have some voice on a development proposal. As long as the issues remain so polarized, a land use policy acceptable to most people is unlikely. We believe the current debate on land use policy may benefit from an examination of the long-established treatment of businesses "affected with a public interest" including, but not limited to, public utilities.

A century ago, in *Munn v. Illinois*, the United States Supreme Court held that Illinois could regulate the prices charged by warehousemen. The plaintiff alleged a "taking." The Court said government can regulate "conduct of its citizens one towards another and the manner in which each shall own his own property, *when such regulation becomes necessary for the public good*." The Court added:

> In their exercise [of these public powers] it has been customary in England from time immemorial, and in this country from its first colonization, to regulate ferries, common carriers, hackmen, bakers, millers, wharfingers, innkeepers, etc., and in so doing to fix a maximum of charge to be made for services rendered, accommodations furnished, and articles sold.

The Court repeated the wisdom of Lord Chief Justice Hale: "[W]hen private property is 'affected with a public interest, it ceases to be *juris privati* only.' "[9]

There is no magical formula in the Anglo-American precedents to determine when a private interest is affected with a public interest and ceases to be *juris privati*. Statutes and cases throughout the United States suggest the breadth of regulation which has been applied to a variety of businesses, commodities, or services. For example, among the various items that have been subject to extensive regulation, including in many instances the regulation of price, the quality of service and, indeed, the prudence of investment and rate of return, are milk, theatre tickets, alcoholic beverages, bread, used cars, agricultural commodities, water, sewer services, natural gas, electricity, telephone and telegraph services, transportation services of all kinds, warehouses, docks, toll bridges, stockyards, ice, steamheating, and cotton ginning, as well as other enterprises.

In *Nebbia v. New York*, the Supreme Court upheld against a due process challenge a New York statute establishing a milk control board with authority to fix minimum and maximum retail prices. The Court stated: "The Constitution does not guarantee the unrestricted privilege to engage in a business or to conduct it as one pleases." The Court also recognized that the selling of milk was not a public utility, but nevertheless concluded that the sale of milk could be subject to state regulation:

> We may as well say at once that the dairy industry is not, in the accepted sense of the phrase, a public utility. We think the appellant is also right in asserting that there is in this case no suggestion of any monopoly or monopolistic practice. It goes without saying that those engaged in the business are in no way dependent upon public grants or franchises for the privilege of conducting their activities. But if, as must be conceded, the industry is subject to regulation in the public interest, what constitutional principle bars the state from correcting existing maladjustments by legislation touching prices? We think there is no such principle.

Due process required only that the law "not be unreasonable, arbitrary or capricious, and that the means selected shall have a real and substantial relation to the object sought to be attained."[10]

Millers and wharfingers, theatre tickets, and used cars can hardly be said to be more affected with a public interest than dealings in and the use of land. Land is a limited if not depleting commodity which is intimately bound up with our public health and welfare. It is a commodity the use and misuse of which can impose enormous public and external costs. Yet land has been treated with a forbearance by the public that is not extended, for example, to the ownership and sale of natural gas or electricity, or the sale of liquor, or the use of the air waves. The ownership of land is often identified with outrageous profits and catastrophic losses, each such consequence more often than not attributable to a spillover from some public act or expenditure. When public surveillance of dealings in and use of scores of other commodities is the accepted responsibility of the states or the national government, the regulation of the use of land should not be left to the caprice and parochial intents of multitudes of local governments, each defining the public welfare in its own image, or in the image of a clutch of neighboring property owners.

Land, and as such its ownership, continues to benefit or suffer, in a variety of quixotic ways, from an ancient inheritance that seems anachronistic in the last years of the Twentieth Century. We propose to examine a few of the current issues in land use policy that might benefit from an extension of the old constitutional doctrine that permits public regulation of a "commodity affected with a public interest," whether or not that commodity or service is labelled a "public utility."

V.

A. Public Scrutiny of Profits and Performance

Alleged windfalls in land development—speculative profits–are a common charge in many sections of the country. The protest is notably strident when the windfalls to landowners are a result of the decisions of public agencies to exercise land use or environmental controls in a particular manner or to make investments of public funds in public facilities which benefit particular land. A number of devices have been suggested to extract from landowners some portion of the public expenditures that increase the value of private land. Among the more common techniques are special assessments, and requirements that the developer dedicate land, improve public facilities, or make payments to public agencies in lieu of dedication or improvement. Vermont has adopted a Land Gains Tax in an effort to discourage land speculation and, not so incidentally, out-of-state developers. The Vermont Supreme Court upheld the tax law and acknowledged that deterrence of land speculation may have been one of the legislative purposes behind the taxes:

> [W]e may take judicial notice of an increasing concern within the State over the use and development of land as a natural resource . . . . Speculation falls within the ambit of such concern as a land use; indeed it has a bearing on many other uses to which the land might be put.[11]

"Recapture of value" recently has concerned those urban planners and transit authorities who note the consequence to market values of land abutting fixed rail transit stops. Although it is not our purpose to choose between specific techniques to recover a share of the profit from these coups, we do suggest that advocates of "recapture" should not have to apologize—let them look to traditional public utility regulation.

The concept of a limitation to "fair rate of return" is not alien to our legal system. The entrepreneur who enjoys a special status because of benefits conferred by the public has been subject to public control over his rate of return for at least a century. In 1923, the United States Supreme Court in *Bluefield Water Works & Improvement Co.,* v. *Public Service Commission of West Virginia* dealt specifically with the issue of the return on investment to which a utility is entitled and concluded that there is no constitutional right to such profits as might be anticipated in other higher profitable or speculative ventures:

> A public utility is entitled to such rates as will permit it to earn a return on the value of the property which it employs for the convenience of the public equal to that generally being made at the same time and in the same general part of the country on investments in other business undertakings which are attended by corresponding risks and uncertainties . . . .[12]

In a subsequent case the Court held that the return can properly be measured on the actual cost of the investment rather than any market or reproduction cost or value. Despite whatever increase in value may accrue to the property of a public utility after an investment has been made, there is no right on the part of the owners to realize that increase at the expense of the ratepayers. Furthermore, it is clear that a fair return is not to be mistaken for a publicly guaranteed rate of return—witness the repeated wipeout of shareholders in railroad reorganizations.

The only examples we have uncovered of direct government regulation of prices affecting private land are rent controls imposed in various parts of the country. Such controls have been upheld as constitutional exercises of governmental authority. The supreme court of New Jersey recently upheld rent controls adopted by the Township of Parsippany-Troy Hills. The court reviewed a number of tests for determining the fair value of rental property and indicated that utility precedents are of value in determining whether rent controls permit a reasonable return to the apartment owner. In discussing the question of what is a "just and reasonable return," the New Jersey court echoed the opinions of other courts that upheld the validity of public regulation of private activity involving personal property or services:

> [T]o be "just and reasonable" a rate of return must be high enough to encourage good management including adequate maintenance of services, to furnish a reward for efficiency, to discourage the flight of capital from the rental housing market, and to enable operators to maintain and support their credit. A just and reasonable return is one which is generally commensurate with returns on investments in other enterprises having corresponding risks. On the other hand it is also one which is not so high as to defeat the purposes of rent control nor permit landlords to demand of tenants more than the fair value of the property and services which are provided. The rate need not be as high as existed prior to regulation nor as high as an investor might obtain by placing his capital elsewhere.[13]

Rent controls, however, have had a rather limited application and do not directly control the often speculative and profitable transactions involving the sale of land. More often than not they have been inconsistent with a public rhetoric directed toward more and better housing.

Decisions by the management of public utilities on capital expenditures are scrutinized for inflated or imprudent investments to assure that customers are not required to pay for facilities or to provide a return on investment in facilities which are not reasonably required to provide adequate service. As one court stated:

> If . . . construction undertaken by the Company is "wasteful," or its expense is unwarranted by the demand probable at the necessary price for service produced by it, or if "proper economies in management are lacking" so that operating expenditures are shown to be excessive or overestimated, unwarranted investments may be excluded from rate base, and unjustified expenditures from the determination of a reasonable return.[14]

In determining the base on which a return is allowed for utility rates, no allowance is permitted in the rate base for the monopoly value of the franchise. A leading text on public utility economics states the general rule: "Although there is no dispute that the monopoly franchise is valuable, it is recognized as having originated in a grant by the public."[15] In land development, to the contrary, the monopoly incident to location near a *public* investment can be a major factor in a windfall return.

Operations of utilities are also scrutinized to assure that some reasonable degree of service is being rendered to the public. When a utility fails to provide adequate service, regulatory agencies may require a utility to make such improvements as are deemed necessary. The obligation to provide adequate service does not mean that a utility must provide the highest possible quality of service, but, rather, that service be reasonable in terms of public demands, costs, and the condition of the utility. In addition, the quality of the service a utility renders the public has been held to be relevant to the question of the allowable return on investment. Where a utility provides poor or inefficient service, it can expect regulatory agencies to be less generous in setting an allowable return on investment. Conversely, "[t]he reasonable rate to be prescribed by a commission may allow an efficiently managed utility much more."[16]

The law is clear that parties making the decision to conduct business vitally affecting the public interest, such as utilities, can be subject to extensive regulation with respect to the quality of the service they provide, the return they will be permitted to earn at the expense of the public, and the reasonableness of the investments they make in conducting the business. It seems reasonable that when public expenditures or the exercise of public authority enhance the value, and consequently the profits, of that vital but limited public resource, land, it is proper that the public exercise some overview of the profit the owner of land will realize from that property. Such oversight should assure that the public not be forced to pay a price which gives the land speculator unreasonable profits attributable to public favors.

The only reason such a suggestion may be shocking is because it is land, not traditional utility or common carrier services, being considered. It is an inadequate rejoinder to assert that utility regulation is based on the need to control an essential natural monopoly such as gas or electricity. That begs the question. Gas and electricity are in competition, both between themselves and with unregulated forms of energy. The finite land which is available clearly is no less essential to society. Why then should transactions in land not be subject to greater and less parochial public scrutiny than is the case today?

The apparent difficulties in transplanting similar public controls to profit, price, and service in land development may be real or they may only appear perplexing because of our historical block concerning transactions in land. Surely, the development of a regulatory system would involve no more obtuse jargon and sanctified formulae than have accompanied the evolution of the regulation of pricing, profit, and quality of service by regulated utilities. Today the developer who proposes a large scale land development under a planned development ordinance must negotiate every aspect of his proposal from allowable densities to contributions of cash or land. There is no reason why he should not also be subject to scrutiny over the prudence of his investment and the rate of his return. The developer should be bound as well to his representations on quality of service. One thing seems sure—such a reform would underscore the need to shift decisions over major land development from the municipality to the state with the former playing the role of advocate, either for or against the proposal, in a state forum.

B. Quotas and Priorities: Quantitative Controls
and Permissible Discrimination

A second and substantially different land use issue might benefit from an examination of the precedents in not only utility but also licensing law. The traditional zoning rationale tells municipalities to take into account "the character of the district."[17] Under traditional land use dogma "more is better." The first intrusion is the excuse, legally, for the next. The presence of one gas station at an intersection is the justification for a second. The first highrise to enter the three-story brownstone neighborhood is the camel's nose under the tent for a wall of highrises. The first half-way house in a neighborhood is often the precursor of another and another. And the rub with the "fair share" low-income housing schemes—even if they do prove to be more than noble proclamations—is that they do not protect the participating communities from the developer who is not a party to an intermunicipal agreement and sees a financial opportunity in exceeding the quota in a particular community. If a developer selects his neighborhood with care, the traditional zoning doctrine which looks to the "character of the neighborhood" will facilitate his effort to break the "fair share" plan. In short, in land use law today there is little law to justify quantitative controls, a concept that may be essential to brake the tendency of the real estate market to congregate.

The concept of quotas is nothing new to licensing law. The first statute in England to provide for a limit on the number of ale houses was Henry VII's law of 1495. Five centuries later, state and municipal governments in the United States have similar authority over dispensers of intoxicating beverages and the presence of five taverns may be a legal basis for a public decision to exclude a sixth. The concept of priorities and quotas—discrimination if you will—when authorized by the public agency, is also well established in public utility law. For example, the number of available radio frequencies is limited. To avoid confusion and interference that could result from attempts by radio broadcasters to utilize frequencies without adequate consideration to the use of the same frequency by others, the United States Congress enacted provisions of the Communications Act of 1934 requiring the licensing of radio broadcasting. The Federal Communications Commission controls the number of radio and television licenses permitted to operate in a given area and the conditions under which the licensees operate.

Perhaps the most graphic and recent examples authorizing public regulatory agencies to establish priorities or quotas regarding the provision of goods and services are the various programs used by natural gas distribution companies to deal with gas shortages by means of a freeze on new attachments to protect existing customers or by a limit on deliveries to existing customers. Among applicants for new gas service, utilities are permitted, even directed to give priority to residential consumers over commercial and industrial users. Such actions are designed to preserve a limited amount of fuel which may be declining in relation to the demand to assure a supply for those residential consumers least able to secure an alternative.

In land use regulation a quota system will, of course, raise difficult problems of equity. Quantitative control over half-way houses or gas stations is relatively easy. If, however, my neighbor obtains permission to build the only high-rise in the block, this undoubtedly confers special privileges on him, but in addition, and unlike the radio license, it may have an adverse impact on the marketability of my neighboring property for a single family home or a duplex. The answer may require a payment to me by the high-rise "licensee" as consideration for my covenant not to develop. In effect, I would share in his development profits.

Existing land use controls do discriminate and establish priorities to the extent they define what uses may be carried out on what land. It is instructive, however, to contrast the experience in land use control systems with public utility regulatory agencies that have authority to establish priorities and to order the regulated utilities to meet the priorities so that the over-all public interest is served. Land use control systems have little muscle in today's world to assure that whatever priorities are set will in fact find expression in actual land use and development beyond precluding non-priority uses or developments. Some recent efforts to require a specified percentage of low and moderate income housing as a condition to approval of a subdivision have not met with success.

We question whether there is a constitutional principle which compels a distinction between the establishment and implementation of priorities and quotas in the sale of electricity or natural gas but not in the sale and development of land.

Occasionally there will be a measure such as the Massachusetts "anti-snob" zoning legislation that permits a qualified developer of low-income housing, with the approval of a state agency, to override local zoning that prevents such housing. Some recent court opinions have suggested that community development controls will not be upheld if they do not accept a "fair share" of housing demand,[18] do not give "the opportunity for the location of appropriate housing for all classes of our citizenry,"[19] or do not balance the local desire to maintain the status quo within the community with regional housing needs. However laudable such judicial responses may be, courts recognize they are unable to effectively cure problems of lack of housing in absence of direct government action. Significant construction of housing for people in all income ranges is unlikely without appropriate carrots or sticks provided by public agencies.

If "fair share" is to become a standard for judging the validity of land use regulations that affect housing, it will be necessary to abandon the "more is better" philosophy and introduce quantitative controls and discrimination. A community which has accepted its "fair share" should not be required to accept more simply because a developer sees an opportunity to make money.

It is possible that selectivity, legitimate discrimination, and quantitative controls, all common to public utility and licensing law, may inject themselves into land use policy by way of environmental law. A developer's right to build homes may depend less upon the zoning he can get than where he stands in line on hookups to the public sewer. The United States Environmental Protection Agency has authority to prohibit local sewage treatment plants from accepting any new connections if the plant does not have adequate capacity to treat additional sewage. Sewer connection moratoria are not uncommon. Indeed, some municipalities have attempted with mixed success to use sewers as one element in a growth control plan. Availability of potable water may also result in severe limitations on growth and development.

Some of the state land use and environmental initiatives designed to protect particularly sensitive ecological areas may provide a justification for selecting and limiting, if not mandating, the quantity as well as the type of development which may take place in designated areas. The New Jersey Coastal Area Facility Review Act, the California Coastal Zone Conservation Act of 1972, the New York Adirondack Park Agency Act, and the Washington Shoreline Management Act are examples of legislation that require the balancing of the need for development with a public interest in preserving areas deemed of some particular significance to the public. For example, the New Jersey law requires development of a comprehensive plan

selected from identified alternative "environmental management strategies
which take into account the paramount need for preserving environmental
values and the legitimate need for economic and residential growth within
the coastal area."[20] Such environmental controls could compel a choice between alternative proposals for development that might in turn introduce a
social purpose by extending a priority to those builders who include some
low-income housing in their developments.

Introduction of a social purpose into land use regulation would bring
regulation into line with public utility law, which has seen regulatory agencies begin to take more and more interest in protecting the right of disadvantaged classes to utility services at reasonable rates. Utility regulatory
agency requirements that "lifeline" services be made available at lower than
normal monthly rates reflect special consideration for the elderly, the poor,
and the infirm. Such services permit customers to receive a bare minimum
amount of electric or telephone service to meet emergencies and basic needs
without having to pay the normal rates which permit middle class subur-
banites to satisfy their desires for a variety of conveniences. Concern for
protection of customers against arbitrary denial or termination of utility
service by utilities over-zealous to protect revenues against nonpayment of
bills has led courts and regulatory agencies to take a more active role in
policing utility credit and service termination practices and in requiring
utilities to adopt more explicit procedural guidelines and safeguards to deal
with credit and bill payment matters.

The usefulness of quotas and priorities in land use controls is not
limited to housing needs. The San Francisco Bay Conservation and
Development Commission (BCDC) recognized the danger of running out of
industrial waterfront sites which do not require additional filling of the Bay.
In order to assure utilization of waterfront sites in a manner consistent with
the over-all objectives of the BCDC plan, the BCDC has established
priorities by designating certain areas exclusively for the use of "water-
related industries."

C. Protection of Existing Development from Economic
Competition

There is a third area where the experience in public utility regulation may
offer some lessons in the formulation of land use policy. Public utility
plants and facilities are expensive private undertakings and it is generally
believed that the public interest is best served if utilities are granted
monopolies to serve specified areas. The reasoning is that the monopoly
permits utility service to be provided economically and efficiently because
the public does not have to pay for the construction and operation of dupli-

cative and costly utility systems. The utility also receives some benefit because it is assured a defined market relatively free of competition with respect to the particular service it provides. In return for its limited monopoly, the utility is subject to regulation with respect to its rates, return on investment and the quality and manner of service it provides. The utility is protected, however, only so long as it provides adequate service; it may be compelled by law to improve service or give up its franchise.

The monopolies granted do not in all instances relieve utilities from competition. Particularly in the energy field, competition is still significant. Electricity may replace gas or oil for heating purposes. For the individual homeowner, however, this freedom to substitute different fuels does not come without expensive alterations to heating equipment that substantially reduces any real competition.

In land use law, the suggestion that regulation may have as a legitimate purpose the protection of existing uses from competition is greeted by the charge that such is improper. Some cases maintain that the use of zoning regulations to control competition is ultra vires or unconstitutional, while others suggest that control of competition cannot be the dominant purpose in zoning. These responses are bemusing in light of the monopolistic consequences of the traditional zoning treatment of nonconforming uses, and the common and accepted litany in zoning cases that apartments may be excluded from single-family districts because, among other consequences, apartments will damage existing single-family property values.

If it is a desirable public policy in the provision of utility services to grant at least limited monopolies in order to avoid wasteful duplication of facilities and resources, there also may be a public interest in a land use policy which seeks to provide more protection than is allowed by traditional zoning dogma against the exploitation for private gain of limited land resources in a manner unnecessarily duplicative of and potentially destructive of existing land uses serving the same community of interest. Suppose, for example, a city with a population of 100,000, an urban center in a rural setting, has seen its central business district deteriorate and decides to remedy the situation. With substantial federal aid and considerable local effort, private and public, it starts to revitalize its central business district. It persuades a major retail chain to rebuild in the run-down central business district. It creates the usual mall, gets a national chain to operate a new hotel and, generally, decides to fight downtown blight. Should the municipality be permitted to use its zoning power to deny a building permit to a developer who wants to construct a regional shopping center on the fringe of the city on the candid basis that the regional shopping center is a threat to the revitalization of its central business district which, in turn, is regarded as essential to the health of the entire city?

It is absurd to deny that zoning regulations have an impact on economic competition whether among commercial or residential developments. Courts that subscribe to the doctrine that zoning may not have as its sole or primary purpose the regulation of business competition are left with the thorny problem of trying to decipher when a zoning ordinance is intended solely or primarily to effect competition. In 1969 a superior court of New Jersey upheld a zoning ordinance which was designed to restrict retail sales to the central business district. The court rejected the claim by the owners of a tract of land located in an outlying area, who wished to construct a supermarket, that the zoning ordinance was unconstitutional. The court held that the municipality had a right to enact measures designed to revitalize the central business area. Although the zoning ordinance might give the central area a virtual monopoly over new retail business, the court did not invalidate the ordinance. It was willing, however, to suggest that the municipality had a right to restrict competition and suggested that the exclusion of competition was simply "an incident or effect of otherwise valid zoning."[21] A California court of appeal upheld a city's denial of a permit to construct an automobile service station. The court accepted the traditional litany that zoning regulation cannot be used to control economic competition, but it stated that "so long as the primary purpose of the zoning ordinance is not to regulate economic competition, but to subserve a valid objective pursuant to a city's police powers, such ordinance is not invalid even though it might have an indirect impact on economic competition."[22]

These and other cases demonstrate that zoning regulation affects competition, but that is not acceptable advocacy to say so. Other courts have recognized that the absence of a public need for a particular use is a valid factor to be considered in judging the reasonableness of a zoning ordinance. But despite such opinions, courts are generally inclined to the proposition that where the declared purpose of land use regulation is to protect specific economic interests the regulation is invalid, but if another "valid" purpose is stated with the incidental effect being to restrict economic competition, the regulation is proper. We suggest there is no legitimate public interest served, beyond the possible encouragement of creative ordinance drafting, in forcing courts to probe the minds of local officials to determine whether a zoning ordinance in fact has as its primary purpose the regulation of economic competition or is intended to achieve other public purposes. Regulation that confers economic benefits is an accepted concept in other areas of law and should be similarly accepted in dealings with land. It seems strange that the character of a single-family neighborhood can be "protected" from a multiple family dwelling, but a central business district cannot be protected from an outlying shopping center. In public utility law the issue would be whether the central business district is providing adequate service. If it is, it will be protected; if it is not, it will be required to shape up or a competitor will be franchised.

A rule of law that flatly rejects the employment of land use regulation to protect existing development from adverse economic competition on the ground that land use policy cannot protect one enterprise from another is not only hypocritical, but also blind to important public concerns as well as to long accepted public policy doctrines. Before the turn of this century, public utility and licensing laws had sanctioned the protection of existing enterprises from uncontrolled competition in appropriate circumstances, not for the purpose of conferring a benefit on the protected enterprises, but because it is believed that some public interest is thereby advanced. The same considerations could be usefully employed in land use law if the mystique surrounding the ownership of land were shed.

D. Land Assembly

A final illustration of an area in land use policy where experience in public utility law may be instructive is the assembly of land, a trying experience for the private entrepreneur. A variety of techniques have been proposed or utilized by public agencies to amass sufficient land to permit development of a single large parcel. Land banking by public agencies has been employed in a number of European countries, particularly Sweden and the Netherlands, and has been widely acclaimed as a mechanism for encouraging orderly urban growth. Advocates of land banking suggest it is a viable means to control urban land sprawl and to assure that land development is soundly planned. The Model Land Development Code approved by the American Law Institute in 1975 contains an article on Land Banking which provides for the creation of a State Land Reserve Agency with authority to acquire land "for the public purpose of achieving the land policy and land planning objectives of this State. . . ."[23] Although still an untried technique in the United States, legislation authorizing land banking in Puerto Rico has been upheld by the Puerto Rico Supreme Court and an appeal to the United States Supreme Court was dismissed.

We surmise, however, that most land development in the United States will continue to be undertaken by private enterprise. Unlike public agencies, private land developers today do not have the power to condemn, nor should they be so endowed, given our present fractured system of control over land development. If, however, some of the old precepts applicable to businesses "affected with a public interest," such as the concept of a limitation to a fair rate of return based on prudent capital investment, a duty to provide adequate facilities and services, and, above all, a consistency of land development with publicly articulated development policies, were introduced into land development, then those *public* standards would be consistent with a system that authorized a state agency to issue a certificate of authority to private enterprise to condemn for the purpose of land assembly, at least in large-scale undertakings. An electric or gas utility may obtain the right to condemn, provided its proposal for development, for example, to construct a new pipeline, is found by an appropriate regulatory authority to be required for the public convenience and necessity. When such a finding is made after an adversary proceeding, the public interest is served by permitting private enterprise to exercise this sovereign power. The sad record of flirtation with new towns is attributable to a multitude of public and private sins, but at least the delays and costs in getting such projects under way would have been substantially reduced had the developers had the certified authority—essential in negotiating—to condemn.

It is ironic that in a tentative draft of the American Law Institute's Model Land Development Code, the Reporters and the Advisory Committee proposed just such a power for developers of large-scale projects provided, first, that the developers assemble a substantial percentage of the land by purchase and second, that their development receive approval from the state planning agency. Because many ALI members were lawyers with utility clients, it was assumed this suggestion would receive a sympathetic response. The idea was squashed decisively by the members of the ALI who reacted not as utility lawyers but as residents of suburban communities. The attitude seemed to be that no land developer should have such authority.

Conclusion

We have suggested that models of regulation of businesses affected with the public interest, including public utilities, may be instructive in dealing with transactions in land. We do not propose that any such regulatory mechanisms could or should be applied wholesale to all land development or transactions in land. There are many practical and conceptual difficulties in the application of licensing and public utility concepts to the development of land or to transactions in land. The variety of interests in land are more subtle and complex than are the interests in the goods and services that are now extensively regulated for prudence of investment, price and quality of service. There is an understandable public interest in assuring a substantial uniformity in the availability of natural gas, electricity, telephone service, or milk. Individuals who trade and invest in land, however, look for various locations, differing amenities, and other characteristics which will make their demands and needs difficult to fit into a uniform public policy. People have different tastes with respect to whether they live on a corner, along a lakeshore, in the middle of a city, in a rural setting, with a south or a north view, near or far away from a school, or any variety of other factors.

The factors that affect the value individuals will place on particular real property may also be of a different nature than those encountered in some of the more traditional systems regulating personal property. Regulatory mechanisms that deal with other commercial enterprises do, however, recognize the need to accommodate varying needs and interests. The rate tariffs of a typical gas, telephone, or electric utility illustrate the wide variation in types of services available and the multitude of price levels which may be charged. Various grades of party line service, private line service, service with unlimited calling privileges in a specified geographic area, extended area service, and a variety of options give the subscriber a wide choice of services depending on how much the individual wants to pay and how many of the services he wants to use.

All transactions in land cannot be subjected to detailed utility-type regulatory oversight; such a system would be intolerable. Nevertheless, the application of such mechanisms to those developments or transactions which exceed a specified dollar amount or acreage would be feasible. The exemption of small transactions from regulation is a familiar concept in American law. Securities laws, both federal and state, contain exemptions with respect to registration requirements for small offerings of securities. Experience under such exemptions suggests they must be carefully designed to assure that the overall public purpose behind regulation is not defeated by activities which are conducted on a small enough scale to escape regulation but which on an incremental basis could undermine the public goals.

The problem of a remedy against a land developer who does not live up to his or her representations or carry out the conditions of his or her license may, as a conceptual matter, seem awkward to put right. Once a building or other improvement is constructed, courts are reluctant to require its removal. Indeed, once land development activity has commenced, it may be impossible to restore natural features of the environment destroyed in the development process. Part of this problem can be dealt with by requiring developers and land speculators to demonstrate their financial and other capabilities as a condition of permission to undertake their activities. Bonding is a common means of protection against default. Licensing of various trades, businesses, and professions, conditioned upon standards concerning the character and responsibility—financial or otherwise—of the licensee, is common. Utilities generally are not permitted to begin their operations and vend their services until a certificate of public convenience and necessity is obtained. In this way the public is able to exercise some oversight to assure that an activity is conducted by someone with the expertise, resources and capability necessary to carry it through.

Analogy to other fields of public interest regulation suggests several other potential remedial devices. For example, licensees under the FCC are subject to periodic review and renewal and their licenses to operate are, at least as a matter of law, revocable. The concept of a forced divestiture of ownership is not unknown to the antitrust laws. The availability of such remedies as non-renewal of a license or divestiture would generate a greater concern by the entrepreneur for compliance with the dictates of the public interest than has been the case under the present system of land use regulation.

As counsel for public utilities, the authors know, and from time to time have shouted, all the usual complaints about utility regulation: the over-regulation, the political pressures and the potential for venality. We believe each of these evils is substantially greater in our disordered system of land use regulation. What our present land use regulation system does not provide, however, is public scrutiny over speculative profits derived from monopoly benefits arising from public expenditures; nor does our system have an effective method for permitting socially desirable discrimination; nor any way to protect what is regarded as a socially desirable investment; nor a method to compel a sharing of the costs of subsidized but socially desirable growth.

We hardly need document the failure of the American system of land use planning and controls to assure that all people have the opportunity to obtain a decent place to live according to their needs and capabilities. That goal requires that a limited supply of land, little of which remains within a reasonable distance from existing jobs, be developed in a manner which takes into account not only the profit motive of the developer, but overall social needs as well. By any measure, land is a commodity that justifies as much if not a greater degree of public scrutiny and accountability by those private interests profiting from public favors, as does telephone service, the sale of liquor, or wharfingering. The courts and legislatures have not hesitated to extend public regulation to these latter items and many others. If we are serious about reform in land use policy, the time has come to replace old rhetoric and exotic proposals with some ideas that have been around for centuries in respect to public regulation of transactions in other commodities far less affected with the public interest than is the case with land.

Notes

1. A. Leopold, *A Sand County Almanc* (1949), p. vii.

2. S. Milsom, *Historical Foundations of the Common Law* (1969), p. 88.

3. F. Pollock and F. Maitland, *The History of English Law* (2d edition, 1898), vol. 2, p. 153.

4. F. Thorpe, *The Constitutional History of the United States* (1901), vol. 1, p. 464.

5. 272 U.S. 365 (1926).

6. Housing Act of 1949, 42 U.S.C. 1441 (1970).

7. Norman Williams, *American Land Planning Law* (1974), vol. 1, paragraph 5.06.

8. 96 S. Ct. 2358 (1976).

9. 94 U.S. 113 (1876).

10. 291 U.S. 502 (1934).

11. *Andrews* v. *Lathrop*, 132 Vt. 256 (1976).

12. 262 U.S. 679 (1923).

13. *Troy Hills Village* v. *Township Council*, 68 N.J. 604 (1975).

14. *New England Tel. and Tel. Co.* v. *State*, 95 N.H. 353 (1949).

15. P. Garfield and W. Lovejoy, *Public Utility Economics* (1964), p. 85.

16. *Missouri ex. rel. Southwestern Bell Tel. Co.* v. *Missouri Public Service Commission,* 262 U.S. 276, 291 (1923) (Brandeis, J., concurring).

17. The Advisory Committee on Zoning, U.S. Department of Commerce, *A Standard State Zoning Enabling Act* (1924), paragraph 3.

18. *Township of Willistown* v. *Chesterdale Farms Inc.,* 462 Pa. 445 (1975).

19. *NAACP* v. *Township of Mount Laurel*, 67 N.J. 151 (1975).

20. N.J. Stat. Ann. paragraph 13:19-16 (West. Supp. 1976-77).

21. *Forte* v. *Borough of Tenafly*, 255 A.2d at 806 (1969).

22. *Van Sicklen* v. *Browne*, 92 Cal. Rptr. at 790 (1971).

23. American Law Institute, *Model Land Development Code* (1975), paragraph 6-101.

Part IV
Ownership

10 Ownership: The Hidden Factor in Land Use Regulation

Frank J. Popper

What most often determines a community's land use? What most often determines its growth? The majority of planners, environmentalists, and government officials would answer these questions by pointing to the land-use regulations they support and administer. On the other hand, most builders, realtors, businessmen and bankers would no less egocentrically point to the market decisions of the development industry.

Both answers, it seems to me, are superficial, although the market one may be somewhat closer to the truth. I would like to argue that the underlying factor in a community's land use and growth is neither the regulation nor the development of its land, but the ownership of it. By ownership, I mean not just the identity of the owners, but also the concentration and value of their holdings and the changes in them over time. Ownership patterns can decisively influence regulatory and market actions, and therefore land use and growth. As we shall see, they have other important social effects as well.

The development industry, whose business it is to deal in the commodity of land, is naturally aware of the significance of land ownership. But many persons whose job it is to regulate land apparently don't know or care about this most basic political and economic fact of the resource they guard. Unlike developers, to whom they seem naive, they are profoundly unaware of the inherent polarity of ownership and regulation. The one aims at private benefit, the other at public benefit. The one means use, the other restraint of use. The objects of ownership and regulation coincide only occasionally. Regulation will only enlist the support of owners when it happens to give them something they want—as, for example, in the case of suburban zoning that upholds property values, excludes unwanted minorities, or takes the growth stance owners prefer.

More frequently, however, ownership and regulation will be diametrically opposed, particularly over the short term. Regulators and owners are natural enemies. But regulators, especially those motivated by some long-term conception of the public interest, rarely grasp the extent of the enmity. So they are usually surprised when technically excellent land-use or environmental controls they propose are rejected, evaded, not enforced,

---

This chapter was originally prepared for publication in *Environmental Comment*, a periodical published by the Urban Land Institute, and is reprinted with permission.

or otherwise made unworkable because of the resistance of owners who don't want to be regulated. The regulators, then, after the fact, attribute their defeats to the machinations of "the big interests."

Yet the size of the resistant interests has little to do with the matter. They resist not because they are big, but because they are owners. The resistant owners need not be large—indeed, most of them are not. A few years ago, in one of the most spectacular planning failures of modern times, a genuinely imaginative and equitable package of land-use and environmental controls was rejected by the small farmers of the Brandywine Creek watershed in exurban Philadelphia. Most of them knew that it would increase property values and amenities. A township supervisor explained to Ann Strong, the leader of the excellent University of Pennsylvania team that designed the plan and thought it had local support, that "The people don't understand communal responsibility toward the land for they are the lords of the land." Another resident said, "If a man's home is his castle, then his land is his fertility. To take away his rights in the land is nothing less than castration."[1]

It is not surprising that Ms. Strong—a most distinguished professor of planning—did not understand the force of these feelings. Planners almost never do. Neither do other regulators. They constantly hear such sentiments not just from small farmers, but also from small suburban and urban homeowners, middle- and large-sized developers, and the gigantic corporations that own vast tracts of the country.

These groups express and act on their sentiments in different ways, of course, but the essential message is the same. All owners feel drawn to their land. They would intrinsically prefer to avoid regulation. They will always fight it. If absolutely necessary, they will accept it, but only in the weakest form possible. It is not a matter of disliking change or paperwork. It is not even necessarily a matter of liking money. It is an instance of the deep human impulse to property, which becomes yet deeper in the context of the American tradition of free-enterprise individualism. But regulators rarely seem to comprehend either the emotional strength of the impulse or the political strength of the tradition.

This incomprehension—more precisely, this obliviousness—hurts regulators in their work, makes them less able to deal with many issues they must face. It means, most strikingly, that they will be insensitive to the effects of concentrated ownership until it is too late to do anything about them. A city, county, or region whose ownership is highly concentrated or becoming so is disproportionately likely to be one where land-use and environmental laws will be subverted by political influence, where assessments will unfairly favor large landowners, where citizen participation won't work, where irresponsible absentee ownership will often ignore the government and people of the community, and where irresponsible local ownership will simply manipulate them.

So, for example, a planner in such a community who tries to devise or implement a zoning ordinance without taking into account its ownership patterns will inevitably accomplish little. If he should begin to understand what is going on, he will typically assume that he can work out a peaceful compromise with the ownership forces. They will sensibly settle for a concession or qualification in the ordinance. By the time he knows better they will have rolled over him. There are too many planners to whom such revelation arrives late. And worse, there are more to whom it never comes.

One of the prime ways for regulators to avoid this obliviousness is to stop clouding their minds with worry about whether land is primarily a resource or a commodity. If we appreciate the significance of ownership, we free ourselves from this cliché riddle. We see immediately that land is primarily a social weapon. It is a means by which its possessors protect their economic, political and other interests. It is a form of power, in some ways the most tangible and primitive form. As such, it will never willingly submit to control and rarely admit of the kind of compromise dear to regulators who have not caught on that they are out of their depth.

If we conceive of land as a social weapon, it follows that land's power whether exerted offensively or defensively, will always advantage—often unintentionally—those who own land at the expense of those who do not. It will generally favor those with more (or more valuable) land over those with less. And in fact instances of the employment of land as a weapon are so numerous, diverse, and far-reaching that they tempt an assertion—that the difference between landowners and the landless is one of the key social divisions in contemporary America. We may not have come that far from feudalism after all. Land ownership determines so much for us. And if we are of the regulatory persuasion, we usually don't realize it.

For example, the well-known difficulties of the energy boom towns of the West are typically attributed to the scale and rapidity of the development needed. But neither this development nor the growth problems it caused would have occurred if the local ownership patterns had not made them possible in the first place. These patterns are nearly always those of high concentration among huge railroads, utilities, oil companies, coal companies, and federal agencies. They mean that a comparatively small number of transactions, made by large outside interests dealing solely among themselves, can overwhelm local government and quickly change the community for the worse.

Thus University of Montana historian K. Ross Toole, visiting Rock Springs, Wyoming, one of the most overcrowded and slum-like of the boom towns, talked to the manager of the local Chamber of Commerce, who said "You look around and you think, why the hell, there's land in every direction." "The problem," Toole writes, "is that the price put on the usable land by the Union Pacific and Bureau of Land Management is so absurdly high, no one can buy any land to build on." And, the manager told him, "we're going to double our population again in four years. You can't keep up with it."² The railroad and the agency almost certainly didn't mean to harm the farmers, ranchers, and transient workers of the town. They were just exercising their land power.

The sad story of the boom towns is an old one, unusual only in degree. Many other localities have found to their sorrow that their concentrated ownership made them vulnerable to rapid changes in land use. A good deal of the voracious growth of Sun Belt cities and Northeastern suburbs since 1945 has been made possible by the fact that large landowners on the urbanizing fringes of these areas have been able to sell off their holdings in huge chunks.

For example, the explosive urbanization of what may be the fastest-growing area of Florida, the coast of Pasco County north of Tampa, came about largely as a consequence of the sale of a single large ranch. Such transactions usually stimulate the local economy. But often—too often in places like Florida and California that in living memory were near-paradises—the sales have also led to irretrievable desecrations of beautiful land, endless miles of sprawl, the permanent loss of some of our best farmland and farmers, and immense strains on local governments and public services. Again, nobody wanted the growth to hurt these places. But the vigorous exercise of ownership power virtually guaranteed that it would. And we aren't by any means done with the growth.

One could cite many other instances where the land weapon has been employed in such a way as to harm the landless and the less landed, sometimes intentionally, sometimes not. These cases occur even when the ownership appears to be more dispersed than it was in Rock Springs or Pasco County. The second-homes boom of the late sixties and early seventies, which irreparably damaged many of the rural communities it hit, is an example. So is the current coal rush in Appalachia and the lower Midwest. So is the long-term rise of agribusiness and the resulting decline of the family farm—particularly the Southern black family farm, whose steady dissolution populated the ghetto.

Another example is the sustained constriction of public access to coasts and shorelines. Yet another is the forestry and other environmental maneuvering of the big timber-and-paper companies. (In 1970 the International Paper Company, hardly a household word outside its industry, was identified as the largest private landowner in the United States.³) Then there are the practices of landlords and speculators in big-city slums and transitional neighborhoods. Or the behavior of companies in company towns. Or the increased "posting" of private forests and farms. Or—an example that ought to shame regulators—the daily exercise of local zoning powers for exclusionary purposes. In all these cases regulators at all levels of government have been nearly impotent against ownership forces. The development industry, a more pragmatic group, has—not always with enthusiasm—accommodated itself to them.[4]

But despite the importance of land ownership, we know surprisingly little about it, especially about how it is concentrated. Regulators, as emphasized, usually aren't interested. Members of the development industry lack research skills or want to keep their results away from competitors. The only research groups that have been interested in ownership issues are Nader-type organizations, investigative reporters, state commissions that are somewhat insulated from local political pressures, and the U.S. Department of Agriculture's Economic Research Service. Together these groups have produced enough ownership studies, most of them on rural localities, to allow us to generalize from their findings.[5]

The most basic finding is that ownership is highly concentrated. Huge timber-and-paper, oil, coal, utility, railroad, and agribusiness companies own a large portion of the nation's private land, and undoubtedly a larger proportion of the best, most productive parts of it. The proportion owned by agribusiness is growing rapidly. Development companies, financial institutions, and manufacturing concerns own surprisingly little rural land, but they apparently hold a great deal of more valuable urban land. Nonlocal, absentee ownership is widespread. It may well be that most of the private land in America is owned by interests from out of state. These findings show precisely why regulators are so powerless against ownership forces, especially in rural areas.

Yet the studies leave a number of other important issues untouched. We know very little about urban ownership and virtually nothing about suburban ownership. We have no reliable studies on whether concentration outside the agricultural sector is increasing or decreasing over time. We have too little information on foreign ownership of American land, as well as on ownership by state and local agencies and by tax-exempt organizations. We don't know enough about underassessment of large holdings and overassessment of small ones. Perhaps worst of all, we have almost no good community-level studies on the social effects of concentrated ownership.[6] There is a great deal of fascinating and practical ownership research waiting to be done.

But is there anything useful that working regulators can do now about ownership? For all their faults, I think the answer is yes. The most essential thing they could do is to start paying attention to it. A simple but effective way to institutionalize such attention would be for the federal and state governments to require that their environmental impact statements deal with the ownership effects of proposed projects. Local zoning and planning boards, as well as state land-use, surface-mining, and public-utilities commissions, could do likewise in their reviews.

Beyond that, one has to concede that American governments generally can't or won't pursue policies deliberately intended to disperse or concentrate ownership. They can, however, try to ensure that their actions and private-sector ones do not cause excessively rapid, socially shattering changes in ownership patterns. Wherever possible, they should brake the rate of such change, whether the changes concentrate or disperse, so as to mitigate their worst social effects—the ones that are most dispossessing.

Thus, for example, federal land-management agencies need not sell or lease much of the West or the Outer Continental Shelf to energy companies right away, or in such large chunks. Other federal and state agencies can give financial and technical aid to communities now on the steep upswing of the energy boom. The federal Coastal Energy Impact Fund is a start in this direction. So are the minerals severance taxes of Montana and North Dakota, which in effect make the energy companies pay boom towns for some of the damage they do. But the communities plainly need much more help.

In a similar vein, we ought to reconsider the federal, state, and local tax policies that offer incentives encouraging the fast conversion of prime agricultural land into strip-development monstrosities like the coast of Pasco County; the anti-speculation Vermont capital-gains and Connecticut conveyancing taxes on land sales might be useful models here.[7] Additionally, we ought not accept as inevitable the disappearance of the family farm from many parts of the country. There are still public measures—subsidies or low-interest loans for qualified families who want to enter farming, government food procurement policies favoring the small farmer, restrictions (such as those in nine Midwestern states) on the size of non-family farm ownership, and real enforcement of the 1902 law requiring that recipients of water from federal irrigation projects in the West get no more than 160 acres' worth and live on or near their farms—that could at least slow the agribusiness takeover.[8]

In more urban settings, we should pursue the various experimental approaches cities around the country have used to slow the conversion of rental apartments into condominiums.[9] We should cast a very cold eye on proposed large urban-redevelopment and urban-renewal projects until we can see how much and how fast they will alter neighborhood ownership patterns. And by both regulatory and tax mechanisms, we should give preference to smaller-scale rehabilitation efforts since they are less likely to wrench ownership patterns rapidly or to uproot neighborhood residents. For too long ownership and its effects have been neglected considerations in land-use regulation and planning. It is time to recognize them for the vital forces they are.

Notes

1. Ann L. Strong, *Private Property and the Public Interest: The Brandywine Experience* (Baltimore: Johns Hopkins University Press, 1975), pp. 169 and 57 respectively.

2. K. Ross Toole, *The Rape of the Great Plains: Northwest America, Cattle and Coal* (Boston: Atlantic-Little, Brown, 1976), pp. 109-110.

3. See Council on Economic Priorities, *Paper Profits: Pollution in the Pulp and Paper Industry* (New York: CEP, 1970), pp. P-1 through P-5.

4. For documentation of many of these examples, see Peter Barnes (ed.), *The People's Land: A Reader on Land Reform in the United States* (Emmaus, Pa.: Rodale Press, 1975).

5. For documentation on these studies and their findings, see Frank Popper, "We've Got to Dig Deeper Into Who Owns Our Land," *Planning,* October 1976.

6. See, however, Walter Goldschmidt, *As You Sow,* (Glencoe, Ill.: The Free Press, 1947; revised edition Montclair, N.J.: Allenheld, Osmun, 1978), a classic of rural sociology that compares two similar small towns in California's San Joaquin Valley, one an agribusiness town and the other a family-farm one, and finds the latter a far superior place to live.

7. On the Vermont tax, see Robert Healy, *Land Use and the States* (Baltimore: Johns Hopkins University Press, 1976), pp. 57-59 and 224. On the Connecticut tax, see William Matuszeski, "Trends in State Land Use Legislation," *Environmental Comment,* September 1976, p. 2.

8. For more on these and similar measures, see The Small Farm Viability Project, *The Family Farm in California* (Sacramento: California Governor's Office of Planning and Research, 1977).

9. On these experiments, see Daniel Lauber, "Let's Put Some Limits on Condo Conversions," *Planning,* September 1977.

11 Property, Liberty, and Land Use Sanctions

Donald R. Denman

The status of land in the last analysis turns about the question of who will make decisions on the use of land and within what sanctions will these decisions be made.

The question of land as commodity or natural resource implies a choice between the consequences of an unfettered market in interest in land and a social acknowledgement that land is a natural resource in danger of being squandered by the irrationality of a free market and uncontrolled property right. This choice of viewpoints, however, is spanned by a deeper question common to both: by whose sanction will decisions about land be made?

This chapter is concerned with certain factors unavoidable in the circumstances of any and all civilized societies, which no answer to this last question can possibly dodge. The question itself is nothing new; men have debated it down the centuries. It may appear novel to us because we have conditioned ourselves to put old conundrums into new forms, and by so doing have confused the nature of what is novel. We kid ourselves that we are opening new avenues of social philosophies because today we speak of decision-makers as if they were a new species of social animal. Our forefathers seem never to have met with them. Yet things were done and actions taken in the older world. Someone must have made decisions to build cities, float fleets, clear and plow the thickets. Whoever these people were, they were decision-makers. Why then the novelty?

Part of the answer is to be found in the curious twists we have taken in our trek toward democracy. Everybody today must have a say in everybody else's affairs. Decision-makers participate: participate, another neologism known of old. The other part of the answer lies in our modern social neurosis. Patent in sociology and other symptoms, our plight bandies us about in bewilderment as we examine ever more deeply the viscera and thought processes of society and its relationships. Societies in the past appear to have been as healthy if not healthier than our own without the incessant probings and uncoverings. Today we hold vast, international congresses on human settlements where our grandfathers and their progenitors would have used time, energy, and intelligence to build homes—to get on with the job, make decisions and act on them, and leave the formulation of mathematical functions to the mathematicians.

The world indeed is a smaller place. We live packed more closely together and bounce words off satellite orbs in space to shorten the distance of speech. There is indeed a difference between the old world and the new; a difference that causes us to be less incurious about ourselves. But the participation and the probings are by no means the full explanation for the existence of the new decision-makers. The main cause is the novel way of looking at ourselves that we have picked up from the stance of post-World War II economics. Indirectly, John Maynard Keynes is the father of the modern decision-makers in the West. He taught the Western world to have regard for the economic behavior of mass man and to do so at a time when the socialist countries had devised, through state planning, ways of giving practical expression to the notion that land and other resources of production should be vested in the people at large. The cult of macroeconomics fused with state planning introduced a hierarchy of decision-making processes. Officials and planners of various kinds were making decisions at elevated levels that affected subordinate level activities in groups and individual persons. People began to feel as if their lives were not their own. They sought out the decision-makers to counter them with others more to their liking.

The Positive Power

One of the strange anomalies of the modern world, with its obsessions with decision-making, is its neglect of the property power: the right of property, either over a thing owned or as an abstract interest or estate in the thing that is the power to use, to dispose of, and to alienate. Decisions made for the use of resources and the deployment of men on a mass scale must engender in the mind of he who makes them an indifference, not to say impatience, toward lesser interests and aspirations, especially those of individual persons. Paramount decisions also and obviously have endowed the decision-makers, the planners, with a false sense of power. To make a decision, however, on how the land, water, and minerals of a nation will be used is of no consequence in the ultimate event unless he who makes the decision has the power of execution also. The positive power to execute is synonymous with the power to use, dispose of, and alienate—the property power. Now inasmuch as the planners of global strategies and schemes have no such power to wield, they prefer (or, so it would appear from the past, have preferred) to turn an indifferent shoulder to those who have the power. However it is, the facts remain: the property power is the only positive power and the holders of it the only decision-makers equipped to take action. For some the power to use and dispose of is a managerial power over resources so handled. That is so, but it does not get away from the universality of the power of property. Managerial power can be accepted either as a form of the property power in itself or as a derivative of that power. Planners do not employ managers over the resources that are the subjects of state and regional plans. The owners of the resources employ the managers; the managers are the agents of the owners or of the holders of the property right.

This dichotomy between planning power and property is more clearly marked in the realm of land use and the use of natural resources than in the use of the complex structures of capital. In respect to land, planners have tended to react to the contention that ascribes to them at best nothing more than negative powers by threatening the ultimate expedient of land nationalization. They are blind to see how wondrously their reaction is an endorsement of the very thesis they are trying to confound. Land nationalization is itself another ambiguity. If by it is meant the transfer of the title of ownership in the land to an executive department or corporation of the state and for the purpose of planning the use of resources, then such nationalization simply demonstrates the need for a change of proprietorship in the land; a necessity to substitute for the owner who is opposed to the planners' ideas an owner who is compliant with them. Without a change in land titles, nothing will be done on the hoped for lines of the planners—for they themselves are impotent.

The First Law of Proprietary Magnitudes

Thus we see the positive aspect of the property power. But to understand how this power operates in an economy and a body social, we must relate it to the holders of it, for no power is greater than the ability of those who wield it to exploit its full potential.

We do not have to delve far into the mysteries of psychology to perceive that a decision is a fusion of human will and consciousness, neither of which at the level of fundamentals can but reside in an individual person. All consciousness must be unitary, if will is to lead to decision and decision to action.

Where a decision has to be made by more than one center of unitary consciousness, an impasse can ensue if the wills behind the intention do not accord with one another. Action that must rely on decision will not take place unless time is allowed for a consensus of wills to form and for the consensus to express itself. The measure of adjustment and the time of adjustment are clogs on the competency of action and execution. All this is of practical consequence when we weigh the facts and merits that distinguish individual and communal titles to property rights.

A corollary of these inescapable fundamentals is a proprietary law—the first law of proprietary magnitudes. This law states that the degree of competence with which the power of decision-making inherent in the property power is used moves in indirect ratio to the number of joint owners. Aristotle's dictum—that which is most common has the least care bestowed upon it—is substantiated not only in the indifference of commoners toward what they hold in common, but in the inability of the many to reach decisions in time to ensure expeditious action in care and management. If in political theory the greatest power is postulated to rest in the will of the people, the paradox follows from the first law of proprietary magnitudes that the people's title must be the least competent. Indeed, the people's title must run far beyond the lowest threshold of the competence of ownership and into the realm where sheer numbers spell impotency in the expression of will in action.

It is one of the given phenomena of nature that will and consciousness operate on the plane of individual persons, of real men and real women, and only there. Logically, no group or loose association of men, let alone the people at large, can have a will, for with them there is no unitary consciousness. Political theorists on the left may not be happy with nature as she is, nor ready to accept her—she is so undemocratic. Unanimous decisions of a number of individual persons are not the expressions of communal will or consciousness existing as something transcendental and apart from the individual will and light of consciousness resident in each member of the group or association. Perhaps the greatest travesty of truth in our times is the claim of the dictator, or indeed of an elected minister of state, that in thinking and acting and doing each and every hour, he is working the will of the people. If he is human (and sometimes we can but guardedly give him the benefit of the doubt), what is done is the outcome of his own decision and no one else's. One man may give in to the overbearing will of another; but the very act of giving in is an act of voluntary will on the part of the dominated. Referenda in the form of questions put to everybody can be conducted and counts made of the number and type of answers and the sum of responses expressed percentagewise. But what do the sums add up to? Nothing other than the exercise of individual will and consciousness. There is no people's will, no community will as an existence apart from these realities.

These truths led the ancient lawyers into strange byways of the imagination. They could see how direct was the relationship between persons and the power of property. Mine and thine were personal adjectives. Property power was so obviously personal power that the ancients maintained that only persons could hold property. And yet there they were in the Middle Ages, surrounded with priors and monks, masters and fellows of colleges, burgesses and mayors of cities; groups, associations, colleges, claiming in the name of the college or city or institution to hold property interests and estates in land. How could this be? Only persons can hold land. How could a loose association, a grouping of men behave as if together they were a real person? The ancients were if nothing else practical, logical folk: they went in search of something they called "bodiliness" and came by trial and error to speak of certain associations as corporate, as corporations, and thus created at law a fiction, a *persona ficta*. So fundamentally grounded is property power in the personal category that the ancients had to create fictitious persons to hold communal titles to it. Because we cannot get away from the personal in the power syndrome of the human condition, society throws up its kings and dictators, presidents and princes to personify the impersonal will of the people.

The Second Law of Proprietary Magnitudes

We have seen how by the first law of proprietary magnitudes title to ownership in the people is the most incompetent, even to the point of impotency. We must now look at this truth in another light, illuminated from another quarter by what is the second law of proprietary magnitudes.

This, the second law, stands upon the simple truth that no man is divine; no man is omnicompetent; no minister of state can himself farm all the land all the time. In short, there are limits to what the human mind can do, even in this computer age. Looking at the use of land in any civilization, we see a wide variety of human activity; some intense, some extensive. The greater the degree of intensity, the more exacting will be the tasks involved, and in the interests of efficiency, the smaller should be the proprietary land unit and the physical range of the responsibilities of ownership.

Simple herding on the hills can make sense over hundreds, even over thousands of acres; but in the heart of a modern city, so intensive may activities be that responsibility in manager or owner has perforce to be limited to square meters. No one man could himself use fully every house, shop, office, and factory clustered on an acre in the heart of a city. This relationship between the competence of human actions, the intensity of human activity, and the measure of land space leads us to the second law of proprietary magnitudes. The law is this: the physical extent of land most conducive to competent, effective decision-making and action is a function of the intensity of human activity over the land implicit in the rights of property over that land and vested in the one who makes the decisions. The relationship can be expressed symbolically as:

$$O_s = f(i)$$

where O_s is the optimum size of the unit of proprietorship, the proprietary land unit, and (i) an index of the intensity of human activity to the degree that the property rights over the land permit. Put another way: the optimum physical size of a proprietary land unit changes inversely with the intensity of human activity on the land of the unit within the sanction of its rights of property.

The optimum size of a proprietary land unit, like the optimum size of any other decision-making unit, is an ideal to which approaches and adjustments are continually made. It must not be confused with the de facto unit. Only in an ideal world are the two coterminous. In the real world of human activity, the human factor, as variable and indeterminate as human personality itself, is the dominant influence; and because it is, standard optima—sizes of labor forces, fixed assets, and land—are exceedingly elusive. Agriculture is a favorite sporting ground for hunting capricious optima; once upon a time in the United Kingdom the optimum was 700 acres of arable land, but it is now reduced to 450 acres if not altogether abandoned in favor of man-day standards and stocking optima, sizes that vary within their categories according to whether the intended end is management rewards, gross profit margins, or some other desideratum.

Adjusting for Optima

While universally valid optima are difficult to establish, the optimum size of the decision-making unit is usually subjectively known, however vaguely, to the decision-maker. In the nature of things, he will be restless with second best and be ever wanting to reach the optimum. In the expression $O_s = f(i)$, if the human activity is too great, ways will be sought to reduce the size of the actual unit so as to conform with O_s. Usually the units are fashioned to fit the activity, a reason why market gardens are in the main smaller holdings than arable farms. Circumstances often preclude the optima. Population increase making for congestion of housing reduces the size of the de facto housing unit below the optimum.

Proprietary land units are protean and can change in numerous ways, not only in physical size but in the range, nature, and potency of the property rights that constitute them. Thus it is possible for the (i) factor in the equation to be manipulated by reducing or inceasing the content of the property rights. If, for example, the owner of a fee simple estate on the fringe of a developing township were to go in for building shops where previously he had been farming, it would be impossible and absurd for him to occupy all the shops he built as the owner of the fee simple estate in them. The range of rights pertaining to a fee simple in possession could not be exercised by an individual person in more than two of the shops. In the notation of our equation, (i) would be too intense to make $O_s > (n)$ shops where $n = 2$. But the fee simple owner of the farmland could cut out of his fee simple derivative interests as leases and convey each shop to a lessee. So doing, the builder would retain the fee simple estate but it would be in reversion, the reversion being contingent upon the leases of the shops. Now the human activity (i) would be reduced to rent collecting, the maintenance of roads and buildings, and other acts of estate management, an intensity sufficient for O_s to be 200 shops. The degree of activity (i) can be so slight, as with the notional vestige of the paramount seignory of the feudal ladder vesting in the Crown under English law, that in principle the proprietary land unit can with ease be a whole realm.

The ownership by the Crown in England of the notional paramount seignory stands in marked contrast to the vesting of all rights of ownership in land in the peoples of a nation, as attempted where collectivist politics are practiced. Reading the equation in those circumstances, shows (i) so intense that O_s is far outdistanced by the state, the de facto unit, and unless adjustments of one kind or another are made, management of the national land and resources is reduced to an absurdity.

In collectivist administrations, much play is made with management. The communal element becomes the notional. Power in large measure passes to committees and soviets sufficiently small to make possible decisions that continue the passing of autonomy downward and into the individual hands of managers of farms and factories. At that stage, what becomes of critical import is the exact nature of the managerial power. It has to be of a flexibility and authority supple enough to enable decisions to be taken as economic efficiency will require. In the notation of the equation, (i) is managerial responsibility within the competence of an individual person and O_s a unit that is accommodated to that competence. So written, the unit O_s resembles a proprietary land unit and the activity (i) the exercise of property rights of some kind. This is how revisers of Marxist practicalities saw it in Czechoslovakia. Economic facts had required the state to delegate power and reduce (i) to managerial proportions so as to give to the recipients of it a sanction that resembled property power. Here was an instance where the absurdity of (i) equaling all the activities of all the people all the time could not in any way be identified with a single or even a few individuals. Either power had to be delegated "by the people" into hands of bureaucrats, and broken down so that each official had no more of it than he could handle efficiently; or assignments, bona fide and real, had to be made of the state titles into the hands of individuals or small groups, syndicates, and collectives of various kinds and shades. Orthodoxy resisted this latter. But it is noteworthy that in recent years, since 1968, just such assignments of proprietary rights have been made in Eastern European countries. Proprietorships have been created in collective farms, proprietorships where the farming activity over the unit, the collective, O_s, is capable of being efficiently handled by the members of the collective. The supreme collective, the state, has had to shed its power and move toward the personal in proprietorship, in accordance with nature and her dictates: not all the way, for the group is still communal, but so far as to reduce (i) to the reasonable competence of an executive committee reporting to members of a collective farm on the daily activities of the enterprise.

This account of actual happenings in certain socialist countries illustrates a pattern by which the conditions for the equation $O_s = f(i)$ can be attained where at the outset and in theory (i) is all the activities of all the people all the time as owners of land and resources, and O_s takes the dimension of the state itself. The pattern assumes four general forms:

1. Ownership is assigned to a collective farm or factory syndicate, and there is a reduction of O_s to a dimension that makes possible the efficient use of the land or resource owned jointly by the members of the collective or syndicate, operating through powers delegated to an executive board of committee. The element of inefficiency, which by virtue of the first law of proprietary magnitudes is inherent in such communal tenure, can be dealt with, in theory and ideally, by including the time-consuming deliberations of the executive among those items of human activity performed by the group, as (i).
2. Alternatively, the power given to a syndicate may not be unequivocally ownership power but a delegated autonomy to be exercised by managers. This is the case of the state farms . . . and similar state enterprises. A central committee of the national executive, ostensibly responsible for a relatively vast unit of resources, brings activity somewhere within what is possible by delegating authority to managerial units and thus reducing the activity of the central committee. The size of the central committee's unit is unaltered, but by the diminution of activity, the magnitude of (i) is manufactured more or less to satisfy O_s for the central committee. The managerial units will themselves be arranged so that the size of each is an optimum for the managerial responsibilities and the operations to be performed.
3. A third possibility modifies the value of (i) by reducing the number of committee members of an executive instead of delegating the powers of the committee; in this way greater efficiency is gained by cutting down the activities of the debating executive.
4. A fourth alternative grants derivative property powers to individual persons from and in the name of a central committee that may be enlarged for the purpose. This creates an arrangement similar to a reversion contingent upon leaseholds—the interest that then remains in the hands of the central committee is O_s in relation to the activities of these quasi-reversioners.

Modes of Influence

Property power is above all things autonomous: in action, the expression of self-conscious will. Its incidence is sporadic, scattered among persons and the groupings of persons. It is characteristically peculiar to those who hold title to it, exclusive to the writ of ownership or its equivalent, and its affinities lie closer to the sympathies of private law than to those of public law. Where the state is sole owner, the public law controlling directly the affairs of the state shapes also the form of the property power. But in mixed economies of the nonsocialist world, and indeed nowadays in the socialist countries with their fast changing outlooks, an important divide runs between property power, its freedom of expression and action, and that imperium of the state that governs directly or indirectly the use of property power. How, it may be asked, does government maneuver the voluntary response of the holders of property power in line with its policies? The one answer we cannot allow is the appropriation of land titles by the state. Our ex post facto assumptions preclude this, for by such a process the question is not answered but rendered nugatory. Nor should we burke the question and suppose there are no general answers but only those that must await on particular and local circumstances.

There are general answers, and these have been categorized into a system of modes of influence. There are two main categories: indirect and direct forms of influence. Modes of indirect influence subdivide into those that encourage voluntary responses along lines favored by government and its planners—as with the farm support prices policy of postwar Britain, with its deliberate encouragement to landowners and farmers to invest in agriculture and the improvement of farmland—and modes that discourage actions, as with the recent monetary policies in Britain and the brake they put upon the development of urban land. Modes of direct influence in their turn subdivide according to the manner in which express controls are imposed upon the use of property power. Either they are embodied in the text of statute law, there to be read by any who would seek the law, or control is put in the hands of an official with discretion to adjudicate upon cases and give a directive. In either of these two ways, the force of the property power is contained.

For property power over land resources there are three further subcategories, which differ according to the type of control imposed. Land use controls fall into one subcategory and can themselves run in four distinct channels: controls prohibiting the use of land for specified purposes, land use zoning procedures imposing general permission for the development of areas and withholding it from other areas, the direct control of structures by building regulations, and control over the provision of roads and access facilities. A second subcategory imposes control over the shape, size, and other attributes of proprietary land units by which the degree of maneuverability within land units is affected. A final subcategory includes those controls that determine what kind of person is permitted to own and hold proprietary land units: for instance, there has lingered in Britain a tradition that puts investment in land by the colleges of Oxford and Cambridge under government control, so that land owned by these colleges would be affected in its use by the proprietary character of the owners and the oversight of their affairs by the Ministry of Agriculture, Fisheries and Food.

Conclusion

The theme of this chapter has been the place of property power in the decision-making processes of society, and it has sought to bring out the personal and the positive in property power. Incidental to the theme and in pursuit of its logic, mention has been made of the unit of decision-making in which property power resides to determine the use of land, its development, and its tenure. This unit, the proprietary land unit, is of critical purport to a systematic understanding of the use of property power as a determinant of land use. It is a particular variety within the genre of decision-making entities or units that provides the structural frame of an economy. The firm and the household are notable examples of other varieties. Fortunately, the concept of the proprietary land unit as an identifiable, sui generis unit within the economy is a novel one, and in attempting a definition of it we are not faced with the difficulties of sorting out clashing and ambiguous definitions culled from a large literature, a tiresome exercise only too well known to authors handling themes on the firm or the household.

There is no time in this chapter to develop a full study of the characteristics of this unit. Essentially, however, the proprietary land unit is the fundamental criterion in the understanding of land use, in the same way that economists have used the firm and the household as basic units in economic structure through which to study the forces of society to generate and distribute wealth.

Part V
Government

12 Value Premises for Planning and Public Policy: The Historical Context

Samuel P. Hays

Conventional wisdom would suggest that certain aspects of our government are relatively neutral in their value preferences. While the main political choices, we are told in our high school civics classes for example, are worked out in the legislature, administrative and judicial bodies merely administer and interpret the laws. These are carried out, so the implication runs, in an atmosphere not of value conflict but of disinterested judgment. As the images are elaborated further, not only governmental administration but planning as well take on the connotations of being scientific, objective, and without value preferences. These functions are carried out by the experts; their only qualifications are their detailed knowledge of the subject and, therefore, their ability to bring the capabilities of disinterested experts to bear on public problems.

One knows hardly where such views come from. There are a host of possible speculations. But the fact remains that a closer look, often carried out by academic observers, but also frequently expressed by participants in these affairs, reveals a persistent set of value choices even in the most objective and expert of governmental functions. Planning is one of these. What could be more neutral than merely to forecast the future and set forth the possible options for getting there? And yet we are all fully aware that any projection of the future is analyzed in terms of what we want for the future, that there is as wide a variety of options for the future as for the present, and that the choices in values in current public affairs spill over directly into the choices in values about the future.

It is often hard to ferret all this out. In planning there is a layer of empirical data, increasingly complex and beyond the comprehension of most citizens, manipulated by computers and displayed in terms of models often powerful as much by the force of their aesthetic elegance as by their appropriate descriptions of reality, and organized and presented with sufficient expertise so as to frighten away all but the initiated. Where are the values in all this? It is not too much to say that one of the major political tasks of the present day is to cut through this weight of expertise, to lay bare the value implications of planning so that the public can understand the choices that are being suggested and make intelligent decisions about them. One of the most pervasive political impulses of the world of expertise is to drive the context of decision-making underground, beyond the purview of the general public, by imbedding it in enormous and complicated detail that makes it all but impossible to grab hold of. Those who wish a more open system of decision-making have a challenging task of bringing to the fore the choices involved in the way a problem is defined, the selection of variables to be measured, the weights to be assigned to the variables, and the treatment of the unmeasurable.

I will provide some preliminary remarks about all this in the context of regional planning, doing so by focusing on the historical development of planning. The purpose will not be just to provide a background for present activities, but to enhance a sensitivity to the value assumptions in planning itself.

Four Basic Assumptions

Let me begin with my own assumptions.[1] There are four. First, planning is an aspect of the search for social control. Planning is not simply a disinterested hobby. It would not be undertaken were it not for the fact that someone, somewhere, wants the future to turn out in a way that it might not do so otherwise. It assumes that the normal course of events, let run with individual and institutional choices apart from those who plan, has implications that one does not approve. Perhaps the problem is one of certain values not being taken into account; the environmental impact statements under the National Environmental Policy Act (NEPA) require an "interdisciplinary" analysis of the impact of major federal actions, and the courts have interpreted this broadly, arguing that a wide variety of factors must be seriously considered. Or perhaps the problem is one of the short-run versus the long-run. An action may achieve one thing next year but damage the possibility of achieving something else ten years from now. Thus, planning is injected into the picture in order to bring about a different future, to control it. The heart of planning is the search for control. If we are to understand planning correctly as a historical phenomenon, we must understand the long-run development in the search for and practice of control over broad social forces.

Second, as a result of the drive for social control, planning is deeply bound up with values and goals. Few of us desire control just for the sake of control; we desire it for a purpose. Control is linked to ends and purposes, and the choices as to which ends and purposes we prefer are the factors that clearly define the social and political relevance of our search for control through planning. A variety of choices are involved in planning. There is, for example, the outline of the "system" for which one plans, the universe that one projects into the future, from which there is output and into which there is input. Is the focus on growth or stability; on enhancement of quality or quantity of life? What are the variables that are to be taken into account? In land use, do we give as strong a focus in our variables to degrees and types of natural lands as to developed lands, with a view to defining the problem as a proper balance between the two? What are the weights to be given to the variables, and especially what weights are to be given to non-quantifiable variables? Perhaps our task is to work into the planning scheme variables that are not capable of being assigned quantities, such as the aesthetic quality of clean air and the capability of long-distance visibility. The value premises in planning can be observed rather readily by focusing on these choices in each major phase of the planning process.

Third, planning is not just a public or governmental activity. In fact, the initial planning in the United States was carried out by private corporations, and I think it would not be too far off to say that despite our common association of planning with governments, still today far more planning takes place within the private corporate realm than by government. Corporations are institutional systems of long-run social control. That is their primary function. The initial planning arose when corporations, because of their huge capital investments at stake, sought to predict the future—future markets, for example, and, as time went on, an increasingly extensive range of factors impinging on corporate decisions. When governments became involved in planning, they copied the steps already taken by private corporations, and with considerable interchange and remarkable similarity between the two. The larger the corporate system, the more it developed a fit in outlook with the larger governmental system. There are, of course, differences in objectives as between private and public planning agencies and yet there are many similarities. Both desire to develop control over the future through planning; often those futures have many features that are strikingly similar.

Finally, planning is never divorced from power. The aim of planning is not merely to carry out an interesting exercise, although many model builders do often emphasize the "elegance" and aesthetic qualities of their models rather than their larger consequences. Planning, for the most part, is closely related to institutional power. Those who wish to control the future wish not merely to know about it but also to have the capability of making it turn out the way they wish. Such capability is dependent primarily upon institutional power. Today the major sources of institutional power are private corporations and governments. Those who seek long-run social control inevitably attach themselves to one or another of these sets of institutions. It should be no wonder, as a result, that one of the perennial focal points of analysis in American growth and development is the degree to which private and public corporate institutions fuse in their search for social control and planning or come into competition. Whichever happens, the process of planning remains intimately bound up with the exercise of large-scale institutional power.

The Increasing Scale of Human Organization

So much for assumptions. Planning is an integral part of the value choices we make for control of the future, and it is intimately bound up with the development of power so as to implement that desire to control. How has all this evolved in twentieth century America, as our industrial, urban, administrative society has grown? I will focus primarily on observations that pinpoint changes in the value premises in planning and will focus on the urban and regional level.

Planning at the urban and regional level is intimately bound up with changes in the scale of social organization, one of the most persistent tendencies of modern society. Historical tendencies within the city and also within the region mark the replacement of smaller-scale activities by larger-scale ones, and the absorption of smaller institutions by larger. One can trace this in a variety of phenomena.

We speak of the nineteenth century city as a pedestrian city, one in which work, home, and leisure activities were all within walking distance of each other.[2] With time, cheaper transportation in the form of the horsecar, the mechanically powered streetcar, and the automobile, and cheap communications in the form of the telephone, changed the scale over which human relationships were established. Even more striking, however, was the way in which the smaller context of life in the early city was dominated by neighborhood and community-scale institutions that, with time, gave way increasingly to larger-scale institutions. One can trace this in the shift from the artisan-craftsman working in downstairs rooms and living in the upstairs to the large factory that needed more space and moved from one outer perimeter of the city to another with each stage of urban growth. It can also be traced in the shift from the smaller consumer-focused retail neighborhood store to the supermarket and shopping center.

The increasing scale of life reorganized public functions on a larger and larger scale. In the mid-nineteenth century, the most striking instances were the fire and police systems.[3] Formerly organized at the ward and community level, these developed into citywide systems after 1850. Frequently, the key change involved the installation of new technology that required a citywide context; the neighborhood fire company could not finance the new pump and hook-and-ladder trucks or a telegraph system for fire and police communications that required a citywide coordinated network. New citywide fire and police administrations recruited personnel through tests for skill and training rather than on a community, friends-and-neighbors basis; they established centralized system control and replaced the community organization of these services.

Similar changes took place in welfare, health, and education. Prior to the mid-nineteenth century, welfare activities took place often at the community or ward level. In Pittsburgh, for example, local aldermen, who were petty judicial officials, became involved in a wide variety of community social problems. Often they dealt in a very personal way with intrafamily or interfamily affairs, such as altercations between husband and wife or between neighbors. They became involved in problems of child neglect and the conditions of widows and orphans. Gradually, over the years, these problems were treated by institutions at a larger level of social organization as first private groups and then governmental agencies developed a variety of welfare programs.[4]

Education underwent the most dramatic change. In the mid-nineteenth century, the focus of education was the elementary ward school. By the end of the century, major steps were underway to replace this with a citywide system of administration. The initial step came with the establishment of the high school, usually one for the entire city and often called Central High School. While elementary schools remained under the control of ward-elected officials, the high school was administered by the citywide board and helped to establish a citywide focus to educational administration. Gradually this expanded, invading the autonomy of the ward elementary school and bringing about an extensive abandonment of the ward school system in favor of centralization.[5]

Changes such as these brought about a similar shift in general urban government in which earlier ward systems of representation were replaced with citywide representation. Formerly, each ward had its own member on city council where councilmen spoke for the communities that had elected them. By the early twentieth century, a shift was well under way toward councils composed of representatives elected citywide to represent the entire city. Not every city went that route completely. Some retained ward representation, but with larger ward units; others combined at-large and ward representation. The city of Pittsburgh, in 1911, went completely from a ward to a citywide system.[6]

These, then, are some of the details in a long-range urban process in which large-scale activities and large-scale administration over a persistently wider geographical area replaced a smaller scale of organization. The details as to why this all came about have not been very well worked out. Yet one aspect of it seems clear. Those who sought to organize government over a large scale were people who had already been active in a similar large-scale organization of private affairs. Two such groups were businessmen and professionals. Businessmen involved had been active in efforts to increase the scale of activities over which business was organized. Professionals, such as doctors, lawyers, architects, and educators utilized large-scale perspectives rather than smaller-scale and more "parochial" points of view. A doctor concerned with the control of disease had a universal perspective; he was concerned with disease not just in a particular ward, but in the entire city. The increasing empirical bent of the professions generated a universalist system of analysis; this gave rise to a similarly universalist preference in administration—and in planning.

These same processes of social change, from small-scale to large-scale contexts of organization in economic and political affairs, took place in rural as well as urban areas. Here activities carried on at the township and community level became reorganized into larger countywide and statewide systems. Changes in the organization of schools and roads in the twentieth century are two examples. Schools, formerly operated at the township level under the jurisdiction of township trustees, went through reorganizations both in administration and in physical facilities. Roads, also formerly supervised by local officials, had been conceived of as servicing the rural community, linking farm and church and store and market, constituting a means of relating people on a small scale. In the twentieth century this gave way to a state highway system, operated under a state commission, with power of eminent domain, which constructed a state system of hard-surfaced roads that linked cities over wide geographical areas. A statewide system of transportation had replaced a local one.

In both these cases, schools and roads, the historical process was one of initiative taken by cities to reorder the affairs of a larger region and of an entire state. The drive for "good roads" and for state highway administrations came from cities that wished to have more rapid transportation to other cities and for whom the more traditional jurisdictions over roads constituted a barrier to larger-scale action. The state highway commission and eminent domain constituted the instruments of political power through which they achieved their objectives. Changes in school administration were urban inspired. Advanced ideas as to what constituted improvements in teaching and curricula came from the urban areas, as did the notion that larger tax bases were essential in order to provide funds for educational innovations. They favored larger-scale administration and management and gradually, over the years, succeeded in imposing their ideas upon a more reluctant countryside.

The development of planning must be understood within this context of the shift from smaller to larger scale. Amid this process of change, planners associated themselves with those who sought to increase the scale of institutional development. Planning has almost invariably involved the assertion that better action on a wide variety of fronts required larger systems of administration and control. As the city replaced the ward as the context of action, the focus of change moved to the larger metropolitan area and a drive arose for countywide planning and later multicounty. Planning has not been associated, on the other hand, with the drive to create smaller units of human activity, to reduce the scale of human relationships, or to decentralize the patterns of human interaction. The values in planning have been associated with the politics of overcoming the resistance of smaller-scale institutions to the drive for larger-scale organization and action. Planning has supported the sociological analyses common to the proponents of larger-scale systems, which assert the wisdom of the larger system and seek to understand the "irrationalities" of opposition to it.[7] Within a mode of thought such as this, the larger-scale system is considered to be "rational" and implicitly valid, while opposition is understood in terms of nonrational or "emotional" factors.

One remaining facet of the change remains to be described. We can well consider the drive for large-scale systems as a broad, historical force in American society that is innovative or radical. Those in business, in government, and the professions who have provided the impulse toward larger-scale affairs, have wrought wholesale changes in American social, economic, and political life. They have constituted a revolutionary force in American society. Those who have resisted these changes and who have asserted the validity of past ways and past smaller-scale forms of social organization have been the conservatives, the defenders of tradition. American history is a constant series of struggles between such radicals and conservatives, and amid this planners have associated themselves with those bringing about innovations. They have played an important role in the twentieth century effort to make such radical change respectable and to discredit the conservative defense of smaller-scale life.

Changes in Social Values

Planning today, then, must be understood in terms of the historical tension between larger-scale and smaller-scale contexts of life. It must also be understood in terms of changes in social values, and especially the emerging values of environmental quality and their tension with development values.

Planning first emerged, in both private industry and government, as part of a drive for greater efficiency in development. It constituted an effort to avoid the wastefulness of short-run decisions and to enhance efficiency in the use of resources, natural and human, for development purposes.[8] It focused on long-run processes and the need to adjust current action to long-run goals. The typical planning document has been one that predicts the future in terms of growth of some social force, such as population or employable people, and then predicts the level of activity that is needed in order to provide for such matters as employment or social services. The entire process was geared to economic development and the development of public services in such a way as to bring them about in a more orderly and efficient manner. Such an approach, it should be emphasized, did not question the values of growth in material development or in social services but was tied merely to the question of how they were to be achieved—in terms of long-run plans rather than short-run pressures.

In more recent years, however, a new set of values has emerged to challenge development values. These are embodied in the new phrase "environmental quality." The precise meaning of this is not always clear. But it does involve two ideas: first, there is a new dimension to the constant search for a better standard of living, which people describe as qualitative rather than in terms of material goods, and second, that a major element of this quality in standard of living is environmental, that is, the surroundings at home, work, or play, which can either make life more pleasant or more degraded. This drive for improvement of the quality of one's environment is symbolized by such institutions as the Council on Environmental Quality.[9]

It might be well to emphasize environmental quality values as part of larger historical tendencies with which they are associated. They did not emerge full-blown in the late 1960s to form the "environmental movement." On the contrary, they represent some historic changes in social values that have grown over the years and that have appeared in many and varied forms, including, but not limited to, environmental quality. One aspect of the drive is the constant tendency toward smaller families as material standards of living rise. This is a choice for quality instead of quantity, a choice that scarce family income will go not toward providing a minimal standard of living for more children, but a higher quality of life for fewer children. Another is the drive toward the suburbs, a process that has gone on in our cities for several centuries. That drive constitutes a search for quality of living space, for more space within the house so that individuals might have more privacy, and more space outside the house. The street life of the urban community, with its constant press of people and noise and dirt was unacceptable to many people who sought a higher degree of personal privacy, more space, and quieter conditions in more "natural" circumstances.[10]

These values have brought new considerations into the analysis of the past, present, and future of human communities, which differ markedly from those implicit in development and development planning. What is space to be used for? For intensive development alone, or for the amenities of undeveloped lands? Should air, water, and land be used for waste disposal, as a receptacle in which the wastes of our urban-industrial society are thrown, or should it be used to improve the quality of life and standard of living? These values, in turn, have come into conflict with development.

It is no longer an issue of whether or not growth will be more efficient, as was the thrust of the conservation movement in the early twentieth century, but of whether or not environmental values will be maximized in balance with material development. Heretofore, the major issues have been over the efficiency of development and delivery of services. But now the issue is changed as considerations of environmental quality cannot be absorbed into new twists to development, but act so as to compromise development in the first place.

A distinction should be made in order to clarify the historical process, one between environmental effects and environmental goals. Analysis in terms of environmental effects is the framework of the environmental impact statements required by the National Environmental Policy Act of 1969 and some thirteen state environmental impact analysis programs.[11] The focus is on the conditions surrounding development. What is its environmental impact? This must be analyzed in a broad fashion, in the federal law in terms of an "interdisciplinary analysis," and alternative types of development must be set forth. Such an approach does not deal with environmental goals directly, but only tangentially, as implicit but unspecified elements in the impact analysis. This is only a halfway step toward the consideration of environmental goals. Full recognition of such goals would require that they be planned for on a coordinated basis with development goals. For the most part, this is not yet done. There is some statewide planning in terms of identifying, measuring, and establishing environmental goals. There are qualitative standards set forth as objectives in air and water laws. And in one state there is a requirement for open-space planning. Thus, we are in the midst of a historical process, a struggle for policymakers to give new values full consideration as goals and not to consider them only as derivative by-products of development.[12]

The new environmental thrust has had an extensive impact on planning as the values of environmental quality have been brought into the planning process. In the past, planning has been linked closely with development values. It is still very common to find planning and development carried out by the same commission, for example, in the area of the Appalachian Regional Commission.[13] Even if the two are separated, the major theme of planning still remains that of how best to accommodate development smoothly. Predictions of growth, of population, of economic activities, constitute the needs, the givens, the natural imperatives of the social order, and planning is tied up with the way in which it can be done more smoothly.

But clearly, the environmental quality emphasis is creating a change in mood. Almost every environmental issue is a very specific instance of a larger planning controversy between growth and quality, and these issues have not been ignored by the planning community. The historical sequence of planning documents reflects the gradual entrance of matters of environmental quality, especially in terms of open space. Land use plans financed now by federal funds are very different from earlier documents.[14] While not all county planning, or even most, has moved in this direction, a number have. Some of the most effective land use plans in terms of environmental quality goals are undertaken by private rather than public agencies.[15] And planning for air and water quality implications of land use, although fostered by recent federal air and water laws, has barely got off the ground.[16] We are in the midst of a long-run process worth watchdogging in some detail, for it involves the way in which deep-seated changes in values become institutionalized in the planning process.

One of the most significant aspects of these changes consists of the way in which problems are defined for description and analysis. Environmental quality values have given rise to many new ways of looking at the world and have opened up a wide range of new phenomena to be examined, measured, and described. The impact on planning is to create new choices in problem definition, description of variables, and weights to be attached to them when selecting goals to which to apply scarce resources. There are a number of these new perspectives; they illustrate the way in which planning may or may not respond to new values.

There is, for example, the concept of the desirability of an appropriate balance between developed and undeveloped land areas. Howard and Eugene Odum have argued for this approach. In a land use model for the state of Georgia, an attempt was made to determine the percentage of acreage that should remain undeveloped in order to provide the necessary biological processes to accommodate and sustain development on the remainder.[17] Or there is the concept of irreversibility and the analysis of development in terms of the degree to which it involves reversibility—"open option" land—or irreversibility. Energy analysis has taken many new forms. There is the concept of net energy, that we must measure energy production not in gross terms but in terms of the balance between the energy output and the energy required to produce that output.[18] The implication is that one should not produce energy if the energy cost, that is, the energy required to produce it, is more than that produced. It may well take more energy to mine coal in Montana and ship it to Cleveland to burn in generating electric power than is represented by the resulting electricity. Or there is the concept of embodied energy, that every product represents a certain amount of energy required to produce it from raw material to finished product, and that products should be described in terms of embodied energy so that consumers could make choices with respect to energy consumption. Or there is the concept of energy productivity, that is, of the amount of product, of GNP, that is created by a given amount of energy. Until 1966, the energy cost of our GNP had gone down steadily, but since then it has gone up.[19]

A systems analysis of the natural water cycle is increasingly used that emphasizes the effect of upstream paving on percolation, water table replenishment, and downstream flooding, or the effect of large-scale sewage transfer of water and channelization on acquifer replenishment.[20] A new form of population analysis emphasizes that, in terms of human pressure on resources rather than mere numbers per square mile, the United States is one of the most densely populated areas of the world and India one of the least densely populated.[21] Or there is the new analysis of urban diseconomies, the added costs that come with population growth. One such approach indicates that up until about 100,000 population the per capita cost of running a city declines, and after that it rises.[22] Each of these approaches constitutes a new mode of analysis with reference to the relationship between people and their environment. Each involves a choice as to how one defines a social problem. And each one leads to choices about variables, about the weight given to particular variables, and often to nonquantifiable variables. The National Environmental Policy Act of 1969 stressed the need to emphasize these variables and especially those customarily not quantified. This is a particular institutional expression of the desire to expand the range of planning to values not normally taken into account.

New environmental quality values have had considerable impact upon planning, but the full range of the impact is yet to be seen. While one can observe that in the historical tension between larger and smaller scale in human context planning has persistently been associated with the former rather than the latter, one can also observe that planning has been receptive to emerging environmental quality values. In the future it may well stand effectively in the middle between development and quality values and mediate between them.

Statewide Environmental Planning and Management

These two historical processes with which planning has been intimately associated have converged to focus on statewide environmental planning and management. This constitutes a separate phenomenon, and its development provides a third useful context through which to examine the value premises of planning.

Environmental concerns and programs have brought a new emphasis to state planning. A wide range of values connected with the use of land, air, and water, growing out of federal programs in these fields, is generating new plans and management capabilities at the state level. This has developed in a particular political context in which state environmental planning has been associated with the peculiar environmental concerns of urban areas and has given rise to a planning process that often implies the manipulation of the rural community to achieve the environmental goals of the city. The state environmental planning process has become the city and metropolitan planning process writ large, representing a stage in historical development in which urban and state concerns become almost synonomous. Thus, state environmental planning does not express primarily the protection of the environmental quality of rural, less developed areas against the environmental loads of the city, but, in fact, serves as an instrument of the urban environmental thrust—often to the disadvantage of the countryside.

Statewide planning has constituted a persistent phenomenon in the twentieth century. Earlier I mentioned highway planning, which began prior to World War I; that was an important early instance. Other cases developed over the years, such as the state police and the state park systems, both of which evolved in the years prior to World War II. But here I am interested in the new phase of state administration and planning that environmental concerns have brought about. Federal air and water programs have relied upon states as the instruments of enforcement of federal standards. A major aim of these programs has been to generate state capabilities to gather data and supervise action. A federal land use program would develop a similar approach for land, and land use implications of air and water laws, yet to be developed fully, would do likewise. All this has given rise to statewide rather than merely citywide or metropolitan programs and planning and thus has enhanced a statewide context of thought, planning, and action.

This may seem obvious enough. But its larger political context requires closer attention. It relates not simply to the growth of statewide planning, but to the use of such planning by cites to transfer many of their environmental problems to the countryside. The state has become not merely an instrument by which cities develop programs to improve their own environment. It is often a means whereby cities mitigate those problems by utilizing the countryside to absorb some of the environmental degradation created by their high levels of resource pressure.

The siting of energy facilities provides a dramatic illustration. On the surface, energy facility siting involves simply the desire of energy companies to locate a power plant, onshore installations connected with offshore drilling or oil importation, or energy parks. These proposed installations have met intense opposition throughout the nation. In some cases they threaten to disrupt long-standing rural and small town communities; in others they interfere with the amenities of summer and vacation homes and recreational activities. In such instances energy companies have attempted to use states and the power of state governments to enforce siting through state programs that override local veto power. When this has been slow to achieve, demands are made that the federal government obtain the power to override state opposition to siting. And this, in turn, leads to land use planning proposals, supported by energy companies, in order to provide areas for new generating capacity, very similar to the way in which industrial promoters seek county planning in order to carve out land for industrial sites.

The political context of energy siting constitutes more than merely the initiative from utilities. It represents the city reaching out to the larger region to use it for its own purposes. Urban consumers demand greater amounts of energy. Why not develop energy industries in the city or on its periphery? Cities don't want them there. They create too much air pollution, as in Los Angeles, and as a result utilities move to the Four Corners area. Or they are too risky, as in the case of nuclear power installations, which recent court decisions require be located some distance from urban centers. Or they produce other environmental results that cities don't want. So rural areas become prime "sacrifice areas" for large-scale installations to provide energy for cities. Out of this emerges a pattern of political relationships in which urban areas of the nation favor such energy development and rural areas, which are called upon to accept the brunt of environmental impact, are opposed. Rural areas resist being used by the city for its own economic growth and development.

The case of energy installation is only part of a larger context of relationships between city and country involving the use of air, water, and land "out there." One such traditional issue is the use of flood storage reservoirs in which rural land is acquired, by eminent domain power, for the protection of cities against flood damage; it would be quite possible to prevent flood damage by controlling settlement patterns of the city without using rural land. Or other examples: the use of solid waste disposal sites for urban solid waste in the countryside rather then recycling; the removal of industrial plants to areas of cleaner air, permitting air deterioration there; or the creation of water pollution through urban-based demands for coal mining without sufficient control of environmental effects. In all such instances, the major context of political controversy involves a more highly developed area preferring not to absorb the cost of environmental impact itself, instead seeking to export that cost elsewhere.

Where does state planning fit into all this? The use of the countryside by the city has historically been one of the major sources of increasing state functions. Cities inevitably wish to utilize land, commodity resources, air and water that are beyond its borders, and such use has given rise to resistance within the countryside. At each such step the city has called upon the state for the power to make possible the use of the countryside because it is the most accessible governmental jurisdiction through which the city can realize its objectives. In the nineteenth century, a host of right-of-way issues concerning plank roads and toll bridges and, later, railroads involved this kind of struggle. The development of twentieth century highways continued the pattern. And now the same pattern is involved in environmental controversy. Large-scale developers seek large-scale units of authority and power in order to override local units. Planning becomes a matter of alternatives within the state as a whole, and choices are made within the statewide universe of planning.

The rural community becomes the source of opposition to this planning because it is forced to modify its land use practices and programs to satisfy external demands. That community seeks to defend past ways, customary institutions, and urges that the more radical and far-reaching transformations of the wider society be checked so as to protect the values of the local community. There is opposition to becoming a "sacrifice area" and cynicism about the attempt to make large-scale development more palatable by describing them in more appealing terms such as "energy parks." Thus, there is organized reaction in Montana and Wyoming to strip mining, in New Hampshire to onshore facilities for oil importation, and in Pennsylvania to energy parks.[23] All are protective in tone, and all seek to maintain established ways of life against disruption.

In this political stance, the rural community is reinforced in its opposition by urbanites who seek to enhance environmental quality values similar to those desired by people in the countryside. Many of these have second homes in the countryside, purchased specifically to secure the environmental values they find missing in the cities.[24] Others are vacationers there or use the countryside for its environmental qualities of cleaner air and water and more open and natural land than they find in the cities. They constitute an urban-based political force in support of those rural groups who seek to protect the same values in the less developed regions; they become a force seeking to restrain the urban-based demands upon rural areas. A considerable portion of the urban environmental movement represents this particular political thrust.

There is implicit in these issues a new form of cost analysis involving the external costs imposed by cities. We have become familiar with the argument that industries should internalize the external costs that their pollution imposes on the community. A similar argument could be made about urban-based environmental pressures. The city is a "growth machine" that imposes burdens on the wider environment beyond the city that appear in the form of costs.[25] Should not these costs be absorbed by the city? If urban dwellers are responsible for the environmental load on the country, should not they pay the cost of recycling their solid waste, locating energy facilities near cities, or fully recycle their water?

To what extent has state environmental planning been capable of expressing the values of environmental quality that these forces in the countryside are espousing? This is one of the most interesting aspects of both the politics of environmental quality and the value-role of planners. Planning to protect environmental quality values has moved forward more in specialized cases than in a comprehensive fashion. Areas of traditional special environmental values, such as the Adirondacks in New York, have been the most important vehicles for their support and expression.[26] New concerns, such as scenic rivers, as well as the interest in natural areas, have provided other vehicles. In some states, wild area and wilderness area programs do likewise. But these do not touch the broad-based problem of environmental quality in the rural countryside, and the values that cleaner air and water and more open space represent for people living there.

It seems that the "no significant deterioration" clauses of the federal clean air and clean water laws will provide one of the first opportunities for general policy formulation with respect to such matters. The land use implications of both provisions are clear and enormous. By and large, state planners have not rushed to take up the no significant deterioration aspects of either federal program; the Environmental Protection Agency has been even more reluctant. The role of planners in these programs will provide another opportunity to observe the relationship between planning and emerging social values in twentieth century America.

Conclusion

An analysis of the values inherent in planning focuses on a set of long-run historical circumstances. There is an emerging set of values and preferences amid the public at large, growing slowly but having the force of long-run cultural change, that is producing deep-seated changes in how problems are defined, what is observed, and what is described and analyzed. But this is taking place within an equally important historical context of increasing scale as the institutional framework of analysis and action. Planning, therefore, now faces the possibility of utilizing the instruments of large-scale manipulation in order to give expression to emerging values that inevitably are defined in terms of the quality of life in the community. Drives to maintain ecological integrity and to enhance environmental quality draw the context of action back to a smaller level of human life and scale. The open-space community in the metropolitan area and the natural environment community in the wider countryside join in giving emphasis to the quality of life in daily human living. This is the current drama in the role of values in regional planning.

Notes

1. These assumptions have been elaborated in a larger context in Samuel P. Hays, "The New Organizational Society," in Jerry Israel (ed.), *Building the Organizational Society* (New York: Free Press, 1972), pp. 1-15.

2. Transformations of scale in urban life are dealt with more fully in Samuel P. Hays, "The Changing Political Structure of the City in Industrial America," *Journal of Urban History*, 1 (no. 1): 1974, pp. 6-38. Similar patterns of change are elaborated in a recent work, Social Science Panel, National Academy of Sciences—National Academy of Engineering, *Toward An Understanding of Metropolitan America* (Washington, D.C.: National Academy of Engineering, 1974).

3. For an example of change in police systems see Roger Lane, *Policing The City: Boston, 1822-1885* (Cambridge, Mass.: Harvard University Press, 1967).

4. These changes are dealt with in Susan Kleinberg, "Technology's Stepdaughters: The Impact of Industrialization upon Workingclass Women, Pittsburgh, 1865-1890" (Ph.D. dissertation, University of Pittsburgh, 1973), see, especially, chap. 5, pp. 125-70.

5. Several recent studies have explored these changes in education. See for example, David B. Tyack, *The One Best System: A History of American Urban Education* (Cambridge, Mass.: Harvard University Press, 1974).

6. For an elaboration of this theme see Samuel P. Hays, "The Politics of Reform in Municipal Government in the Progressive Era," *Pacific Northwest Quarterly*, 55 (no. 4): October 1964, pp. 157-69.

7. A good example of this approach is Basil G. Zimmer and Amos H. Hawley, *Metropolitan Area Schools: Resistance to District Reorganization* (Beverly Hills, Cal.: Sage Publications, 1968), which focuses on the "irrational" opposition to school consolidation.

8. This theme, as demonstrated in the early twentieth century resource conservation movement is elaborated in Samuel P. Hays, *Conservation and the Gospel of Efficiency: The Progressive Conservation Movement* (Cambridge, Mass.: Harvard University Press, 1958).

9. This analysis of the environmental movement is elaborated more fully in Samuel P. Hays, "The Limits to Growth Issue: An Historical Perspective," in Chester L. Cooper (ed.), *Growth in America* (Westport, Conn.: Greenwood, 1976).

10. Street life and crowdedness were acceptable to many established urban dwellers, but was less so to later generations. For some observations on this see Herbert Gans, *The Urban Villagers* (New York: Free Press, 1962), pp. 19-24.

11. Environmental effects analysis can be followed most effectively in the pages of "102 Monitor," published by the U.S. Government Printing Office, Washington, D.C., for the Council on Environmental Quality.

12. Some states have mandates to develop environmental planning, but these have not progressed very far. See, for example, Department of Environmental Resources, Commonwealth of Pennsylvania, *Environmental Master Plan: Planning Survey Report* (Harrisburg, Pa., 1973).

13. Thus, for example, there is in Pennsylvania the Northwest Pennsylvania Regional Planning and Development Commission as one of a number of regional groupings in the state.

14. See, as one example, "A Preliminary Report" on land use for Crawford County, Pa., prepared by Beckman, Yoder and Seay, Inc., Wexford, Pa., 1972.

15. One such privately financed plan, sponsored by the Western Pennsylvania Conservancy, Pittsburgh, Pa., is William J. Curry III et al., *The Laurel Hill Study* (Pittsburgh, Pa., 1975).

16. See, for example, John J. Roberts, Edward J. Croke, and Samuel Booras, "A Critical Review of the Effect of Air Pollution Control Regulations on Land Use Planning," *Journal of the Air Pollution Control Association*, 25-5: May 1975, pp. 500-20.

17. Eugene P. Odum, "Optimum Population and Environment: A Georgian Microcosm," *Current History*, June 1970, pp. 355-65.

18. For a governmental report in this vein see *Transition, A Report to the Oregon Energy Council Prepared by the Office of Energy Research and Planning,* Office of the Governor, State of Oregon, Eugene, January 1975.

19. See Lee E. Erickson, "A Review of Forecasts for U.S. Energy Consumption in 1980 and 2000," in Barry Commoner, Howard Bokensbaum, and Michael Corr (eds.), *Energy and Human Welfare—A Critical Analysis*, vol. 3, *Human Welfare: The End Use for Power* (New York: Macmillan, 1975), pp. 11-16.

20. An example of this approach is Environmental Studies Institute, Carnegie-Mellon University, *Girty's Run: A Study in Urban Watershed Management* (Pittsburgh, 1974).

21. Wayne Davis, "Overpopulated America," *New Republic,* 162: January 20, 1970, pp. 13-15.

22. Eric G. Johnson et al., *Is Population Growth Good for Boulder Citizens?* 2nd ed. (Boulder, Colo.: ZPG, 1971). For another study in a similar vein see Richard C. Bradley, *The Costs of Urban Growth: Observations and Judgments* (Pikes Peak, Colo.: Pikes Peak Area Council of Governments, 1973).

23. Details of this opposition for cases in the Mountain-Plains states can be followed in *High Country News* published in Lander, Wyoming. Data from the recent case of energy park proposals in Pennsylvania comes from newspaper coverage in the ten candidate site areas, in the author's files.

24. These values are described in Mary Keys Watson, "Behavorial and Environmental Aspects of Recreational Land Sales" (Ph.D. dissertation, The Pennsylvania State University, 1975), pp. 211-60.

25. Harvey Molotch, "The City as a Growth Machine," mimeo, University of California, Santa Barbara, July 1973.

26. Temporary Study Commission on the Future of the Adirondacks, *The Future of the Adirondacks* 2 vol., Blue Mountain Lake, N.Y.: (The Adirondack Museum, 1971).

13 A National Land Use Policy: Its Formal Characteristics

Wesley H. Gould

"History, reduced to its basics, is one real estate transaction after another."[1] Written with reference to Moses Cleaveland's purchase of Indian rights to the Western Reserve in Northeastern Ohio, George E. Condon's statement, without excessive exaggeration, provides insight into a variety of historical occurrences ranging from the age of migrations in the late Roman Empire and the territorial exchanges and acquisitions of modern states to agricultural change, industrial plant location, and the growth of urbanized areas. Such events and their various impacts on land have not been totally divorced from government actions, even though such actions often have not been taken with primary concern for land and its use.

Basic though land ownership may be, more important are the uses to which land is put, whether by the owner (public or private), the tenant, or someone in a trustee or agency role. Misuse of land can bear a relationship to the decline of civilization and the fall of states—for instance, Spain's decline, after much arable land was destroyed as a consequence of large-scale deforestation, from the ranks of the Great Powers.[2] Such misuse of land reflects a failure to view land, like civilization, as a heritage held in trust for future generations.

Closest to home, and most clearly visible to those who can observe complexities, is urbanization and its many effects on the land. Sprawl eats up increasing amounts of acreage with each additional mile's ring around the core.[3] Yet many who observe the sprawl, to say nothing of those who contribute to it, seem quite indifferent to its impact on the ecology, the food chain, and agriculture. Living in dependence upon technology, modern man in general has become increasingly unconcerned about land. "The chain of dependence upon technology lengthens and with it the distance between the individual and the physical basis of survival."[4]

Land use policy and one of its correlates, urban policy, have been fragmented at best. Such well-publicized demand as there now is for an integrated policy has been for a national urban policy. For a national land use policy the demand has been weaker and less persistent. Yet, as P. Nijkamp succinctly states it, "The absence of an effective land-use policy . . . renders an effective urban policy impossible."[5]

167

The Complexity of Planning

Town and country, buildings and land, humans and other forms of life—all are parts of the same complex system. To formulate separate policies and programs for each part of the system risks taking insufficient account of the interactions among the parts, not all of them visible to humans as they interact with each other and with their immediate environment. Today's system is global. Its patterns of interaction reflect an underlying complexity that renders single solutions ineffective. Even combinations of interrelated policies and programs run the seemingly unlikely risk of doing the right things in the wrong combination.[6]

Planning and its implementation in principle should avert the dysfunctions of unidimensional programs and wrong combinations of programs. Planning should be conceived not strictly as mapping and zoning but, like English structure plans and strategic plans, as a set of policy statements concerned about economic and social as well as land use matters.[7] This does not mean that a "grand design" conceived at one point in time could be effective or even adhered to amid changing circumstances—such circumstances themselves impose the need for ever-present monitoring, feedback, and adaptation. What it does mean is that planning has little chance of being effective if its related segments are so compartmentalized that complementarity is forsaken.

Unfortunately, even in regard to land use alone, compartmentalization has been the norm. With rare exceptions, such as the South Hampshire Structure Plan of 1972, there has been little effort to plan the urban and rural environments as one even for a single county. The reason for this is that planning has traditionally been conceived of as town planning. Even with the introduction of the "new towns" approach and the green belt method of containing sprawl, both the concepts and the practices of land use planning have retained an urban flavor. The positive side of land use planning reflects the concepts of urban growth and urban economic development. Its negative side—where not to build—bounds the planner's horizon in respect to the countryside and itself embraces an urban outlook in the form of containment of urban sprawl."[8]

In spite of physical planners' urban bias and limited view of protected countryside areas as inherently changeless, countrysides have not gone totally unplanned. Even when not taking the initiative, government was involved in the process. For historical perspective one need only think back to the English Statute of Bridges of 1530 and 1531, the Highway Acts of 1555 and 1562, the many Acts of Parliament enabling enclosures to take place from the late fifteenth century into the nineteenth century, and the removal of people from the Scottish Highlands from the late eighteenth to the mid-nineteenth century in order to make room for the more profitable Great Cheviot sheep.[9] More recently, powerful resource planning agencies, such as the Ministry of Agriculture, the Forestry Commission, and the Nature Conservancy Council, each with its own system of legislation and finance, have shaped the use and appearance of the English countryside. Today, especially in the south and east, hedgerows, originally intended to protect against wind erosion, have been broken down.[10]

In the United States there is a similar history of government agency involvement. Government policies have promoted homesteading, railroads, highway building, mining, the establishment of national and state parks and forests, wildlife protection and management, rural electrification, soil conservation, irrigation, and agricultural extension services. All have altered the landscape.

More recently, in the San Francisco, New York, and Cleveland urban areas, legislation has brought the Golden Gate, Gateway, and Cuyahoga National Recreation Areas into being under the control of the National Park Service. The last of these entails major land purchases to spare an unspoiled area from the industrial, commercial, and residential development converging on it from Cleveland and Akron.[11]

The preceding examples indicate the reality of planning for rural areas by resource agencies. They also illustrate its fragmentation and its separation from planning for urban areas (even though such planning impacts upon urban areas, most visibly in the case of transportation linkages). Less obvious, but implicit in the variety of programs for rural areas, are the conflicting claims to rural space put forward by the farmer, the part-time farmer especially near conurbations, the seeker of recreation, the electric power company, pipeline companies, and water authorities, among others.

Conflicting demands for rural space, coupled with the establishment of separate agencies serving different clienteles, not only increase fragmentation of rural resource management and its related, even if often incidental, land use planning but also, because the cycles are not congruent, add complexity along the time dimension. Three basic rhythms or cycles illustrate the time complexity in the human world, excluding the additional complications arising from the differing lengths of generations among nonhuman species: (1) the daily rhythm of the urban, artifactual world; (2) the yearly rhythm of the agrarian world; and (3) the generation rhythm (30 years or more) of the human ecological world.[12] Furthermore, anyone who considers these three basic rhythms in terms of both activities and populations of actors will recognize that neither the activities nor the populations, nor therefore the rhythms, are bounded by local demarcations such as property lines, political boundaries, or watersheds. They entail the circulation of goods, money, and people on national and international scales.

The National Context

Land use policy, countryside policy, and urban policy are now much more national matters than they used to be. In addition, the nation-state is a part of an increasingly interdependent globe that includes firms making investment decisions in land outside the jurisdiction of the nation in which the land is located.

National intervention in urban policy lags behind the emergence of problems of national scope. For example, despite comparatively early awareness in England of a need for town planning for reasons of public health, the Ministry of Housing and Local Government dates only from 1951. The United States Department of Housing and Urban Development was established in 1965. Canada's federal Ministry of Urban Affairs came into being in 1971. In each case there was an accumulation of serious problems before an organization was established to deal with them in some interrelated manner.

In the urban policy area and other areas such as agriculture, there is at least the recognition that some problems require a comprehensive approach. However, such organizational indicators as the placing of transportation in a separate department and the creation of separate Water Authorities in England and Wales under the local government reorganization of the early 1970s demonstrate that a particularist bias may enter a supposedly comprehensive national approach. A particularist bias tends to dominate land use matters so that the very organization of government tends to reinforce those private and public claims upon land that are compatible with specific agency missions.

National policies neither embrace land use on a comprehensive basis nor provide an organization charged with undertaking a comprehensive approach to land use. In the United States, efforts to enact a federal land use bill have foundered on numerous obstacles. For example, in 1974 the House of Representatives Rules Committee deferred consideration of a land use bill indefinitely after the bill had passed the Senate, 64-21, and been approved, 26-11, by the House Committee on the Interior.[13]

Rather than a national land use policy as an instrument helping to harmonize agricultural policy, woodland policy, economic policy, transportation policy, energy policy, and a still nonexistent national urban policy, we have a melange of piecemeal programs that affect communities and the countryside. One consequence is that initiating and extending municipal services occurs less according to policies and priorities than as a result of the mere force of developers' presence.[14]

In federal systems the probability of a melange of policies and programs is increased by the constitutional allocation of powers to states and provinces. In Canada the allocation of powers is more significant for land use matters than in the United States. Provincial control of natural resources under the British North America Act enabled British Columbia to impede ratification of the Columbia River Treaty and thereby compel Canada and the United States to renegotiate it in the early 1960s. The Columbia River Treaty case tells us that federal constitutions can be powerful fragmenting forces. The same can be said about state constitutions that provide for municipal home rule.

Three forms of fragmentation can be identified. One is the vertical fragmentation that is established by the constitutional allocation of powers. A second form is horizontal when political boundaries or administrative boundaries of a geographical nature limit the territorial range of authoritative decisions. In this case the governmental units are at the same level, for example, cities. A third form, usually but not necessarily horizontal, is functional fragmentation within a particular level of government, although it also occurs between levels of government not because of constitutional allocations but because one level staked out a field of action first or because of different choices of priorities.

Functional fragmentation is of particular concern because of its presence at whatever level of government is deemed to be the most appropriate maker of land use policy. It impedes the capacity to think in terms of an entire system, that is, to think in terms of the relationship of all parts to each other and to the whole. Of course, the totality of desired knowledge is not to be had. But the inescapable problem of insufficient knowledge is compounded by functional specialization to increase uncertainty for both public and private actors and thereby to ensure malfunctioning rural, suburban, and urban societies and economies.[15]

Additional difficulties arise when functional specialization occurs between levels of government. An American example of functional specialization between levels is found in the national government's preoccupation with economic matters while physical planning, including land use, is largely left to states and local governments. In such a situation, if national government moves into physical planning, as occurred when Congress authorized the National Park Service to create the Cuyahoga National Recreation Area, debate can shift from a problem-solving focus to jurisdictional issues about which government has the right to do what. Since the capabilities of subnational units are limited by national economic and fiscal policies and by national use of tax resources, diversion of effort into jurisdictional debate can be wasteful.

Complicating the matter today is the fact that national government no longer can orient policies toward economic self-sufficiency. Moreover, nations are interdependent in realms other than the economic, even though that is the most prominent aspect considered in policymaking. For example, there have been predictions that in the next century most of the world will be dependent on the United States, Canada, and Australia for food, just as many countries are now dependent on the Arab states for oil. In such a situation, national government's role can be reduced to that of broker. Multinational enterprises can also impose broker status even in regard to land use. Just as the exploitation of natural resources created continental management and control problems for both public and private actors in North American countries,[16] now land development in the United States includes many foreign-based firms among the participants.

Even where the broker's role is all that is available to a national government, experience, such as that of the American states in attempting to cope with the economic malaise that began in 1929, tells us that subnational units cannot go it alone.[17] What cannot be done by subnational units would seem to require transfer to the national level. But if national government is to develop and implement a coherent policy that, among other things, overcomes intergovernmental differences and agency conflicts, it is essential to know the characteristics of a national policy.

National Land Use Policy Characteristics

If a national land use policy is to do more than merely ratify what others have decided, it cannot take the form of day-to-day reaction to whatever is happening. True, a government cannot ignore what is happening. But when overwhelmed by the immediate, the time and effort of policymakers will be exhausted by matters better dealt with at subordinate administrative levels. Policy then is likely to express only the sum of small decisions. In part this is an organizational problem, but it is also a matter of conceptualization, attitude, and motivation.

Brian Berry identified four modes of planning that are essentially modes of policymaking.[18] The most common mode is ameliorative problem-solving. Nothing is done until problems arise or undesirable dysfunctions are perceived. At best, the approach is reactive or curative.

The second mode of planning is allocative trend-modifying, a future-oriented method of reactive problem-solving. Projecting present trends into the future with the purpose of preserving existing values, regulatory mechanisms are devised to modify trends.

Third, exploitive opportunity-seeking undertakes analyses to find new growth opportunities with analytical stress upon feasibility and risk. This is the approach of the corporate planner, the private risk-taker and speculator, the real estate developer, the industrialist, the public entrepreneur acting on behalf of private interests, and the national leader exercising development leadership.

Berry's fourth mode of planning, normative goal-orientation, is based on an image of a desired future to be reached either by means of policies and plans intended to guide the system toward the selected goals or by changing the system if it is presently incapable of reaching the goals. Because this system requires the cybernetic controls of monitoring, feedback, and adaptation, Berry regards the normative goal-orientation mode as possible only when a society can achieve closure of means and ends by acquiring sufficient coercive power to ensure that inputs actually produce the outputs desired. Berry's necessary condition seems too harshly antidemocratic to fit traditional Anglo-American thought. Even so—but preferably with more persuasion than coercion—if land is not to be sacrificed to inappropriate technologies or to greed, some authority requires the capacity to proceed toward desirable ends. Berry's fourth approach at least embraces the initiative required to replace reaction with policy that is oriented to something socially more useful than exploitive opportunity-seeking.

Berry's typology of planning specifies only one major characteristic of planning, namely, *goals.* Other main characteristics of a national land use policy include a *comprehensive scope,* an *integrated character, discrimination* or (if one prefers) *selectivity, continuity,* and a *suitable locus of decision-making.* In the absence of any of these characteristics, there cannot be a true national land use policy.

Goals

Without goals, one can go nowhere, slowly or speedily, but can only drift with the tide of millions of small decisions. In one context related to land, the tide of small decisions is called "the market." For a society without a clear idea of goals, courses of action are indeterminate. Purposeless planning results—a set of means without ends.

Means without ends lead to the drift that is associated with the so-called goal of "growth" or "development." This alleged goal is really a process upon which no limits have been set. No outcome is envisaged save, perhaps, avoiding economic depression or protecting certain people's investments.

In system terms, growth for its own sake is an excess of positive feedback combined with a shortage of negative feedback, at least until in a finite world nature supplies the latter. Wisdom advises heeding an observation by the English Joint Planning Team responsible for developing a strategy for the Counties of Cheshire, Lancashire, Merseyside, and Greater Manchester:

> We see no justification for trying to put the clock back to the region's heyday of rapid growth when for a century the North West itself was one of the most favoured regions of the country. Having experienced the environmental consequences of that period of unrestrained rapid growth it is unlikely that the people of the North West would wish to have it repeated.[19]

The Joint Planning Team also objected to numerical standards that associate population growth with success and population decline with failure and lack of confidence. The team argued for

> A change of attitude towards our criteria for judging success. Growth should not be seen as an end in itself—it is more important to ensure a good standard of life for the people of the region, however many or few they are.[20]

To ensure a good standard of life it is necessary to treat land as more than a place to stuff people, buildings, and businesses. Under that concept, land is but a commodity to be exchanged and built on for profit, while people are reduced to being conduits for the flow of money. Unless both people and land are conceived differently—the people as personalities to be cherished and the land as a source of life and a heritage to be transmitted unabused to the generations yet to be born—a good standard of life is neither to be expected for many nor to endure far into the future.

The heritage concept of land suggests that rural planning should embrace more than land use and treat land use as requiring more than a "hands-off" approach. The absence of integrated positive planning for rural areas has led to the decline of village life and the disruption of local status hierarchies, among other consequences. In other cases, villages have expanded at the cost of open space and fragile areas.

A positive approach to rural planning would include treating outstanding, rare, or fragile areas—ecological, cultural, or historic—as fixed and inviolate, to be properly managed and to be a core around which agricultural and urban uses would revolve and relate in a system of priorities that, whenever possible, would prefer agricultural uses.[21] One goal would then be established—a goal expressing the heritage concept of land.

To date, green belts are the closest thing to inviolate open space, particularly when firmly defended as the West Cheshire Green Belt was protected by the Wirral Borough Council against such encroachments as the BBC proposal to build a television tower.[22] Yet, green belts are really afterthoughts rather than the open space around which English cities were built. Moreover, some green belts have had their edges nibbled off. This has been the case, for example, in Buckinghamshire and might well happen in the Toronto Region's designated Parkway Belt West and the open space core of the Netherlands' Randstad, which was planned as a circle from east of Rotterdam to Utrecht, closed toward the coast and open in the southeast.[23]

Protection of land and landscape can be a goal realizable either by negative action, such as refusal of planning permission for structures in a green belt, or by positive efforts to promote rural uses. However, an isolated concern for protecting land is unlikely to be fruitful. There is need to be comprehensive in a sense that embraces much more of a society's life than do the traditional concerns of the physical planner.

Comprehensiveness

There is a great deal of interdependence among issues and among the forces acting upon a given territory. Land use policy, settlement policy, urban policy, and agricultural policy are inextricably embedded in a national and international economy. As Davidson and Wibberley observe, "If Britain can recover her position as a relatively wealthy nation with a secure external trading balance then she will gain the maximum degree of flexibility in relation to land use matters."[24]

British experience is illustrative. At the beginning of the 1970s, Britain saw a major rural need to be the retirement of marginal agricultural land. But when the terms of world agricultural trade turned against Britain, an adverse balance of payments became chronic and, further complicating the situation, the cost of oil rose, it became necessary to continue to support agricuture in the hills and uplands. In short, the balance of payments tied land use to foreign policy.

Linking land use and foreign policy is beyond the capacity of subnational governments. But those matters that are open to subnational control also require comprehensive treatment. For example, the Central Lancashire New Town, based on the three existing towns of Preston, Chorley, and Leyland, was planned in isolation without either the benefits or the constraints of a regional plan. Moreover, the original assumptions were invalidated by population drains from Merseyside and Greater Manchester that reduced needs for overspill housing. As a corrective measure, the Strategic Plan for the North West proposed a Mersey Belt strategy with the Central Lancashire New Town held in reserve until the late 1980s or early 1990s.[25]

Land banking is another technique best conducted in the setting of a broader strategy. Britain's Community Land Act is of questionable value. The Act was passed at a time not only of financial constraint but also of a shortage of valuers and planners. The latter, a manpower and educational deficiency, was acknowledged as early as the introduction of the 1974 White Paper but without indication of what would be done.[26]

In contrast, Saskatoon made effective use of land banking by retaining land obtained during the Depression through tax default. While other cities sold such land and reduced taxes, Saskatoon used it to direct development onto city land and control its form, replaced developed sites with other sites within and outside the city, and implemented an excellent community planning scheme. The city worked with private developers who gained the advantage of not having to keep funds tied up in undeveloped land or pay speculators' prices.[27] The Saskatoon authorities did not have unusual foresight but, not knowing in 1945 what to do with their land, chose the cautious course of waiting until they could formulate a broad strategy.

The Saskatoon experience with land banking is an exception. But it illustrates the value of comprehensive approach even at the local level. Among other things, exorbitant prices for the original land bank were avoided and the private sector was persuaded to cooperate. Policymaking and planning were not purely reactive and curative.

Integration

Comprehensiveness refers to the range or scope of actions and interactions to be embraced by a goal-oriented policy. Its corollary is integration, that is, the bringing together of the several segments of policy in a manner that minimizes conflict among the segments and enables them to reinforce each other in the pursuit of posited goals.

To say that policy should have an integrated character is to recognize the need for a process of synthesis. Synthesis is the pulling together, harmonizing, and reconciling of parts in order to make a whole. With attention to interdependencies, one synthesizes in order to avoid the self-defeating fragmentation arising from random, ad hoc policy decisions.

Saskatoon did more than simply produce a plan. Its elected officials and bureaucrats acted along several dimensions, comprehensive in scope. They also integrated policy segments dealing with such things as distances to schools, open space, and bus stops. They obtained land outside the city limits in order to control land use and development on a scale reflecting the interactions of city, suburb, and countryside.

A recent attempt to integrate a range of policy segments is reflected in the approved Regional Official Policies Plan (December 7, 1976) of the Regional Municipality of Waterloo, Ontario. The effort to integrate is most evident in the chapters on land utilization policy, settlement patterns, and environmental policy. The Waterloo planners' concern for settlement patterns links their policy with national policy to the extent that national policy may try to determine what particular cities and their regions should do in the national economy, express preferences about where people should live and work, and make decisions on immigration.

The harmonization implied by integration does not require that everything move in the same direction, but that there be reciprocal movements so combined as to enable the whole to move in a controlled manner. Earlier it was suggested that the pursuit of growth for its own sake has produced an excess of positive feedback and a shortage of negative feedback. Progress or movement cannot occur if both are present in equal strength to nullify each other. Both must be present if there is to be a controlled movement forward—but present in the right proportions. The engine that propels a vehicle has reciprocating parts that are so integrated that thrust and counterthrust interact both to move a vehicle and to permit controlling it.

From the need to mix positive and negative feedback, one can infer a need for choice. Choice imposes the burden of establishing priorities related to goals and needs. Since needs are not equal, meeting them requires the policymaker to be discriminatory when necessary.

Discrimination (Selectivity)

Seemingly, national land use policy has to be discriminatory in the nature of things, given differences in soil composition, terrain, water supply, and such. However, in light of such things as the overgrowth of Arizona cities relative to the water supply, there seems to have been a lack of discrimination based on nature's constraints. Nor does there appear to have been much discrimination exercised on the basis of a deliberate decision about a region's appropriate role in the national economy.

The need for discrimination arises in part from the uniqueness of individual regions and their cities. It also arises from financial constraints and the available supply of high caliber manpower—limits that prevent doing everything desired at once for every region and city except by spreading resources too thinly to be effective.

British regional policy has been discriminatory. In this century policy has favored the South East and the London region, thereby fostering the decline of Liverpool, Manchester, and other northern cities. Birmingham and the West Midlands have been discriminated against by a Whitehall policy embracing the assumption that the region would continue to have a strong metals, automobile, and engineering economy and be capable of supporting more needy regions.[28]

Discrimination among regions in Great Britain now takes the forms of permanent eligibility for assistance and favoritism in public investment. The first action of this sort occurred in 1963 when the North East (centered on Newcastle-upon-Tyne) and Central Scotland were designated as growth areas. In 1974 the Government included Merseyside, parts of North Wales, Edinburgh, Cardiff, and Chesterfield among the assisted areas.[29]

A land use corollary to the discriminatory feature of growth area policy is found in an October 1973 circular to local authorities from the Secretary of State for the Environment. The circular refers to "white land" in the development plans then in use. In growth areas, planning applications for building on such land are to be considered with a strong presumption in favor of housing. The presumption is to be overridden only if there are exceptional planning objections, for example, good agricultural land, high landscape value. Outside growth areas, this presumption is not to apply and "white land" is to be used for housing only if it is a natural extension of existing development and is compatible therewith in size, character, location, and setting.[30] In this case, not a policy of growth anywhere but a discriminatory growth policy provides some protection for land.

In the United States, discriminatory initiative at the federal level seems to rest with congressional committee chairmen, with some mitigation through trade-offs. The most evident result has been the movement of industry and federal spending to the Sunbelt. One can trace the beginnings of such a movement to the 1930s when, because of the inadequacies of state and local action in Depression conditions, the federal government moved into activities previously within the domain of subnational governmental units. The idea of using the federal government to transfer funds from the North to the South originally carried virtually the connotation of charity. The effect on land use was secondary, largely in the form of recreational areas where power projects created artificial lakes. In postwar affluence, the transfer policy has become increasingly discriminatory to the point of being viewed as a threat to Northeastern and Midwestern regions. In this case, policy displays not only a discriminatory aspect but also the characteristic of continuity.

Continuity

Without continuity, which is not identical with permanence, policy is absent. Fits and starts, stops and changes, may constitute government activity without reflecting policy. Even though short-term considerations and related actions are inevitable, strategy, and so policy, requires a longer-range element.

Policy ought not to be just the product of decisions taken at various moments on the basis of transient claims and demands. It ought to be conceived as something related to a trajectory of time, particularly since the policy itself is not the goal but a means of attaining a goal in the future. The passage of time is critical—a basic reason why the implementation of policy requires continuous monitoring and feedback.

Time is of the essence because policy deals with matters not disposed of overnight. In regard to land use, it deals, among other things, with the slow processes of land assembly, design, building, and reforestation. Land policy also contends with incongruent cycles of activity like the "rhythms" referred to above—the daily urban rhythm, the annual agrarian rhythm, and the generational ecological rhythm. Policy changes not meshed with nature but derived from ideological or political considerations undermine continuity and, with it, goals—thus undermining policy itself.

Where can one turn for policymaking continuity? Certainly not to political parties and elected officials in a democratic system, unless successive electoral victories reduce the frequency of change of governmental control. In the absence of political durability, the most likely source of continuity is the bureaucracy. The bureaucracy will be on the job longer than any elected official and so can win long-term battles with politicians. Moreover, it is involved with far more of the information and other ingredients of policy decisions. For example, early in 1966 Richard Crossman, then British Minister of Housing and Local Government, found himself helpless when confronted with a paper prepared by his Permanent Secretary, Dame Evelyn Sharp, and circulated to all relevant departments. Even though the Minister had not read it, the document had the status of an agreed official paper with unanimity in Cabinet ensured, thereby precluding changes by the minister.[31] This incident, one of many, suggests that if the status of land is to become something more than that of a commodity, change must be accomplished by a long process in which the bureaucracy is early won over to a new concept not only to formulate policy but also to lend it continuity. There remains the question of the political decisions which, with or without new legislation, are required if land is to acquire a new status for which the bureaucracy can provide continuity.

Locus of Decision-making

Where in government might there be a chance of formulating an integrated, comprehensive land use policy that embraces the value judgment that land is a heritage temporarily held in trust by its users? Answering that question requires turning again to the problems of allocation of powers between levels of government and of functional fragmentation. A new term, senior government, will be introduced to cover both national government and a subnational government when, as in Canada, such a unit has final constitutional authority over natural resources.

Although one can hardly argue with the proposition that certain aspects of land use control should be dealt with at the local level in order to take advantage of special local knowledge, one should heed the warning of *The Guardian* (Manchester) that any national scheme, such as the then proposed Community Land Act, that has to be administered by local authorities risks failure through attrition or deliberate disuse.[32] Failure to use local planning authority or incompetent use thereof may require a senior government to intervene by exercising detailed control over planning at the cost of work overload, delay, and local resentment and resistance. Ontario is an example. As Peter Silcox, the Commissioner for the Essex County Restructuring Study, wrote:

> I am opposed to the exercise of such detailed supervision by provincial authorities but find it extremely difficult to argue with the case currently

made for it. In a situation where no municipality outside the City of Wind-
sor employs a single expert staff member with continuing responsibility for
a planning programme and the County Land Division Committee and local
Committees of Adjustment lack the advice of such a person, what else is
one to expect.[33]

Furthermore, can one expect the larger issues that are involved in cases
like that of the Niagara fruitlands to be always clearly understood by local
officials? About 27,500 acres between the Niagara Escarpment and Lake
Ontario provide optimum conditions for the growth of tender fruit, grapes,
and, conflictingly, cities. Niagara accounts for 80 percent of Canada's
grapes, 55 percent of its cherries, and 75 percent of its peaches. Besides the
fact that loss of this fruitland increases Canada's dependence on imports,
the value of the land and its product increases as fruitland in the United
States, especially in California, receives heavy pressure from urban growth.
Let property taxes rise too high, however, as well as the price paid with the
intention of subsequent urban development, and land is idled indefinitely to
become a breeding ground for insects and a source of disease for surrounding fruit farms.[34]

Planners in the service of the Regional Municipality of Niagara, basing
themselves on a 1973 Regional Council policy statement, would have
limited the area designated for urban expansion to 5,000 acres. The
Regional Planning Committee and the Council raised the total to 8,000
acres in the Official Plan submitted to the Minister of Housing. Told to cut
back the area for urban expansion, Niagara authorities resubmitted the plan
in 1976 with the total set at 7,600, a reduction of only 400 acres. On
February 16, 1977, the Minister of Housing announced that there must be a
reduction of 3,000 acres, with urban development to be above the Escarpment, away from the best fruitland.[35] Niagara officials were not pleased
with this display of the Ontario Government's control over land use, nor
with the minister's obvious priority on the provincial and national interests,
important though these are.

Ontario exercises a control over land use through its control over
municipalities. Except for certain areas such as the Parkway Belt West and
the Niagara Escarpment from the Niagara River to Georgian Bay, it has no
land use plan as such, and in this respect it resembles American states.

By 1975, seventeen American states had enacted various land planning
and control measures. But only Hawaii has overcome the opposition of
special interests and zoned all its territory for urban, rural, agricultural, or
conservation uses.

At the federal level, as noted earlier, land use legislation ran into a congressional procedural roadblock. Yet, given the national and international
extent of activities bearing upon land and the effects of inadvertent national
land use programs, such as, the interstate highway program, it seems

evident that land use should not be isolated from the formation of national policy as a whole.

Were land use to become a major concern of the American federal administration, decision power must be placed somewhere. The objective should be to have a structure of authority that inhibits the tendency of agencies to go their separate ways, nullifying each other's efforts because of their functional or mission-oriented views. As is well known, the usual structure of government produces departments in need of coordination at their highest levels.

If there is no way to structure an administration so that one department can authoritatively formulate a national land use policy that is a derivative of a general, broader national policy, then policymaking must take place at the White House. This does not mean that the president and his aides should be immersed in the details of land use. Rather, it means that only the president and the higher ranking members of his staff are in a position to formulate generalized directives about land use that relate it to the total American system and the interdependence of its parts. But in the final analysis, whatever the gain in coordination of separate departments, little benefit will come to the land unless a concept of land as a heritage held in trust holds sway at the White House, in the bureaucracy, and among the public.

Attitudes and Values

A fundamental question might be stated as follows: On what basis does a government assume the right to deny any part of open, rural space to the developer or the highway builder? This question poses the problem of creating, more solidly than environmentalists have yet done, a climate of opinion that is fully aware of the significance of land. In a democratic system that we still value, this question is crucial if democracy is not to allow the sustenance of life to deteriorate beyond redemption.

The imperative for democracy is embraced in a Toronto editorial based on a report that between 1970 and 1975 Ontario farmland vanished at the rate of 26 acres per hour:

> We have reached the point where a citizen is no longer free to do what he wants with his land, and if the citizen must give up that right, then government must be ready with a just and wise plan for the use of land in the best interests of all.[36]

What is justice is a difficult question, usually answered subjectively. Even so, given the seriousness of the land use and related problems, an attempt to embrace the issue of justice when tackling the land use problem is inescapable. Useful guidance was provided by Lord Goodwin, Chairman of England's Housing Corporation. "The rights of the citizen must be protected, so the rights of one citizen would have to be protected in a most elaborate, meticulous fashion, quite regardless of what happens to the rest of the citizenry." Thus, in biting manner, Lord Goodwin referred to the claims and demands of developers and speculators before proceeding to his main point. "What I am quite sure is that the processes of civic justice demand that we do disregard and override some of the facetious rights of a man who thinks he should assert them, not knowingly, but, in fact, to the detriment of the community."[37]

Land use relationships and their legal buttresses tend to express ideals, assumptions, and beliefs about social order. The current ethos gives dominance to economic considerations and thus renders public policy auxiliary to economic forces, the most influential of which has been economic growth and its accompanying philosophy. The resultant motivation has been toward actions damaging to land and ultimately to the human species. Without a new attitude toward land, motivation to act with greater care for land is not to be expected at the national, subnational, or private level.

It is intriguing to consider the difference between British and American attitudes toward planning and land use. A comparative study of rural-urban fringe areas near Bristol, England, and near Columbus, Ohio, is revealing. In regard to choice of residential neighborhood, it was found that Americans sought a good school system but the English did not. In contrast, the English sought nearness of open country, while Americans did not.[38] Perhaps there lies the American mental roadblock.

The American seems not to value the countryside as much as does the Englishman. Moreover, not having a Stonehenge, a Salisbury Cathedral, a Warwick Castle, or a Tintern Abbey to visit, the American's time perspective does not extend far beyond the here and now. An extended time perspective is the essence of the concept of land as a heritage held in trust. As Harold Nicolson once wrote:

> Not only have [Americans] no sense of the past: they have no sense of the future. They do not plant avenues for their great-grandchildren. This gives them not merely an absence of past roots but of future roots also. It gives a ghastly feeling of provisionality: "Chicago's ever-changing sky-line.[39]

Notes

1. George E. Condon, *Cleveland: The Best Kept Secret* (New York: Doubleday, 1967), p. 11.

2. Tom Dale and Vernon Gill Carter, *Topsoil and Civilization* (Norman: University of Oklahoma Press, 1955); Hans J. Morgenthau, *Politics*

Among Nations: The Struggle for Power and Peace, 5th ed. (New York: Knopf, 1972), p. 116.

3. A. Allan Schmid, *Converting Land from Rural to Urban Uses* (Baltimore: Johns Hopkins University Press, 1968), p. 42.

4. Paul B. Sears, *The Ecology of Man* (Eugene: Oregon State System of Higher Education, 1957), p. 35.

5. P. Nijkamp, "Urbanization Policy: Plans and Possibilities," *Planning and Development in the Netherlands*, 9 (no. 2): 1977, p. 128.

6. R.S. Lang, *Nova Scotia Municipal and Regional Planning in the Seventies: Report/Evaluation of the Town Planning Act Review* (Halifax: Nova Scotia Department of Municipal Affairs and Central Mortgage and Housing Corporation, 1972), pp. 305-06.

7. Planning Advisory Group, *The Future of Development Plans* (London: HMSO, 1965), pp. 21-25.

8. Joan Davidson and Gerald Wibberley, *Planning and the Rural Environment* (Oxford: Pergamon, 1977), pp. 3, 22-23, 173; J.R. Wright, W.M. Braithwaite, and R.R. Forster, *Planning for Urban Recreational Open Space: Towards Community-Specific Standards* (Toronto: Ontario Ministry of Housing, 1976), p. 42.

9. Edward Hyams, *The Changing Face of Britain* (St. Albans, Eng.: Paladin, 1977), pp. 99-106. See also John Prebble, *The Highland Clearances* (Harmondsworth, Eng.: Penguin, 1969); K.B. Smellie, *A History of Local Government*, rev. ed. (London: Unwin, 1968), p. 12.

10. Davidson and Wibberley, *Planning and the Rural Environment*, pp. 22-23, 80-81; Hyams, *Changing Face of Britain*, p. 229.

11. *Cleveland Plain Dealer*, September 29, 1976; *Detroit Free Press*, June 19, 1977.

12. W.J.G. van Mourik, "Physical Planning in Rural Areas—Policy Resolutions of the Netherlands Government 1977," *Planning and Development in the Netherlands*, 9 (no. 2): 1977, p. 140.

13. *New York Times*, February 28, 1974.

14. N.H. Lithwick, *Urban Canada: Problems and Prospects—A Report for the Honourable R.K. Andras, Minister Responsible for Housing* (Ottawa: Central Mortgage and Housing Corporation, 1970), pp. 170, 174.

15. On uncertainty as a by-product of government intervention, see J.R. Markusen and D.T. Scheffman, *Speculation and Monopoly in Urban Development: Analytical Foundations with Evidence for Toronto* (Toronto and Buffalo: University of Toronto Press, 1977), pp. 125-27.

16. Wesley L. Gould, "Metals, Oil, and Natural Gas: Some Problems of Canadian-American Co-operation," in David R. Deener (ed.), *Canada-United States Treaty Relations* (Durham, N.C.: Duke University Press, 1963), pp. 151-84; Jacob Spelt, *Urban Development in South-Central Ontario* (Toronto: McClelland and Stewart, 1972), *passim*.

17. *Strategic Plan for the North West: SPNW Joint Planning Team Report 1973* (London: HMSO, 1974), p. 31.

18. Brian J.L. Berry, *The Human Consequences of Urbanization: Divergent Paths in the Urban Experience of the Twentieth Century* (New York: St. Martin's Press, 1973), pp. 178-79.

19. *Strategic Plan for the North West*, p. 32.

20. *Ibid.*, p. 31.

21. Wright, Braithwaite, and Forster, *Planning for Urban Recreational Open Space*, pp. 28, 40-41; L.O. Gertler, *Regional Planning in Canada: A Planner's Testament* (Montreal: Harvest House, 1972), pp. 124-25; William Serrin in the *New York Times*, April 27, 1978.

22. *Liverpool Echo*, February 10, 1975; *Hoylake News and Advertiser*, January 16 and February 6, 1975.

23. *The Guardian* (Manchester), November 20, 1974; *Development Planning in Ontario: The Parkway Belt West* (Toronto: Ministry of Treasury, Economics and Intergovernmental Affairs, June 1973); Jac P. Thijsse, *Rim-City Holland: Problems of a Metropolis in the Making* (Amsterdam: Delta International Publication Foundation, 1959).

24. Davidson and Wibberley, *Planning and the Rural Environment*, p. 32.

25. *The Guardian* (Manchester), November 4, 1974.

26. *Ibid.*, October 28, 1974. See also the letter of D.R. Denman to *The Times* (London), November 6, 1974.

27. Boyce Richardson, *The Future of Canadian Cities* (Toronto: New Press, 1972), pp. 98-101, 123-24.

28. West Midlands County Council, *A Time for Action: Economic and Social Trends in the West Midlands* (September, 1974), esp. pp. 5-6, 14, 22.

29. *Labour Weekly Reporter*, September 16, 1974.

30. *The Times* (London), October 3, 1973.

31. Richard Crossman, *The Diaries of a Cabinet Minister,* vol. 1, *Minister of Housing, 1964-66* (London: Hamish Hamilton and Jonathan Cape, 1975), p. 441.

32. *The Guardian* (Manchester), September 13, 1974.

33. Peter Silcox, *Essex County Local Government Restructuring Study: Final Report* (June 1976), p. 189.

34. Ralph R. Krueger, "Changing Land-Use Patterns in the Niagara Fruit Belt," *Transactions of the Royal Canadian Institute*, Part 2 (October 1959), pp. 114-15.

35. G. Keith Bain, "Proposed Official Plan for the Regional Municipality of Niagara—A Confrontation over the Preservation of Agricultural Land," presented at the symposium, "The Face of America: This Land in the Year 2000." University of Michigan, May 1977; *Globe and Mail* (Toronto), August 23, 26, 1976.

36. *Globe and Mail* (Toronto), August 26, 1975.

37. *Daily Telegraph* (London), October 29, 1974.

38. H.E. Bracey, *Neighbours on New Estates and Subdivisions in England and the U.S.A.* (London: Routledge, 1964).

39. Harold Nicolson, *Diaries and Letters, 1930-1939*, Nigel Nicolson (ed.) (London: Collins, 1969), p. 135.

14 Law and Land: The Ecology and Sociology of Land Use Planning

Lynton K. Caldwell

If people pressure is excluded as common and basic to most problems of the human environment, land use is our largest and most fundamental set of environmental problems.[1] Land use presents environmental problems for three reasons. The first is because improvident human uses may degrade the quality of the land, diminishing its ability to sustain life and causing it to degrade the quality of air and water. The second reason is because human uses often conflict and require public action to resolve differences. The third reason is that the management of land in our society is vested in large numbers of proprietors whose preferred uses may be inconsistent with the preservation of the land or the welfare of society and over whose decisions society has very limited influence.

Contrary to some skeptical opinions, land use must be placed on the agenda of public policy. This is not only because its various aspects require public decisions, but also because it is linked to almost every other major social and ecological problem, for example to energy, climate, transportation, housing, urbanization, agriculture, health, recreation, and the protection of plant and animal life.

Yet, relative to its importance, we have had little success in developing effective land use policy. Have we attacked land use as a policy problem from the wrong perspective? Have we misinterpreted the problem? Have our methods of solution been inadequate or inappropriate? If the answer to these questions is "yes," then what responses are required if those aspects of land use planning necessary to the continuing social and ecological well-being of our society are to be realized?

A Problem for Policy

Many of our programs and proposals relating to land use appear to contain the cause of their frustration. We seem to have built negating components into many of our land use policies. This has seldom been a calculated risk. It may best be described as inadvertent—caused because we have been looking at the problem from the wrong end. But misconception of a problem leads to its misinterpretation, and action based on mistaken premises cannot realistically be expected to prove effective. How can we develop land use policy that is not self-defeating? Perhaps the way is not to attempt statutory authorization comprehensive enough to meet policy objectives, but rather to focus upon specific actions and behaviors that incidentally affect or involve the misuse of land. Our purpose here is to consider why this may be the most promising approach to policy problem of land use in the United States, avoiding the trap of self-defeating legislation.

Perhaps we can better understand how to develop a new and more effective approach if we understand how we arrived at our present formulation of land law and policy. To find out how to succeed, it may be helpful to see where we have failed.

Law expresses culturally derived principles and relationships and in the main is necessarily conservative, for its purpose has been to stabilize and regularize relationships and rights so as to make them predictable and reliable guides to behavior. Law is intended to expressly confirm patterns of accepted behavior and to provide means for resolving conflicts among principles as variously interpreted.

For historical reasons, man-land relationships are numerous, complex, and often inconsistent—representing in subtle and often unapparent ways the accretion of centuries of custom. The present law thus contains many residual principles, doctrines, and assumptions pertaining (1) directly to rights of land use and ownership and (2) more general principles applicable to land use and ownership (for example, laches and adverse possession). This historicity explains why the conservative field of land law embodies popular beliefs and accommodates behaviors derived from a long past.

Land law in the United States evolved from West European—largely English—precedent, in which land tenure relationships had for hundreds of years been the basis of political power, social structure, and economic rights.[2] In medieval culture, land ownership or tenure was a requisite to a larger degree of freedom.[3] Lack of personal rights in land use tended to correlate with lack of control over one's personal life. Land and personal freedom became especially associated in the minds of settlers in America. A free market approach to land as a commodity became a basic element in the concept of economic freedom in contradistinction to feudal and communal servitudes and encumbrances characteristic of medieval law.

Thus when rational, nonhistorical approches are made to present day land use problems, they often run head-on into a psychological wall of obdurate incompatible attitudes and behavior patterns. The intense emotional hostility with which many people react to almost any land use control measure cannot generally be explained wholly by reference to economic self-interest. Very old ethical assumptions regarding human relationships to land reinforce perceived self-interests. Motives for land holding are numerous and diverse. They need not be explicit to pose formidable barriers to a rational consideration of land use policy. Landowners, especially small owners, have often reacted violently to changes in law and policy that seem clearly to have been in their economic interest.[4]

A Stacked Deck

The game of land use politics is played with a deck of cards stacked by "history." Although abstract, this metaphor is nevertheless accurate. The properties of the several suits in the deck, which we may term (1) behavior, (2) economics, and (3) ideology, are more often the cumulative result of historical practice than a deliberate rigging of the game by interested players. Of course the interests of particular social classes and economic groups have been incorporated into law and practice. It is hardly exceptional for people to seek to institutionalize, and thus to protect, their interests as they perceive them. And when, for whatever reasons, the larger society acquiesces in policies that favor some of its members more than others, the resulting arrangements may be taken as consensual in the society. This consensus need not be truly voluntary; people may accept as "given" arrangements that they see no prospect of changing, especially if the arrangements are of long standing, reinforced by habitual behavior, social status, and political power. One need no more than observe that the composition of the American deck in the land use policy game is culture-specific to American experience. In other cultures the values of the cards may be different. For example, social consensus may not favor individual preemption or even control of land. In societies as contrasting as those representing nomadic pastoralism, communal agriculture, or Marxist socialism, the cards may be stacked against individual ownership or possession of land or against certain ways of using land. In the United States the cards, with few exceptions, favor the individual or corporate proprietor of land.

A major suit in the land use policy deck is behavior, and the shuffle in America has provided few means for its comprehensive planning or control. "Behavior" should here be read as *the generally accepted practice of people* without regard to rationale or approval. For example, it is a time-honored practice in much of rural America to dump old automobile bodies, defunct refrigerators, bedsprings, and miscellaneous refuse in woodland ravines and along the banks of streams. Not all rural Americans accept the practice as desirable, but many would not personally attempt to interfere, nor would they favor public prohibition provided that the owner of the trash dumped it on his own land. Only if and when a nuisance, generated by the dumping, can be shown to harm neighbors or the community in certain specified ways can the particular behavior affecting land be effectively questioned. Even then, it is seldom the land use practice that is challenged; the effort is rather to force abatement of the nuisance. The gully-washing of one farmer's misused land may give no cause for complaint to his neighbors until their drainage ditches are blocked by sediment from his eroding acres. Other behaviors often immune to policy interference include (1) destruction of wildlife habitat, (2) value impairment of an aesthetic or unconventional nature, (3) speculation—land treated solely as a commodity.[6] Behind the behaviors lie ideological explanations or justifications, but these rationales are rarely invoked as the behaviors, per se, are seldom challenged; legal action is more often directed toward after-the-fact correction of their allegedly harmful effects. And too often "after the fact" means ecologically too late!

The behavioral approach to land, especially as a commodity, leads directly to its economic significance. Here again the political cards are stacked against comprehensive policy. Economics may be aptly described as a "rational" science, but its rationality is of a limited kind, and not all economic behaviors are fully "rational." What seems rational for an individual human with a restricted life span may not be rational as defined by long-term community needs and values. And it is easier for the individual landowner to analyze and evaluate available options for the uses of his proprietary rights in land than for society to discover and agree upon its own long-term needs and values in relation to his land.

Reconciliation of short-term, long-term, and individual social rationalities has been attempted by public agencies, notably by the courts, in public "takings" of private landed property for public purposes.[7] Where national parks or monuments have been established in populated areas, a phase-out period is now normally provided, assuring present occupants of lifetime possession, but consummating the transfer to public control whenever a "turnover" in possession is for any reason occasioned. Favorable as this type of arrangement may appear to be for the occupants, it is nevertheless often rejected, sometimes for reasons of sentiment (for example, leaving a family heritage to heirs) but as often perhaps because of economic loss, demonstrable or conjectured.[8] For example, there may be a great economic advantage in possession of an "inholding" surrounded by a state or national park or forest. The inholding owner or occupant may obtain, as a consequence of public investment, extraordinary protection from economic competition from other landholders and from damage occasioned by misuses of their lands—economic, aesthetic, or ecological. But of course the government may not always be a "good" proprietary neighbor.[9]

There are some "wild" cards in the economic suit however. These include unforeseen or unforeseeable changes in land values resulting from, for example, oil or gas strikes, highway construction, or radical changes in community life-styles, such as a craze for second homes. These shifts in the values of otherwise unchanged parcels of land cause the windfalls and wipeouts addressed by Donald Hagman and others.[10] They create interlinking problems of law and economics and often arise because the right hand of public policy, concerned for example, with highway construction or low-cost housing, is oblivious or indifferent to what the left hand may be doing with respect to taxation, resource conservation, or environmental quality control. Land is thus a medium through which the consequences of certain value changes may be projected upon individual land users and owners and indirectly upon society at large.

Were economics, like physics, a conceptually unified science, a generally reliable calculus might be developed to measure and allocate the costs of changes in the valuation and uses of land. But economics consists of not one, but many, schools of theory and analysis. And although there are principles of economic behavior upon which nearly all economists agree, debates over economic policy soon arrive at the juncture at which an answer must be given to the question "whose economics should prevail?" And the answer accepted may bear heavily upon the subsequent direction of policy development.

The task of sorting out and trying to reconcile differing values in land and its uses is, or should be, one of the principal miseries of land use planners. Like the searchers for miracle drugs in medicine, planners have sought for practical, acceptable legal devices to accommodate and adjust value conflicts over land and to clear the way for rational planning. For a short time, the concept of transferable development rights was seen by some land planners as a "magic bullet" that would obviate much of the conflict resulting from the imposition of legal restraints upon hitherto acceptable economic uses of land.[11] Transfer of development rights has proved to be a selectively helpful tool of land use planning and control, but it does not answer all needs and circumstances.

An obvious difficulty in finding equitable solutions to conflicts in value preferences is that the values are not always, or even often, commensurable. The constraints that some people wish to impose upon economically motivated uses of land may be aesthetic, ecological, or ethical. Even if one were to accept the hypotheses that everyone has his price, and that even the most deeply and intensely held ethical value can be reduced to monetary terms, the proposition would not help the policy planner if enough people perversely rejected its validity. Problems of land use policy choice cannot be solved through economic reductionism unless some means are found to persuade almost everyone to accept a translation of all values into econometric terms. The prospect for this conversion in an age of apparently increasing ecological and aesthetic awareness would appear to be poor.

A third suit in the political deck whose cards may reinforce, weaken, or cancel the value of behavioral and economic cards is the ideological. Here one finds the ethical beliefs and aesthetic values that may or may not be translatable into economic terms but may also either censure or legitimize economic behavior. Most behavior in any society, including economic behavior, is in some sense legitimized by the prevailing ideology. Thus it is logical in our culture to "own" or to "buy" land in a way that is in effect quite different from acquiring possession over given quantities of air, water, or sunlight. What is usually acquired are "rights" to transitory and specified uses of these hard-to-hold resources. One buys a "view" on a hillside subdivision, but may lose it if obstructed by high-rise buildings or defaced by chimney stacks or electric power lines. One buys measurable quantities of water only to lose them in use.

Some legal principles of long-standing application to property rights pertaining to land (for example, laches and adverse possession) have discriminated heavily against groups and individuals deficient in power or knowledge. These legal doctrines grew out of a social ideology that, among other things, did not question capital punishment for offenses now regarded as misdemeanors and denied to women most economic and many personal rights. Although no legal principle or doctrine can continue indefinitely to be regarded as more valid or persuasive than the social ideology that sustains it, a legal principle that has become questionable theoretically may continue to be sustainable practically until supplanted by a feasible alternative. Several interrelated reasons explain this with particular reference to land law in the United States.

For one, ideological change in American society has largely been issue specific, not comprehensive. Reform movements characteristically have been directed to specific discovered abuses, not toward the social system as a whole. For another, the law, being conservative in tendency, is not likely to change in the absence of pressure upon some specific effect or provision. A third reason is the complex set of interrelationships involving land, law, and economics manifest in the traditional emotional aura surrounding the concept of ownership. Land is widely regarded as our most important commodity, and transactions affecting its disposition and use are almost invariably locked into the real estate triangle of landowner, moneylender, and lawyer (at bar and on the bench).[12] The law governing land ownership and uses is thus strongly reinforced by linked and convergent interests. In many communities, the real estate triangle is the most potent single fact of politics.

It should not be surprising, therefore, that broadly based land use policies that are not consistent with generally accepted and mutually advantageous relationships among landlords, lenders, and lawyers are likely to encounter resistance. Many of the concerns motivating policy changes in land laws fall outside the real estate triangle and do not serve the interests that it symbolically represents. The objectives of land use reform today are characteristically sociological or ecological; their economic rationales tend to be those of communities rather than of individuals, but their impacts may be felt by land-owning persons. Even when the proposed reforms could benefit individual proprietors, the advantages are not always specified or clarified in a manner adequate to overcome a generalized fear of loss of control.

Present day attacks upon the traditional structure of land use law are moreover far from consistent with one another. Some are mutually antagonistic. The sociological objectives of some reformers, for example, to promote racial and economic diversification within communities, to break down various forms of de facto segregation, have sometimes run counter to ecological objectives such as the preservation of open space and the control of population densities.[13] The aesthetic values of harmony in cultural and natural landscapes that reformers, often including landowners, attempt to protect through changes in traditional law may conflict with other changes sought by advocates of massive public technologies who object to legal provisions that slow progress or increase costs by protecting "rights" of individual landowners or occupants.[14]

In sum, land use problems are people problems. The critical issues and disputes have often more to do with the implications and consequences of particular uses than with the uses themselves. It is accordingly difficult or impossible to draft statutory declarations of land use policy at less than a very high level of generality. High level generalities unless expressive of strong emotional bias are notoriously poor catalysts of popular enthusiasm and support. On the land use issue in America, the emotion is largely weighted against long-term comprehensiveness, supporting individual rights against social infringement, real or fancied. If comprehensive land use policy is sought, a problem of strategy must be faced.

Needed—A Strategy

A strategy may be described as a plan of action designed to achieve a generalized goal by increasing proponents and diminishing opponents. In our society a public strategy will be most effective if overt and honest, not covert or dissembling. To win friends by straightforward efforts to help people reconcile their short-term interests with the longer term needs and interests of society cannot fairly be described as subversive, and that is what an effective strategy for land use policy must achieve.

In the United States, most statutory proposals for comprehensive land use planning have attracted too few allies to offset hard-core opposition. It is plausible that, if fairly understood, legislation such as the National Land Use Planning Assistance Act (S. 3354, 1970, and its successors) would be favored by a majority of the national electorate. Federal legislation was three times recommended by President Nixon and adopted by the Senate.[15] At the state level, comprehensive planning has been enacted for limited and specific purposes—for example by initiative in California (Proposition 20: The California Coast: environmental preservation and public access)[16] and by legislative action in Vermont.[17] But this state legislation has been largely confined to areas of conspicuous vulnerability—the coastal zone and land adjacent to lakes and streams. Legislation requiring restoration of strip-mined land has been enacted in many states, but its uneven effectiveness prompted demands for federal legislation.[18] More inclusive measures might win approval if they could be debated and could come to a vote. But the commonly successful strategy of the opposition has been to prevent land use planning measures from reaching the legislature as a whole by "bottling them up" in committee. Thus consideration of general federal land use legislation has repeatedly been blocked by the Rules Committee of the House of Representatives.[19]

The hard-core opposition to comprehensive land use policies may not be as formidable numerically as it is strategically. Its principal cohorts are the real estate lobby, the building trades, mortgage and land investment companies, and development interests generally. Their stakes in land use policy are their preferred economic futures. Their legal responsibilities have little bearing upon the social or ecological consequences of their actions. There are, moreover, few practicable ways to hold land developers accountable for their actions other than bonding for specific performance.[20] For many land abuses, the only remedy is prevention. Prevention implies constraints upon landowner, user, and developer, obviously diminishing their economic freedom in relation to the uses of the land.

Owners are not necessarily disadvantaged, even economically, by land use controls and may be advantaged. For example, owners wishing to retain lands in farms, forests, or for residential use can be protected against pressure to develop accompanied by increased tax assessments.[21] But land-owners can be frightened by the prospect of unspecified and unforeseeable consequences of changes in their legal rights that comprehensive land use planning might entail. The hard core of unconvertible opposition to public control over land use has effectively exploited this uneasiness. Its success may be the most significant single reason for the general failure of the comprehensive approach thus far.

If comprehensiveness in land use policy is necessary to its effectiveness, but not attainable by statute, a different approach must be sought. The pragmatic approach that many jurisdictions have begun to follow has been to focus efforts on specific aspects of land use and environmental objectives, for example, through implementation of Section 208 of the 1972 amendments to the Federal Water Pollution Control Act.[22] The unhappy consequences of ad hoc approaches to land use policies and controls have provided some of the most convincing arguments for comprehensiveness in planning.[23] It can hardly be too strongly emphasized, however, that the *goal* of comprehensiveness does not imply a particular method of planning. Its extremes may be highly centralized or broadly participatory, but it is more likely to be truly comprehensive if it is the latter.

A major rationale for a federal land use planning assistance act was illustrated by a series of transparent overlay maps prepared for a hearing before the Senate Committee on Interior and Insular Affairs on March 24, 1970, pursuant to S. 3354.[24] These overlays depicted existing and some projected land uses by the federal agencies. Points of competition, contradiction, and conflict were made explicit. The maps indicated localities in which tax dollars were being spent by federal agencies, in effect, to negate one another's efforts. Lack of coordination in land use planning was obviously costly in both dollars and program effectiveness. Prudent public investment in land and public works required a degree of comprehensiveness in planning and control sufficient to reconcile and coordinate existing and proposed usage. It made poor logic for Congress to grant public works funds to the states for airports, highways, land and water conservation, and similar land-related purposes when most states made no effort to see that the land use effects of these and other projects were not mutually contradictory. But this logic alone was insufficient to obtain legislation that would have assisted statewide land use planning.

One should understand, however, that separate attack upon particular land use problems does not afford a practical alternative to a comprehensive statutory planning unless two conditions are present. The first is that particular action be taken within a broad perspective and evaluation of land use interrelationships and priorities. The second is that there be some operational institution or agency to make this assessment and to obtain, by whatever means appropriate, results consistent with long-range public welfare. These two conditions are essential components of a strategy to obtain by a skillful combination of existing means the policy comprehensiveness heretofore unobtainable through broad statutory authorization.

This alternative approach to policy need not negate nor evade the general body of legal principles governing land use and tenure. It need not be prejudicial to the proprietary rights of a person—individual or corporate—in land with an important exception. Exercise of these rights ought not be permitted to impair or destroy the integrity or self-renewing capabilities of natural ecosystems or human communities without the strongest social justification subject to review by those who must in various ways bear the cost of resulting damage. This is a large exception, but one consistent with the concept of an inherent power in government to protect the public health, safety, and general welfare.

An effective strategy for comprehensive land use planning must enlist the support of a critical mass among persons who have traditionally opposed the planning concept. These include, principally, persons holding proprietary interests in land for these, as Donald Denman has reminded us, are the primary land use planners.[25] It has been a failure-inducing paradox of many land use planning proposals that no clear or appropriate role was provided for these primary planners. A strategy is needed that will avoid uniting landowners against planning and will bring as many of them as respect ecological and cultural values into an influential and constructive role in the planning process.

An effective strategy of implementation does, however, imply a well conceived and concerted set of objectives—in effect a plan that is comprehensive in the scope of its consideration and intended results, but flexible and opportunity-seeking with respect to practical means. In theory, although rarely in practice, political party platforms afford a rough analogy. They set forth a set of (sometimes) interrelated goals indicating an intended direction of policy, but are usually noncommittal as to means. It is, of course, commonplace for candidates for the offices of state governor or president to declare in favor of policy objectives without specifying a particular course of action. To fit together pieces of authorized action to form a coherent and consistent policy may be regarded as effective administration; it may be called policy making by implementation.

Implementing a Strategy

Any effective strategy must provide answers to three questions: *What* is the strategy? *Who* is to implement it? and *How* is the strategy to be implemented?

Our definition of strategy has been a consensus building plan of action, directed in this instance *toward* ecologically sustainable patterns of land use, yielding optimal levels of human satisfaction. Obviously this is not a self-explanatory definition. The expressions "ecologically sustainable patterns" and "optimal levels of satisfaction" do not represent broadly understood criteria in our society. Although their meanings may incorporate significant and even objectively demonstrable findings of fact, and to this extent may be called "scientific," they may also contain subjective preferential aspects that are not demonstrably right or wrong in an ethical or scientific sense. Optimal satisfactions may most easily be isolated through discovering those circumstances that almost no one would regard as optimal. For example, exhausted soil fertility or water supply would hardly be regarded under any circumstance as optimal. Optimality might be posited as a goal and some of its major parameters identified through objective analysis. But its ultimate meaning as a goal of policy would have to be discovered through the implementation of an optimum seeking strategy, for, there appears no other way that in societies holding multiple values, consensual definitions of optimality can be achieved.[26]

The balancing of values by the courts may be regarded as a practical effort to approximate optimality.[27] But equitable balancing is compromised by the parameters of the case under review. Posterity may not have standing in court, and the implications of the controversy may extend to social and ecological considerations beyond those reviewable in the court.

Practices that are ecologically sustainable, meaning protective of the self-renewing capabilities of ecosystems, including those serving the ecological needs of people, are more easily defined and verified than are propositions regarding optimality. Their validity may be established by demonstrable cause-effect relationships, regardless of human preference or value. Some people may prefer to exercise property rights in ways that pollute estuaries and destroy wetlands in disregard of ecological consequences. Their intentions, in principle, may not necessarily be destructive, but those consequences follow regardless of what people value or prefer. Strategy therefore also calls for making explicit and widely understood the interrelationships among natural systems, including the systems that man contrives through the manipulation of natural forces. This strategy assumes that man can be persuaded to act more often in his own interest in a manner consistent with that of his fellows and posterity to the extent that he understands the probable consequences of his actions. No strategy can wholly offset ignorance, stupidity, or perversity. Human destructiveness has many causes—some scarcely understood. A strategy is, after all, an effort to advance human purpose; in our context it is a corrective, not a panacea, for the limitations of human altruism and intelligence.[28]

The causes and characteristics of land use problems indicate who should be involved in their solution. The traditional base for land use decisions has been the real estate triangle of landlord, lender, and lawyer, with the speculator and developer playing roles intermediate among the three principles. And because decisions within the triangle have historically been made largely exclusive of general public interests or external costs, public authority has been interposed to afford at least minimal protection to the community. Land use controls, notably zoning, have been the generally accepted forms of public involvement in land use policy.[29] But conventional methods have been widely criticized as ineffective and clearly have not prevented many of our worst land abuses, including many perpetrated by governmental agencies.[30]

Among the more obvious weaknesses of conventional public controls are these: *first,* the owners and users of land are seldom involved in representative or constructive ways that are open and protective of the public interest, *second,* the policy machinery is easily captured by economically focused development interests that preempt representation of proprietary interests in land, and *third,* no systematic way is provided for scientific or cultural considerations to influence the decision process. In many communities these circumstances have been conducive to skulduggery, conspiracy, favoritism, and a bad name for land use planning. Zoning and planning boards are often dominated by persons whose interest in land is almost wholly in short-term economic profit. The interests of small landed proprietors are often overridden in favor of big developers, builders, speculators, and government public works agencies. Development interests may numerically represent a small minority in a community, the proprietors a much larger number. But the development interests invoke the magic symbols of jobs, economic growth, and especially of increased taxable assessments, whereas the individual landowner is likely to be seeking protection for preferred private uses of his property. Stability rather than growth may as often be his objective.

Land use control, therefore, has tended to be a manipulative and adversary process, with little long-range regard for its effect upon the community, state, or nation. When the big public and industrial eminent domain decision-makers enter the process to obtain rights of way, power plant sites, airports, or housing tracts, they have characteristically done so with advanced plans, narrowly focused on their economic missions, without significant public input, and ably defended by lawyers and economists. Invariably, the public interest is invoked, in addition to theoretical economic justification for overriding the preferences of adversely affected communities and property owners.[31] The bureaucratic and industrial enterprisers define the public interest in terms consistent with their missions and assume with good logic that the courts will entertain a presumption in their favor. Under the present structure of land use decision-making, it is logical to assume that duly constituted representatives of the public such as the Bureau of Reclamation, Tennessee Valley Authority, and the Federal Highway Administration are more broadly representative of the public interest than any probable combination of individual landowners or users. It is similarly logical to assume that a legislative grant of eminent domain to power and mining corporations confirms their interpretations of public convenience and necessity as more valid than any combination of citizens short of an electoral majority. Courts may not agree that this assumption holds in a particular land use or environmental dispute.[32] Recent legislation, such as the National Environmental Policy Act of 1969, have injected a new set of considerations into the land use policy process.[33] Nevertheless the political cards continue to be stacked against the ecological and sociocultural values that this legislation was designed to protect.

The matter of *who* is involved in the decision process significantly influences its outcome. If land use policy is to serve comprehensive long-range and ecologically defensible values, the structuring of participation in the decision process must be consistent with this purpose. The excessive influence of the real estate triangle and of the narrowly focused eminent domain decision-makers needs to be leavened by participation from the full range of interests in land use. These include landowners and many users, representatives of the affected and concerned public that does not own land, and scientists, engineers, and environmental planners with special knowledge and operational skills pertaining to the utilization and conservation of land and its associated resources.

In simple language, a workable strategy for comprehensive land use planning calls for a greatly broadened base of real and not superficial or symbolic participation. Institutional arrangements are required that will go as far as formalities can toward ensuring this broad participation. To serve its purpose, however, this participation must be informed, and this implies a learning experience for the participants. Finally, it must result in demonstrable accomplishment, in action and not mere rhetoric.

Only to the extent that participation makes a difference in the outcomes of land use decisions will it be possible to sustain a broad spectrum of disinterested involvement. The interests within the real estate triangle ensure *their* participation. The bank balances of developers and builders ensure their readiness to sit past midnight in sessions of planning boards—this public business is their business—its outcomes determine their economic futures. Paradoxically, the individual and relatively small landed proprietor is often the most vocal opponent of public land use planning. A free enterprise bias may persuade him that the representatives of the real estate interests are his allies and protectors. This dubious proposition has been cultivated by real estate lobbyists, reinforced by the often heavy-handed and uncomprehended behavior of governmental planning and development agencies, and sharpened by a sense of powerlessness among individual landowners. Powerlessness breeds fear that broadly inclusive statutory controls over land will be used to the landowners' disadvantage. The historical record of government land policy, at all jurisdictional levels, tends to confirm rather than refute the fear. The private development sector may threaten the values of many individual landowners, but it often obtains compliance through the persuasive power of money, whereas government more often must resort to administrative regulations or judgments-at-law.

Who implements a land use planning strategy depends greatly on how the decision processes of society are organized. We have argued that our comprehensiveness in the scope of land policy requires the participation of large numbers of people involved in or affected by land use decisions. How to obtain this participation in an appropriate, constructive, and responsible manner is a major aspect of the land use policy problem.

The *how* of implementation therefore includes the building of an institutionalized public coalition to accomplish the purpose of comprehensive land use planning that, within the limits of ecological fact and social value, is broadly consensual. To achieve an operative consensus that is democratically constituted and scientifically informed, it is necessary that the substance of the consensus, however minimal, be explicit and that a critical mass of civic leadership is committed to it.

The consensus would be agreement regarding preferred future states of the environment with particular reference to the effects of land use decisions. Consensus need not imply universal agreement; some measure of conflict is safely predictable. My thesis, however, is that consensus is more widely and surely achieved through the experience of persons representing the broadest range of concern with land use. Brought together on boards or commissions, these persons may find a level of consensus through coping with land use problems against a background of generally accepted preferences. To plan toward preferred outcomes implies some structuring of the decision process so that a connection is established between what is decided in particular cases and the preferred outcomes. A major purpose here is to avoid the tyranny of small decisions that, taken incrementally, foreclose future options. Gradually emerging from this collaborative decision process should appear the elements of a democratic and realistic land use plan, not asserted prematurely by statute or expert opinion, but evolved through a broadly representative and responsible effort to approximate land use wisdom.

To effectively serve its purpose, this process must be characterized by order, system, and directedness. A weakness of conventional land use controls has been their superficial neutrality and ad hoc modification. Zoning and subdivision controls, for example, have proved to be unreliable instruments of land use policy, most "effective" where they are least needed, but of dubious protection against powerful socioeconomic pressure.[34] These controls are especially vulnerable to forces for change, for they represent a barricade or status quo psychology and possess no power to alleviate or redirect the pressures that they were intended to resist.

The *how* aspect of planning land use policy has three interactive components: citizen representation; professional, scientific and technical advice; and administrative implementation.

The first and basic is the structure of representation. Local, regional, and state commissions, broadly representative of the legitimate interests in land use could provide this component. California and Vermont have provided examples of citizen commissions for the review of land use decisions in the vulnerable areas of the coastal zone and the shores of lakes and rivers.[35] These commissions function pursuant to statutory authority, but governors and local executives might appoint advisory and fact finding bodies whose actions could be influential without the force of law. A statutory basis for such bodies would be desirable, however, expressly to define their roles and representative character and to provide, as far as possible, against their misuse.

The need for informed judgment on many land use issues calls for professional, scientific, or technical opinion. Here advisory panels could be useful; some could be continuing, others ad hoc. The study group of the National Research Council on the extension of airport runways into

Jamaica Bay, New York, illustrates the role of this component in the decision not to extend, and its findings may have decisively influenced the outcome.[36]

The administrative component is divided between the secretariat function essential to effective citizen committee work and the executive responsibilities of the public officials responsible for the decisions that make or implement land use policy. These officials include not only general executives such as governors, mayors, and city/county managers, they also, and often more importantly, include the administrators of airport, highway, park, and sanitation programs, among others.

To implement a strategy, these components must constitute an effective network of communication. American civic behavior is long experienced at combining official and unofficial action to serve public needs. Let us accept as plausible that irresponsibility in land use decisions results more from an inadequate system of information and consensus-building than from inadequacies in the law. If so, then to focus corrective efforts on statutory reform to the neglect of building a structure of popular understanding and consent is to attack the policy problem from the wrong end. Statutes are often necessary but per se are insufficient to achieve the purposes of law. Our statutory codes are replete with unenforced or indifferently enforced provisions. Law most effectively administered is usually law that has substantial public support.

The *how* of formulating land use policy includes consideration of what it is about land use that requires attention.[37] Because prevention of misuse is usually more effective than its cure, policy needs to be anticipatory as well as reactive. Both citizen and official bodies need to look at the uses of land, present and prospective, in relation to (1) probabilities, (2) potentialities, and (3) values.

Probabilities

The policy formulating process should search for best estimates of the consequences of socioeconomic or ecological trends affecting land and its uses. To arrive at rational decisions regarding land use, the decision-makers, unofficial as well as official, need to know what will probably happen if they do nothing and the prevailing forces of man and nature work toward their most likely consequences. To obtain this information, the assistance of science is needed. Trends and impacts, and the results toward which they appear to lead, must be compared with those that the society generally prefers. From this survey and comparison it would be possible to identify those policies and practices, public and private, impairing the terrestrial environment. It should be possible to locate the pressure points and more pervasive forces threatening the quality of the terrestrial environment.

   This estimate of probabilities is an important instrument of consensus-building. To arrive at estimates meaningful for policy, analyses of costs and benefits of impending actions are needed. Cost-benefit analysis is a tricky tool of policy. But in principle, and when all true costs are considered and value biases made explicit, it affords a means for discovering who gains what and who loses what in specific land use decisions and policies. In particular, it may help individuals to discover their personal stake in land use decisions and what they have to gain or to lose in particular circumstances. It is plausible that if most landowners and members of the non-land owning public had more realistic understanding of the impact of land use decisions upon themselves, they would be more favorably disposed to comprehensive planning. They might seek an effective voice in public decision and be less easily coopted by the emotion-charged propaganda of liberty lobbies and predatory development interests.

   Few allies are won by recitations of abstract social or ecological costs, but individuals may be aroused by the threat of impositions upon themselves personally. It is plausible that the absence of socio-ecologically rational land use planning is contrary to the interests of most landowners and the general public. But in our society, the burden of proof that planning may be advantageous is on its advocates. Conventional wisdom points to an opposing conclusion.

Potentialities

A second aspect of plan development relates to potentialities or opportunities for optimal land use. It is a point of faith, but not of demonstrable fact, that free market decisions always result in optimal land use. Individual landowners and decision-makers characteristically act upon imperfect knowledge regarding the consequences of their actions. The probable consequences of opportunities overlooked or foreclosed may be ascertained from cost-benefit analysis. No less important is analysis of what might be done to enhance environmental quality and self-renewing productivity through rational land use initiatives.

   Conventional definitions of the scope and substance of the land market may be unduly restrictive. In some respects the land itself, beyond proprietary rights pertaining to it, is a common property resource comparable to air and water. As common property in the sense of societies[1] terrestrial life-support base, all society is involuntarily involved in the land market regardless of the distribution of legal rights over land. In various ways all members of society part with and acquire certain "goods" and "bads" in land regardless of their awareness of participation in this larger quasi-involuntary market process. Yet there are few ways in our society for most of the involuntarily involved public to obtain a voice in what they "buy" and what they "sell." Nevertheless, for many purposes a "free" market in land is an efficient way of implementing land use decisions, and, within a broader framework of comprehensive policy, it could remain the principal tool and conceptual cornerstone of land use decision-making.

Doctrinaire socialization of land ownership and land use decision-making is fraudulent in that it offers per se no unique solutions to most substantive problems of land use policy. It substitutes one form of ownership status for another but cannot guarantee that responsible concern or foresight or wisdom will thereby be enhanced. It is one thing to recognize that there are widespread but differentiated public interests inherent in land use decisions that have certain characteristics of a market and quite another to regard the land as a "commons" in which privileges and responsibilities are equally distributed. No sustainable socialist or communal scheme of land control could for long risk "the tragedy of the commons" in which each user seeks to maximize his advantage, thus destroying the commons for all.

To replace the relatively free system of land use accountability afforded by a socially perfected system of private ownership, a socialized system would need to find an alternative form of motivation. The historical substitutes for personal interest have usually been coercive. In self-styled socialist states, costs and risks of initiative traditionally borne by the owners of land have been assumed by public bureaucracies wholly paid for by the people and ostensibly accountable to them. The people, however, are no longer independent agents; they are part of a hierarchial structure of authority. So called "democratic centralism" has been the most common institutionalized system for socialist land use decision-making. The big centralized state bureaucracies act in the name of the people and fight out their differences behind the closed doors of high political councils. The experience of citizens in trying to review or to challenge the land use decisions of the big federal or enterprise agencies in the U.S. free enterprise framework offers little ground for belief that citizens individually or collectively would significantly influence land use decisions under centralized systems of socialized land ownership.

Values

A third aspect of systematic policy development linking prospects with opportunities is the consideration of values.[38] American politics and public administration have not been characterized by sophistication in value analysis. Values are customarily asserted in dogmatic and simplistic language. Unexamined assertiveness regarding land ownership and land use more often makes for antagonism than it predisposes to cooperation. Value analysis is, however, a necessary precursor to successful coalition building. Conflicts over land use often occur because alternative means are never explored for the reconciliation of apparently conflicting values. It is not always the values that conflict, more often it is the proposed means to their realization. Discovery of what values can be reconciled and what cannot would obviously serve land use planning strategies. Meritorious land use propositions have miscarried because they failed to accommodate legitimate and compatible values, thus making enemies out of persons who could have been counted as friends.

The Essence of Policy

The argument of this chapter has been that the goals of broadly beneficial land use planning are more surely achieved through a progressive and broadly participatory development of policy than through legislative or judicial assertion. The task of strategy is essentially the building of a coalition or critical mass of popular understanding and acceptance. The strategic means include the responsible involvement of all the major interests in society concerned with the consequences of land use decisions. A suitable institutional arrangement to accomplish this purpose would need to be invented, but we are not without models or precedents. Many types of federated citizen action groups, soil and water conservation districts, and neighborhood associations are examples of a multiplicity of institutional arrangements that might afford guidance to the architects of a novel but feasible structure for broadly participatory, but scientifically informed, systems for the implementary development of acceptable land use policies.

An outcome of this strategy should be a generally agreed upon hierarchy of priorities, reflective of a broad range of values and guided by considerations of (1) immediacy of threats to the terrestrial environment, (2) extent of costs of remedial measures, (3) alternative means to the realization of values sought in land, and (4) constructive opportunities for optimizing the values attainable through people-land relationships.

Procedures toward this end include consensus-building through citizen involvement and by making explicit the sociological, ecological, economic, and political consequences of specific policies and actions affecting the land. Unlike most conventional land use controls, this approach is more positive than negative. It would be characterized by citizen-based public initiatives in which landowners, both public and private, would play major roles, within a social content broader than the traditional real estate triangle.

Obviously, not all owners and users of land would benefit from this approach. It is not calculated to serve the interests of speculation or of irretrievably destructive land uses. Yet it preserves and, in principle, extends the market mechanism for land use decisions, but modified to protect this irreplaceable common property resource from exploitation either by an irresponsible socialized ownership or by shortsighted individual owners or users.

To put this strategy into effect would be a major task of political innovation. To build the minimum required base of understanding and consent would require time, reliable and adequate information, and a high order of dedicated persuasiveness. Both the extension and the restriction of freedoms over land usage might be facilitated by the prudent use of incentives and compensatory provisions. Abuses of land use policy are not fairly attributable solely to landlords and land users as some social reformers allege. So-called agrarian reform, whatever its justification, has seldom been motivated by regard for the ecological renewability of the land or for enlarging the values served through uses of the land. More often, the objective has been the destruction of a social class dependent upon control of the land. In our times, redistribution of land to the landless has been swiftly followed by collectivization, once the holders of centralized political power have eliminated independent sources of opposition. Economic power derived from landownership has traditionally been an instrument of political power. But in the independence of the landowner it has also been a brake against the abuse of political power. A broadly distributed pattern of ownership with the size of holdings appropriate to usage and terrain have characterized most societies in which personal freedoms and widespread responsible participation in public decisions have flourished.

What implications does this thesis hold for law? Most importantly it implies that the conservatism of law should reflect the need to conserve land as a basic resource for life-support and a broad range of human values. The growth of scientific knowledge pertinent to land use policy has not yet been adequately accommodated in the law. Policies to protect aquifers, ground water, soil quality, and deposits of essential materials such as sand, gravel, and building stone often run against the grain of the law. Policies to protect the public from hazardous uses of land, as, for example, on floodplains and unstable subsurface terrain, have been handicapped by legal provisions and presumptions that in effect favor the immediate economic interests of the real estate triangle over the long-range interests of the community.

To bring the law more nearly in line with current needs implies more legal research into its present state of inadequacy. Much work has of course been done on various aspects of land law, but there is still need for a systematic taxonomy of problems and related legal provisions that case books do not adequately provide. The need relates as much to what the law does not provide by way of guides for policy as to what may be done under the law as it now stands.

This discourse on law-land relationship began with the proposition that focus on specific land abuses might offer a more meaningful and acceptable approach to land use planning than general statutory authorization, which has historically attracted more opposition than support. Knowledge of specific problems and available remedies is obviously essential to this approach. More than legal research is needed, because the range of land use related problems is very broad. Many of these problems are well known to the people who have experienced them, but the remedies in law or in policy are not always obvious nor are the relative merits of alternatives generally perceived. This survey of the problems and the law of land usage should therefore be designed as much for average citizens and public officials as for lawyers. The primary purpose of this chapter has been to address the practical need for broadened participation in land use decisions; and that implies that more people not professionally trained in the law participate in its interpretation and administration. This development would not be unique to land use policy; citizen participation in public administration and planning has been growing across the spectrum of public affairs.

Complexity and specialization in modern life have increasingly separated the citizen from personal involvement with the law as an instrument of self-government. Alienation of people from their legal system can hardly be healthy for the practice of self-government or for an individual sense of civic responsibility. And although citizen participation in government is now on the increase, signs of popular alienation from government and public affairs have also been increasing, and at a time when precisely the reverse of this trend is needed. If we are to cope effectively with the environmental problems of our times, ways must be found to establish a relationship between people and the law that will be widely regarded as meaningful. Land use is an area of public affairs in which rapprochment between the citizen and the legal system is an essential condition of developing and achieving sound and acceptable policy goals. The linkage between law and land is the public, which now and in the future is unavoidably affected by whatever happens to the land.

Notes

1. A 1974 study by the Environmental Protection Agency cited land use and growth as the two most serious problems: see S. Carter, M. Frost, C. Rubin, and E.L. Sumek, *Environmental Management and Local Government*, prepared by the International Management Association for the EPA (EPA Report no. 600/5-73-016, February 1974).

2. See L. Caldwell, "Rights of Ownership or Rights of Use," *William and Mary Law Review*, 15: 759, 1974; also see F. Horack and V. Nolan, *Land Use Controls* (1955), chap. 1.

3. A. Simpson, *An Introduction to the History of the Land Law* (1961); Horack and Nolan, *Land Use Controls*, pp. 13-17.

4. Schlatter, *Private Property: The History of an Idea*, (London: George Allen & Unwin, 1951).

5. See Jacob H. Beuscher, Robert R. Wright, and Morton Gittelman, *Cases and Materials on Land Use*, 2nd edition (St. Paul, Minn.: West Publishing Co., 1976), chap. 2, "The Law of Nuisance."

6. See, for example, on wildlife destruction: Department of State, *U.S. National Report on the Human Environment* (Department of State Publication 8588, June 1971), pp. 10-12.

7. For example, *Morris County Land Improvement Co. v. Township of Parsippany—Troy Hills*, 40 N.J. 539, 193 A.2d 232 (1963); *Just v. Marinette County*, 56 Wis. 2d 7 201 N.W.2d 761 (1972). For general discussion see F. Grad, *Treatise on Environmental Law*, vol. 2 (New York: M. Bender, 1977), pp. 16-27; Fred P. Bosselman, David Callies, and John Banta, *The Taking Issue: A Study of the Constitutional Limits of Governmental Authority to Regulate the Use of Privately Owned Land Without Paying Compensation to Owners*, prepared for the Council on Environmental Quality and summarized in the Council's 4th Annual Report, 1973, pp. 121-53.

8. See Glen O. Robinson, *The Forest Service: A Study in Public Land Management*, 2d ed. (Baltimore: Johns Hopkins University Press, 1977) for a brief discussion of the history of private land holdings and problems with these holdings. Also see Public Land Law Review Commission, *One Third of the Nation's Land*, chap. 13, "Occupancy Uses" (Washington, D.C.: U.S. Government Printing Office, 1970), for recommendations on occupancy use of public land.

9. For example, in the New York Adirondacks, the Adirondack Park Agency has zoned use of private land in the park into districts based on allowable intensity of use rather than type of use, causing reactions on the part of the local owners complaining about the technical restrictions on their land by the administration of the program itself. Sylvia Lewis, "New York's Adirondacks: Tug of War in the Wilderness," *Planning* (American Society of Planning Officials, 1976), pp.

10. Donald Hagman, and Dean Misczynski (eds.), *Windfalls for Wipeouts: Land Value Capture and Compensation* (Chicago: American Society of Planning Officials, 1978).

11. For good discussion see American Society of Planning Officials (ASPO), Planning Advisory Service, "Transferable Development Rights," Report no. 303 (Chicago, 1975); also see *Transfer of Development Rights Bibliography* (Division of Information and Research, Legislative Services

Agency, Room 128, State House, Trenton, N.J., 1975); John V. Helb, B. Budd Chavooshian, and George H. Nieswand, *Development Rights Bibliography* (New Brunswick, N.J.: Rutgers University, 1976); *Penn Central Transportation Company* v. *City of New York*, 273 N.Y. Ct. Ap. (June 23, 1977).

12. See Raleigh Barlowe, *Land Resource Economics: The Economics of Real Property*, 2d ed. (Englewood Cliffs, N.J.: Prentice-Hall, 1972); Peter J. Lane, *Real Estate and the Environment* (New York: Practicing Law Institute, 1973).

13. See Mary Sullivan Mann, *The Right to Housing: Cost Issues and Remedies in Exclusionary Zonings* (New York: Praeger, 1976); Edward A. Williams, *Open Space, The Choice Before California* (Berkeley, Diablo Press, 1969) (Williams is director of Urban Metro Open Space Study); Mary Anne Guitar, *Property Power: How to Keep the Bulldozer, the Power Line and the Highwayman Away from Your Door* (New York: Doubleday, 1972); and Natural Resources Defense Council, Inc., *Land Use Controls in the U.S.: A Handbook on the Legal Rights of Citizens* (New York: Dial Press, 1977).

14. See *Pennsylvania Coal Co.* v. *Mahon*, 260 U.S. 393 (1922) esp. for rezoning density requirements; *Morse* v. *City of San Louis Obispo*, 247 Cal. Ap.2d 600, 55 Cal. Reptr. 710 (1967); *Hartnett* v. *Austin*, 93 So.2d 86 (Fla. 1956) for shopping centers; and *United* v. *Callsby*, 328 U.S. 265 (1946) for airports.

15. S. 3354 (Jackson) 91st Cong. 2d sess. (1970); S. 3354 (Jackson) 92nd Cong. 1st sess. (1971). Following introduction, Nixon announced in a February 8, 1971, message to Congress on environment that the administration would support its own National Land Use Proposal, S. 992, 92nd Cong. 1st sess. (1971). After ten days of hearing before the Senate's Interior, Banking, Housing, and Urban Affairs and Commerce Committee, S. 632 was passed on September 19, 1972, with amendments. HR7211 (companion bill) was out of the House Interior but not out of Rules. A version almost identical to S. 632 was introduced in January 1973, S. 268 (Jackson) 93rd Cong. 1st sess. 1973, and so was the administration sponsored bill. After six days of hearings, S. 268 passed the Senate. For the legal history see U.S. Senate Committee on Interior and Insular Affairs Report to accompany S. 268, Land Use Policy and Planning Assistance Act., S. Rep. no. 93-197, 93rd Congress, 1st sess. (1973); also F. Grad, *Treatise on Environmental Law*, vol. 2, p. 10-38.

16. California Public Resources Code, sec. 27000 et seq. Proposition 20 required builders of homes on private land that is within 3,000 feet of the ocean to secure a permit with the regional agency. Regional decisions can be vetoed by statewide commissions.

17. See Vermont Statutes Anno. Title 10, sec. 6021 et seq. (Also in *Environmental Reporter—State Solid Waste—Land Use*, sec. 1331,

pp. 2101-09.) Act 250 requires all developments of ten acres or more to have a state permit.

18. For a list of states see F. Grad, *Environmental Law Treatise*, sec. 10.03-.64, fn. 54 (1977). An example of a federal law is the Surface Mining Control and Reclamation Act of 1977. 30 U.S.C. S. 1201 et seq.

19. S. 268 was passed by the U.S. Senate on June 21, 1973 (vote—64-21) and was almost identical to an earlier land use bill (S. 632) passed in September 1972. The House Interior and Insular Affairs Committee reported HR 7211 on August 7, 1972, but the bill was not considered by the House. The House Interior Committee reported HR 10294 in January 1974 by a vote of 26-11, but it was killed by a 9-4 vote of the House Rules Committee on February 26, 1974. Source: Elizabeth Haskell, "Land Use and the Environment: Public Policy Issues," *Environment Reporter*, Monograph no. 20, vol. 5, 1974.

20. "Scarsdale N.Y. once required a builder to put up $80,000 in a cash bond for a minor subdivision." Quoted in: Richard F. Babcock and Fred P. Bosselman, *Exclusionary Zoning: Land Use Regulation and Housing in the 1970s.* (New York: Praeger, 1973), p. 13. Source: Raymond Urguhardt, *A Survey of Local Government Restrictions Affecting Home Building in N.Y. State* (New York: New York Homebuilders' Association, 1966), p. 20.

21. One way is for states to provide use-value assessments or other favorable tax treatment for open space land. See Council on Environmental Quality, *Fifth Annual Report* (Washington, D.C.: U.S. Government Printing Office, 1974). Land is taxed on basis of its current, open space use. For listings of states and further analysis see F. Grad, *Treatise on Environmental Law*, vol. 2, chap. 10, sec. 10.03(6)(b), "Techniques to Encourage Open Space Maintenance."

22. Federal Water Pollution Control Act Amendments of 1972, publication 92-500, title I S. 101(a), 86 Stat 816, 33 U.S.C. S. 1251(2) 1972. The objective of the legislature is "to restore and maintain the chemical, physical and biological integrity of the nation's water." S.1215(a) states that the discharge of pollutants into navigable waters is to be eliminated by 1985. S.208, 33 U.S.C. 1288(a)(1) requires the administrator, after consultation with the appropriate authorities, to publish guidelines on those areas that "as a result of urban industrial concentration or other factors have substantial water quality control problems" S.1288(a)(1). After publication, the governor identifies the areas and twelve days later designates a program [1288(a)(2)]. This amendment, providing for area wide waste treatment management plans and advocating "tough" clean waters approach has significant land use implications. For a good discussion see F. Grad, *Environmental Law Treatise*, vol. 1, Sec. 3.03(3)(6)(1975).

23. For a good general discussion see F. Grad, *Treatise on Environmental Law*, vol. 2, chap. 10: "Land Use Planning and Land Use Controls in the Context of Environmental Protection" (1977), pp. 10-12.

24. "A National Policy for Land," in *National Land Use Policy*, Hearings before the Committee on Interior and Insular Affairs, U.S. Senate, S. 3354, 91st Cong. 2d sess. (March 24 and April 28-9, 1970). Washington, D.C.: U.S. Government Printing Office, 1970.

25. Donald R. Denman and Sylvio Prodano, *Land Use* (London: Allen & Unwin, 1973), especially chap. 8.

26. See Mancur Olson, *The Logic of Collective Action, Public Goods and the Theory of Groups* (Cambridge, Mass.: Harvard University Press, 1971), pp. 27-31.

27. See Eva H. Hanks, A. Dan Tarlock, and John L. Hanks, *Environmental Law and Policy* (American Casebook Series 1976 Supp., St. Paul, Minn.: West Publishing Co.); Norman Williams, Jr., *American Land Planning Law*, vol. 2, "Zoning for Open Space" (New Brunswick, N.J.: Rutgers University, Center for Urban Policy Research, 1978), p. 1133; American Law Institute, *Environmental Law*, vol. 2, p. 447 "The Evolving State of the Judiciary in Land Use Litigation" (Washington, D.C.: American Bar Association Committee on Continuing Professional Education, February 1978).

28. Garrett Hardin, *The Limits of Altruism: An Ecologist's View of Survival* (Bloomington: Indiana University Press, 1977).

29. For example, *Village of Euclid* v. *Ambler Realty Corp.* 272 U.S. 365 (1926); *Baker* v. *City of Milwaukee*, 533 F.2d, 772 (Oregon 1975). For general information see R.M. Anderson, *American Law of Zoning*, 4 vol. (Rochester, N.Y.: Lawyers Co-operative Publishing Co., 1968).; Charles M. Haar, *Land Use Planning: A Case Book on the Use, Misuse & Reuse of Urban Land*, 3rd ed. (Boston: Little, Brown, 1976), pp. 185-223.

30. Highway planning is often cited as an example of the abuses caused by an ad hoc or "mission-oriented" approach. Routing through parks without concern for longer range needs of cities or carving up community neighborhoods indicate the need for a broader policy approach. See Madison: University of Wisconsin Press, *Building the American City: Report of the U.S. National Commission on Urban Problems*, House Doc. 91-34 (Washington, D.C.: U.S. Government Printing Office, 1968), p. 231. Also see Richard F. Babcock, *The Zoning Game* (Madison: University of Wisconsin Press, 1966), and Richard F. Babcock and Fred R. Bosselman, *Exclusionary Zoning* (1973).

31. See Bosselman, Callies, and Banta, *The Taking Issue* (1973); Haar, *Land Use Planning*, chap. 5, "The Government as Land-owner and Redistributor: City Planning as the Public Purpose," (1976).

32. See *Construction Industry Association of Sonoma City* v. *City of Petaluma*, 375 F. Supp. 574 (N.D. Cal. 1914) rev'd 522 F.2d 897 (9th Cir. 1975) Ap. Dis. 96 S. Ct. 1148 (1976); *Golden* v. *Planning Board of Town of Ramapo*, 30 N.Y.2d 359, 285 N.E.2d 291, 334 N.Y.S.2d 138, App. Dis.

408 U.S. 1003 (1972); *City of Eastlake* v. *Forest City Ent. Inc.*, 41 Ohio St.2d 187, 324 N.E.2d 740. (1975) rev'd 96 S. Ct. 2358 (1976).

33. Public Law no. 91-190, January 1, 1970, 83 Stat. 852, 42 U.S.C. 4321-4347 (1970).

34. General texts for reference: F. Grad, *Treatise on Environmental Law*, vol. 2, chap. 10 (1977); Daniel R. Mandelker, *The Zoning Dilemma* (Indianapolis: Bobbs Merrill, 1976); Norman Williams, *American Land Planning Law* (1974). See also Donald G. Hagman, *Public Planning and Control of Urban and Land Development: Cases and Materials* (St. Paul, Minn.: West Publishing Co., 1973), chap. X-12; and Bernhard H. Segan, *Land Use Without Zoning* (Lexington, Mass.: Lexington Books, 1972), p. 247.

35. See California Coastal Zone Conservation Act, Cal. Publication R Section 2700 et seq. (1976 suppl.); and Vermont, Stat. Anno, Title 10, sec. 6001 et seq. (1973, 1975 suppl.). In Vermont, the statute vests permit granting authority in a State Environmental Board assisted by eight District Commissioners, all citizen members except the chairman. Under the California statute, all meetings of the commission are open to the public. Public hearings are required in connection with issuing regulations by the commission. Any person has standing to maintain an action to restrain violations. For analysis see National Resources Defense Council, Inc., *Land Use Controls in the U.S.: A Handbook on the Legal Rights of Citizens*, chaps. 6 and 12 (1977); J. Adams, "Proposition 20: A Citizen Campaign," *Syracuse Law Review* 24:1019 (1973); for general discussion see Douglass Petrillo, "California Coast: The Struggle Today; A Plan for Tomorrow," *Florida State University Law Review*, 4:315 (1976).

36. Jamaica Bay Environmental Study Group, *Jamaica Bay and Kennedy Airport: A Multidisciplinary Environmental Study* (Washington, D.C.: National Academy of Sciences), 1971.

37. For a comprehensive review of research problems see Donald M. McAllister (ed.), *Environment: A New Focus for Land-Use Planning* (Washington, D.C.: National Science Foundation, 1973, NSF/RA/E-74-001).

38. See Richard N.L. Andrews and M.J. Waits, *Environmental Values in Public Decisions: A Research Agenda* (Ann Arbor: School of Natural Resources, University of Michigan, 1978).

15 American Land and Law

John G. Sobetzer

How can you buy or sell the sky, the warmth of the land? The idea is strange to us. If we do not own the freshness of the air and the sparkle of the water how can you buy them?

So spoke Chief Seattle in response to a government request to buy the ancestral lands of the Suquamish tribe in 1854.[1] Such questions, however, would not be asked by a modern landowner. Concerns for the air, water, or land are separated from the land by the modern economic system. As Paul Diesing notes:

> One cultural element after another has been absorbed into the everwidening economy, subjected to the test of economic rationality, rationalized, and turned into a commodity or factor of production. So pervasive has this process been that it now appears that anything can be thought of as a commodity and its value measured by a price. . . . time, land, capital, labor, . . . As these become commodities they are all subject to a process of moral neutralization.[2]

Land, as Diesing points out, is treated by our economic system as a commodity. As a commodity, each parcel of land is treated independently of its neighboring parcels through the predominance of private property rights. Its value, as measured by its price, is derived from its utility as a site for man's activities or as the location of the raw materials industry needs. Decisions concerning its use are, in large part, determined by the operation of the market system and the price it has therein.

The price of land and hence the decisions regarding its use, however, do not reflect the true value of land to our society. People value, as Chief Seattle did, fresh air and clean water. The natural functions that land performs enable us to have clean air and water and thus to have value even though they too are not reflected in the prices of the land parcels. People also value wildlife, open space, scenery, wildness, and a variety of other land elements, which again are not usually reflected in the price of land.

Natural resources, in fact, include the psychic amenity values as well as the natural functions land performs. When land is viewed from the natural resource perspective, not only is price usually misleading—because it usually reflects only the commodity status of land—but so are man-made boundaries of ownership and political jurisdiction because the impacts of

213

activities spill over onto other parcels or jurisdictions. Consequently, the use of a parcel must take into consideration impacts on other land, air, or water. It would make more sense if rights in land were *correlative*—that is, dependent upon and limited by the rights of others. Traditional nuisance and riparian law have always been correlative.

Our economic system, therefore, has overvalued land's status as a commodity and undervalued its status as a natural resource. Similarly, the legal system has overvalued those private property rights that protect and maintain the commodity status of land and undervalued the public and private rights associated with its natural resource status.

The question facing us, therefore, is whether the law can validate an expanding notion of land as a natural resource or whether, particularly through the application of the Fifth Amendment prohibition against the taking of private property without just compensation, it is likely to stand as a barrier.

The "taking" doctrine, although a constitutional prohibition, is not forever unchangeable. On the contrary, it has been able to change in many cases, to accommodate the expanding recognition of the natural resource status of land. An excellent example of this dynamic change can be seen in the regulation of wetland development.

In recent years a variety of studies have discovered that wetlands (swamps, marshes, bogs, and the like) are exceedingly valuable to water quality, maintenance of stream flows and flood control, primary productivity, fish and wildlife habitat, open space, and groundwater supply. Several sources have concluded that wetlands perform functions worth on the average 50-80,000 dollars per acre. Their destruction has deleterious impacts to surrounding areas and throughout the entire watershed. Yet in many states more than two-thirds of existing wetlands have been destroyed; much of the remainder is under heavy development pressure. Wetlands were considered to be valueless if not nuisances, and developers therefore could purchase them at a very low cost and, after filling, sell them for a substantial profit. If restricted, they generally lose speculative profits.

Recognition of the values of wetlands, and the development pressure they were under, convinced many state legislatures to enact wetlands protection statutes. Some of the earliest wetlands statutes, such as Maine's, were struck down as taking without just compensation. The Maine Supreme Court recognized the value of wetlands, but felt that there could be no other result under the "diminution in value" test.[3] This test requires that landowners be compensated whenever they have been deprived of a significant amount of the economic value of their land (that is, of its value as a commodity).[4]

This test evolved at a time when the natural resource status of land received little recognition while the commodity status was predominant.

Police power regulation such as zoning was primarily designed to protect the commodity status of land. Michigan's enabling statute, for example, mentions property values explicitly as a basis for zoning, and the other bases reflect on property values as well. It is not surprising, therefore, that this test would focus on the diminution in economic value to the landowner. It seemed only fair that one landowner should not be forced to suffer undue economic loss in order to benefit others economically. In that case, compensation from the larger beneficiaries will adequately compensate the landowner and prevent the others from receiving benefits at his or her expense.[5]

As the knowledge of the detrimental impacts on others from the inappropriate development of wetlands spread, other states enacted wetlands protection laws; and their courts began to look beyond the commodity status of land and upheld the statutes on a variety of theories. One approach was to inject a public interest factor into the diminution in value test, thereby establishing a balancing test between economic concerns (commodity status) and harm to the public interest (natural resource status). In the case of wetlands, therefore, the demonstrated damage to the natural resource functions of land from development permitted the court to uphold restrictions that destroyed the commodity functions.[6]

Recently, two state supreme courts explicitly recognized the natural resource status of wetlands. After finding that wetlands in their natural state perform functions important to the public, the Wisconsin court stated:

> An owner of land has no absolute and unlimited right to change the essential natural character of his land so as to use it for a purpose for which it was unsuited in its natural state and which injures the rights of others.[7]

These cases suggest that, whenever it can be shown that a land resource in its natural state performs valuable natural resource functions, regulations drafted to protect these functions should be upheld even though economic value is destroyed. The requirement that all land retain its natural function of water retention and groundwater recharge, for instance, should be upheld under this approach because of the deleterious impacts to lakes and streams from runoff.

Another exception to the diminution in value test, the noxious use test, has been widely used to sustain public health and safety and pollution regulations. The theory is simply that no one has a right to continue nuisance uses that are harmful to the public.[8] The problem is that, although defining a case as one for the noxious use tests determines the result, the issue of definition is unresolved. In effect, by relying on such traditional public interests as health, safety, and pollution, the cases really amount to a balancing of the public interest with the private commodity interest. A somewhat similar result was accomplished in other wetland cases by injecting a public interest into the diminution in value test.[9]

Hence the problem is no longer that the natural resource status of land is not being recognized, but defining the limits to it when it conflicts with the commodity status. It might be that a limit could be based upon the changing values of society in land. It would be dynamic and could accommodate both the commodity and natural resource status values in land without unreasonably interfering with exceptions. An approach that reflects a basis in changing public values has been set forth by Philip Soper, who would employ an objective standard to limit "the scope of property rights in accordance with implicit—if not yet legally embraced—expectations of society."[10] Such an approach would justify the recent decision in Massachusetts upholding billboard regulation on aesthetic reasons alone, where previously there had to be an economic reason. The court recognized that land had a status beyond that of a commodity in the community and that the public welfare should be expanded to reflect changes in community values.

Probably the most explicit recognition that all land has a status as a natural resource in addition to its commodity status is the Michigan Environmental Protection Act (MEPA).[11] Under the provisions of this act, no person may pollute, impair, or destroy the natural resources unless they can show that there are no feasible and prudent alternatives *and* that such conduct is consistent with the promotion of the public health, safety, and welfare in light of the state's paramount concern for the protection of its natural resources. This mandate applies to everyone, whether acting on private or public land. Decisions concerning the use of a parcel of land must no longer be based on price alone, but must consider the impacts on the natural functions that affect other land parcels and the public interest. By incorporating the public health, safety, and welfare requirement, MEPA has made provision for changing public values. By relying on the courts to fashion an evolving standard of environmental law to give it substance in a manner similar to the common law, MEPA has made it possible for the change in environmental values in land to be recognized. MEPA has been viewed as placing a public trust in private land; and this trust's content can expand with changing values just as the traditional public trust doctrine has been expanded to reflect new environmental values. This is not to say that from time to time and area to area there will not be problems. Lower state courts in particular may lag behind. As a matter of constitutional law, however, carefully drafted regulations designed to protect an important natural function should not be struck down.

It would appear from these examples, therefore, that the law should not be viewed as an impenetrable barrier to changing the way land is managed in the United States. In part this is because it should not hinder properly drafted regulations that reflect changing public values. In part it is also because the most serious barrier to sound land use is our own subsidization of improper development. Attempts to change the law regarding funding and considerations that go into the building of highways, storm water systems, sanitary sewers, and the like, for instance, do not have to worry about private property rights and the taking issue: they need only be changed by the legislature.

The problem, therefore, goes back to the values our society places on the land. The key to any efforts to improve our management of the land is the development of a land ethic. As Aldo Leopold stated,

> No such ethical and aesthetic premise yet exists for the condition of the land these children must live on. Our children are our signature to the roster of history; our land is merely the place our money was made. There is as yet no social stigma in the possession of a gullied farm, a wrecked forest, or a polluted stream, provided the dividends suffice to send the youngsters to college. Whatever ails the land, the government will fix it.[12]

Or to quote Chief Seattle again:

> You must teach your children that the ground beneath their feet is the ashes of our grandfathers. So that they will respect the land, tell your children that the earth is rich with the lives of our kin. Teach your children what we have taught our children, that the earth is our mother. Whatever befalls the earth, befalls the sons of the earth. If men spit upon the ground they spit upon themselves.

If we change the values and the economic system, the law will reflect this. The barriers are in public attitudes, not in the law by itself.

Notes

1. Taken from an adaptation of a speech given by Chief Seattle. In another part of this prophetic speech he described the white man's approach to land that is still very evident today:

> We know that the white man does not understand our ways. One portion of the land is the same to him as the next, for he is a stranger who comes in the night and takes from the land whatever he needs. The earth is not his brother, but his enemy, and when he has conquered it, he moves on. He leaves his father's graves behind, and he does not care. He kidnaps the earth from his children. He does not care. His father's graves and his children's birthright are forgotten. He treats his mother, the earth, and his brother, the sky, as things to be bought, plundered, sold like sheep or bright beads. His appetite will devour the earth and leave behind only desert.

See Lewis P. Jones (ed.), *Aboriginal American Oratory* (Los Angeles: Southwest Museum, 1965), pp. 98-101.

2. Paul Diesing, *Reason in Society* (Urbana: University of Illinois Press, 1962), chapter 1, note 15.

3. *Maine* v. *Johnson*, 265 A.2d 711 (1970). But see *In Re Spring Valley Development*, 300 A.2d 736 (1973). The court found that in the absence of fill the parcel has no commercial value. Also see two other cases, *Morris County Land Improvement Co.* v. *Parsipanny Troy Hills*, 193 A.2d 232 (1963) and *Bartlett* v. *Zoning Commission*, 282 A.2d 907 (1971).

4. The test was first stated in *Pennsylvania Coal Co.* v. *Mahon*, 260 U.S. 393 (1922).

5. The theory has many other problems. See Philip Soper, "The Constitutional Framework," in *Federal Environmental Law*, ed. E. Dolgin and T. Guilbert (St. Paul, Minn.: West Publishing Co., 1974), pp.

6. *Turnpike Realty Company* v. *Town of Dedham*, 284 N.E.2d 891 (1972) cert. den. 409 U.S. 1108 (1973). *Candlestick Properties, Inc.* v. *San Francisco Bay C.&D. Commission*, 11 Cal. App. 3d 557 (1970). The *Candlestick* case could also be read as stating that the reasonable remaining uses must be measured in terms of natural resource functions as well as economic.

7. *Just* v. *Marinette*, 201 N.W.2d 761 (1972), Wisconsin, and *Sibson* v. *State*, 336 A.2d 239 (1975), New Hampshire. The court distinguished this case from traditional cases by the interrelationship of wetlands to water quality, navigation, fishing, scenic beauty, and other qualities that make up its natural resource status.

8. *Mugler* v. *Kansas*, 123 U.S. 623 (1887); *Hadachek* v. *Sebastion*, 239 U.S. 394 (1915); *Goldblatt* v. *Town of Hempstead*, 369 U.S. 590 (1962). The latter case might even be considered a repudiation of *Pennsylvania Coal*.

9. See note 7. The important natural functions test of *Just* by definition involves public interests that outweigh private. If expanded outside the impacts on air and water to such things as aesthetics, then it must be because it is felt that the overriding public interest has been expanded to include the new purpose.

10. Soper, "The Constitutional Framework," in *Federal Environmental Law*, p. 66. The level at which one approaches expectations could lead to varying results. In the case of wetlands, it could be said that for much of society wetlands were not considered to be of much value. Taking a larger perspective, however, such services as clean water, flood control, and wildlife protection are of considerable value.

11. MCLA 691.1201 et seq. See also art. 4, sec. 52, of the 1963 Michigan Constitution.

12. Aldo Leopold, *A Sand County Almanac* (New York: Ballantine Books, 1970), pp. 201-02.

Select Bibliography
Land: Commodity or Natural Resource?

Peggy Ann Kusnerz

1. Land Use

Anderson, R.M. "Land Use Control." *Syracuse Law Review* 27 (1):167-79, 1976.

Avery, L.J. "Social Control of Land." *Real Property Probate and Trust Journal* 10 (4):602-05, 1975.

Bell, D.E., et al. *Earth Resources Management for Regional Development.* Columbus: Ohio Department of Natural Resources; Washington, D.C.: Appalachian Regional Commission; Columbus: Battelle Columbus Laboratories, September 1974.

Bermingh, J.R. "1974 Land Use Legislation in Colorado." *Denver Law Journal* 51 (4):467-507, 1974.

Bourne, L.S. "Urban Structure and Land Use Decisions." *Annals of the Association of American Geographers* 66 (4):531-47, 1976.

Branfman, E.J., et al. "Measuring Invisible Wall: Land Use Controls and Residential Patterns of Poor." *Yale Law Journal* 82 (3):483-508, 1973.

Browning, Frank. *The Vanishing Land.* New York: Harper & Row, 1975.

Burchell, Robert W. *Future Land Use: Energy, Environmental, and Legal Constraints.* New Brunswick, N.J.: Transaction Books, 1975.

Caldwell, Lynton K. *Man and His Environment: Policy and Administration.* New York: Harper & Row, 1975.

Carter, Luther J. *The Florida Experience: Land and Water Policy in a Growth State.* Baltimore: Johns Hopkins University Press, 1976.

Chisholm, Michael. *Rural Settlement and Land Use: An Essay in Location.* Atlantic Highlands, N.J.: Humanities Press, 1966.

Clark, Colin. *Population Growth and Land Use.* New York: St. Martin's Press, 1977.

Clawson, Marion. "Future of Nonmetropolitan America." *American Scholar* 42 (1): 102-09, 1973.

Clawson, Marion. *Suburban Land Conversion in the United States: An Economic and Governmental Process.* Baltimore: Johns Hopkins University Press, 1977.

Clawson, Marion, et al. *Land for the Future.* Resources for the Future Series. Baltimore: Johns Hopkins University Press, 1960.

Costonis, John J. "Fair Compensation and Accommodation Power: Antidotes for Taking Impasse in Land Use Controversies." *Columbia Law Review* 75 (6):1021-82, 1975.

Curtis, D.C., and McCuen, R.H. "Economic Analysis of Residential Land Use Alternatives." *Journal of the Urban Planning and Development Division-ASCE* 101 (2):109-16, 1975.

Davis, Kenneth P. *Land Use.* New York: McGraw-Hill, 1976.

Delafons, John. *Land Use Controls in the United States.* Cambridge, Mass.: M.I.T. Press, 1969.

Dolce, Philip C., ed. *Suburbia: The American Dream and Dilemma.* New York: Anchor/Doubleday, 1976.

"Fair Housing and Exclusionary Land Use." *Urban Land Institute Research Reports* (1974), M23, PR 3.

Fellmeth, Robert C. *Politics of Land: The Report on Land Use in California.* New York: Grossman, 1973.

Finkler, Earl, and Toner, William J. *Urban Non-growth: City Planning for People.* New York: Praeger, 1976.

Gottdiener, Mark. *Planned Sprawl: Private and Public Interests in Suburbia.* Beverly Hills, Calif.: Sage, 1977.

Green, F.H.W. "Recent Changes in Land Use and Treatment." *Geographical Journal* 142 (March):12-26, 1976.

Greenbie, B.B. *Design for Diversity.* New York: Elsevier-North Holland, 1976.

Halberstadt, Hans. *Urban Alternatives.* 16mm color film, 18 min. Pasadena, Calif.: Arthur Barr Productions, 1977.

Healy, Robert G. *Land Use and the States.* Baltimore: Johns Hopkins University Press, 1976.

Holland, Stuart. *The Regional Problem.* New York: St. Martin's Press, 1977.

Holmes, J.H., ed. *Man and the Environment: Regional Perspectives.* New York: Longman, 1976.

Huemoeller, William A., et al. *Land Use: Ongoing Developments in the North Central Region.* Ames: Iowa State University, 1976.

Hushak, L.J. "Urban Demand for Urban-Rural Fringe Land." *Land Economics* 51 (2):112-23, 1975.

Kamm, Sylvan. *Land Banking: Public Policy Alternatives and Dilemmas.* Washington, D.C.: Urban Institute, 1970.

Kaplan, Samuel. *The Dream Deferred: People, Politics, and Planning in Suburbia.* New York: Seabury Press, 1976.

Kengchon, Charn. *Land Use and Related Topics: A Select Bibliography.* Cambridge, Mass. Institute of Land Policy, 1974.

Kraus, M. "Land Use in a Circular City: Some Numerical Results." *Regional Science and Urban Economics* 6 (4):399-418, 1976.

Little, C. *Challenge of the Land.* Elmsford, N.Y.: Pergamon Press, 1969.

McClellan, Grant S., ed. *Land Use in the U.S.* Bronx, N.Y.: Wilson, 1971.

Mattingle, P.F. "Intensity of Agricultural Land Use Near Cities—Case Study." *Professional Geographer* 24 (1):7-10, 1972.

Mields, H. "Federally Assisted New Communities: New Dimensions in Urban Development." *Urban Land Institute Landmark Report* (1973): 1-278, 1973.

Neering, M., et al. "Stanford Land Use Study." *Socio-Economic Planning Sciences* 6 (4):409-19, 1972.

Robinson, Shepard D. *Land Use Guide for Builders, Developers, and Planners*. Farmington, Mich.: Structures, 1977.

Schweitzer, D.L., et al. "Ensuring Viable Public Land Use Decisions: Some Problems and Suggestions." *Journal of Forestry* 73 (11):705, 1975.

Shomon, Joseph J. *Open Land for Urban America: Acquisition, Safekeeping, and Use*. Baltimore: Johns Hopkins University Press, 1971.

Smith, Edward E., and Riggs, Durward S., eds. *Land Use, Open Space, and the Government Process: The San Francisco Bay Area Experience*. New York: Praeger, 1974.

Strong, Ann L. *Private Property and the Public Interest: The Brandywine Experience*. Baltimore: Johns Hopkins University Press, 1975.

Susskind, Lawrence. *The Land Use Controversy in Massachusetts: Case Studies and Policy Options*. Cambridge, Mass.: M.I.T. Press, 1976.

Vink, A.P. *Land Use in Advancing Agriculture*. New York: Springer-Verlag, 1975.

Watson, J.W., and O'Riordan, T. *American Environment: Perceptions and Policies*. New York: Wiley, 1976.

Whyte, William H. *Securing Open Space for Urban America: Conservation Easements*. Washington, D.C.: Urban Land Institute, 1959.

Whyte, William H. *The Last Landscape*. New York: Doubleday, 1968.

Zube, Ervin H., and Zube, Margaret J., eds. *Changing Rural Landscapes*. Amherst: University of Massachusetts Press, 1977.

2. Land Use: Policy and Planning

Andrews, Richard B., ed. *Urban Land Use Policy*. New York: Free Press, 1972.

Baldwin, M. "Land Use and Land Use Policy: Environmentalists Critique." *Natural Resources* 5 (2):301-07, 1972.

Bartholomew, Harland, and Wood, Jack. *Land Uses in American Cities*. Cambridge, Mass.: Harvard University Press, 1955.

Berger, C.J. "Accommodation Power in Land Use Controversies—Reply." *Columbia Law Review* 76 (5):799-823, 1976.

Birkelback, Aubrey W. *A Sample of New England Land Use*. Cambridge, Mass.: Lincoln Institute Land Policy, 1975.

Bosselman, Fred P. et al. *Land Use Planning: A Guide*. Berkeley, Cal.: University Extension Publications, 1976.

Branch, Melville C. *Urban Air Traffic and City Planning: Case Study of Los Angeles County*. New York: Irvington, 1973.

Capozza, D.R. "Efficiency of Speculation in Urban Land." *Environment and Planning* 8 (4):411-22, 1976.

Colvin, Brenda. *Land and Landscape: Evolution, Design, and Control.* Levittown, N.Y.: Transatlantic Arts, 1971.

Costonis, John J., et al. *Compensation in Land Use Control: A Recommended Accommodation, a Critique, and an Interpretation.* Berkeley: University of California Institute of Governmental Studies, 1977.

Darin-Drabkin, H. *Land Policy and Urban Growth.* Elmsford, N.Y.: Pergamon Press, 1976.

Davis, R.M., et al. "Approach to Trading off Economic and Environmental Values in Industrial Land Use Planning." *Geographical Analysis* 7 (4):397-410, 1975.

Devoy, R.S. "Evaluating Economic and Energy Consequences of Land Use Decisions." *Journal of the Urban Planning and Development Division-ASCE* 102 (1):105-10, 1976.

Dreyfus, D.A. "National Land Use Policy: Is It Needed?" *Journal of the Urban Planning and Development Division-ASCE* 102 (1):9-13, 1976.

Dunning, Glenna. *Periodical/Serial Indexes: Keys to Information on Land Planning.* Monticello, Ill.: Council of Planning Librarians, 1976. (Exchange bibliography no. 1165.)

Eklund, Kent E. "A Social Access Explanation for Community Land Use Evaluations." *Land Economics* 53:78-96, February 1977.

Freund, Eric C. "Land Use Policy for the U.S.: A Major Political Enigma." *Illinois Business Review* 33:6-8, December 1976.

Groves, D.L., and McCart, G.D. "Land Use Planning and Community." *Long Range Planning* 9 (2):83-87, 1976.

Gustafson, G.C., and Wallace, L.T. "Differential-Assessment as Land Use Policy—California Case." *Journal of the American Institute of Planners* 41 (6):379-89, 1975.

Haar, Charles M. *Land Use Planning: A Casebook on the Use, Misuse, and Re-Use of Urban Land.* Boston: Little, Brown, 1976.

Harriss, C. Lowell, ed. *The Good Earth of America: Planning Our Land Use.* Englewood Cliffs, N.J.: Prentice-Hall, 1974.

Haskell, F.K. "National Land Use Policy." *Natural Resources Lawyer* 7 (2):257-62, 1974.

Hess, David, ed. *Bibliography of State Land Resources Planning, 1960-1974: Indexed by Year, Topic, State, and Agency.* Monticello, Ill.: Council of Planning Librarians, 1977.

Hess, David, ed. *Bibliography of State Land Resources Planning, 1970-1975: Indexed by Topic, Year, State, Agency.* Monticello, Ill.: Council of Planning Librarians, 1975.

Hulchanski, John D. *Citizen Participation in Urban and Regional Planning: A Comprehensive Bibliography.* Monticello, Ill.: Council of Planning Librarians, 1977.

An Introduction to the Los Angeles Land Use Planning and Management Subsystem. Los Angeles Department of City Planning, 1975.

Jorvig, R. "Land Use Policy: Toward a New Land Ethic—Remarks." *Natural Resources Lawyer* 7 (2):285-90, 1974.

Kieffer, F.V. *An Annotated Bibliography of Geology and Land Use Planning.* Monticello, Ill.: Council of Planning Librarians, 1977.

Land: State Alternatives for Planning and Management. A Task Force Report. Council of State Governments, Lexington, Ky., 1975.

Land Use Planning. Washington, D.C.: National Academy of Sciences, National Research Council, 1975.

Landman, G.B., et al. "Flood Control in Oklahoma: Example of Land Use Preceding Land Use Planning." *Oklahoma Law Review* 29 (1):16-64, 1976.

Lassey, William R. *Planning in Rural Environment.* New York: McGraw-Hill, 1977.

Lewis, P.H. "Land Use and Land Use Policy: Statewide Inventory. Wisconsin Story." *Natural Resources* 5 (2):282-96, 1972.

Libby, L.W. "Land Use Policy: Implications for Commercial Agriculture." *American Journal of Agricultural Economics* 56 (5): 1143-52, 1974.

Listokin, David. *Land Use Controls: Present Problems and Future Reform.* New Brunswick, N.J.: Transaction Books, 1974.

Lockwood, S.C. "Issue Based Land Use Planning Process." *Journal of the Urban Planning and Development Division-ASCE* 102 (1):41-47, 1976.

Lovejoy, Derek, ed. *Land Use and Landscape Planning.* New York: Barnes & Noble Books, 1973.

Lustig, M. "Social Evaluation of Land Use Controls." *Journal of the Urban Planning and Development Division-ASCE* 102 (1):111-15, 1976.

McDowell, B.D. "Intergovernmental Guidance of Land Use and Growth." *Journal of the Urban Planning and Development Division-ASCE* 102 (1):15-23, 1976.

McGee, G.W. "Land Use and Land Use Policy Challenge from Capitol." *Natural Resources* 5 (2):321-29, 1972.

Mandelker, Daniel R. "Role of Local Comprehensive Plan in Land Use Regulation." *Michigan Law Review* 74 (5):899-973, 1976.

Mark, S.M. "Development of a Comprehensive State Land Use Plan." *Urban Lawyer* 7 (2):310-18, 1975.

Morison, F.H. "Land Use and Land Use Policy: Critique from Colorado Viewpoint." *Natural Resources* 5 (2):296-301, 1972.

Muth, Richard F. *Cities and Housing: The Spatial Pattern of Urban Residential Land Use.* Chicago: University of Chicago Press, 1969.

Neuburger, H., and Wilcox, J. "Economic Appraisal of Land Use Plans." *Journal of Transport Economics and Policy* 10 (3):227-36, 1976.

Notess, C.B. "Summary of Land Use Policy Papers." *Journal of the Urban Planning and Development Division-ASCE* 102 (1):147-55, 1976.

Rose, Jerome G., ed. *Foundations of Land Use Planning*. New Brunswick, N.J.: Center for Urban Policy Research, 1975.

Scott, R. "Land Use and Growth Management: Comment for Professionals." *Problems, Trends*. 3 vols. Washington, D.C.: Urban Land Institute, 1975.

Shaffer, R.E. "Citizen Involvement in Land Use Planning: Tool and an Example." *Journal of Soil and Water Conservation* 30 (5):211-14, 1975.

Stahl, D. "Changes in Private Sector." *Journal of the Urban Planning and Development Division-ASCE* 102 (1):25-27, 1976.

Stegman, M.A. "National Housing and Land Use Policy Conflicts." *Journal of Urban Law* 49 (4):629-66, 1972.

Thomas, R.D. "Directing Development: Florida's Experiment in Land Use Management." *Growth and Change* 6 (2):29-35, 1975.

Trevaski, J.P. "National Land Use Policy." *Real Property, Probate and Trust Journal* 9 (4):639-41, 1974.

Veri, Albert R., et al. *The Resource Buffer Plan: A Conceptual Land Use Study*. Washington, D.C.: Conservation Foundation, 1973.

Witherspoon, Robert E., et al. *Mixed Use Development: New Ways of Land Use*. Washington, D.C.: Urban Land Institute, 1976.

Young, J.W., et al. *Land Use, Energy Flow, and Policy Making in Society*. Davis, Cal.: Institute of Ecology, University of California, 1975.

3. Models and Methods of Land Use Planning

Alexande, I.C. "Multivariate Techniques in Land Use Studies: Case of Information Analysis." *Regional Studies* 6 (1):93-103, 1972.

Bammi, D. "Land Use Planning: Optimizing Model." *Omega-International Journal of Management Science* 3 (5):583-94, 1975.

Barber, G.M. "Land Use Plan Design Via Interactive Multiple Objective Programming." *Environment and Planning* 8 (6):625-36, 1976.

Bathke, W.L., and Haney, W.A., eds. *Land Management in the 70's: Concepts and Models*. San Francisco: San Francisco Press, 1972.

Batty, M. "Recent Developments in Land Use Modelling: Review of British Research." *Urban Studies* 9 (2):151-77, 1972.

Beckmann, M.J. "Thunen V Revisited: Neoclassical Land Use Model." *Swedish Journal of Economics* 74 (1):1-6, 1972.

Berechman, J. "Toward a Land Use Planning Model for New Towns." *International Journal of Systems Science* 7 (2):225-39, 1976.

Brown, H. James, et al. "Empirical Models of Urban Land Use." *Journal of the American Institute of Planners* 40 (3):212-15, 1974.

Davies, R.L. "Structural Models of Retail Distribution: Analogies with Settlement and Urban Land Use Theories." *Transactions of the Institute of British Geographers* 1972 (57):59-82, 1972.

Dickey, J.W. *Urban Land Use Models*. Monticello, Ill.: Council of Planning Librarians, 1976. (Exchange bibliography no. 959.)

Dickey, J.W., and Azola, M.P. "Adaptive Programming Technique for Sequencing Highway Improvements to Affect Land Use Growth." *Regional Studies* 6 (3):331-42, 1972.

Douglas, J.J. "Use of a Modified Input-Output Multiplier for Land Use Evaluation." *Australian Journal of Agricultural Economics* 17 (1):68-72, 1973.

Ervin, O.L. *Application of the Delphi Method to Regional Land Use Forecasting*. Tenn.: Oak Ridge National Laboratory, Energy Research and Development Administration, 1976.

Found, William C. *A Theoretical Approach to Rural Land Use Patterns*. New York: St. Martin's Press, 1971.

Gautam, N.C. "Aerial Photo-Interpretation Techniques for Classifying Urban Land Use." *Photogrammetric Engineering and Remote Sensing* 42 (6):815-22, 1976.

Gibson, J.A., and Timmons, J.F. "Information Needs and Models for Land Use Planning." *American Journal of Agricultural Economics* 58 (5):902-13, 1976.

Hecock, Richard D., and Rooney, John F. *Land Use Changes and Reservoir Development: An Application of Land Use Information Systems*. Stillwater, Okla.: Oklahoma State University, Department of Geography, 1976.

Huang, W., and Hogg, H.C. "Estimating Land Use Patterns: Separable Programming Approach." *Agricultural Economics Research* 28 (1):22-33, 1976.

Hundemann, Audrey S. *Remote Sensing for Natural Resource, Environmental and Regional Planning*. Springfield, Va.: National Technical Information Service, 1976.

Jameson, David L. *Ecosystem Impacts of Urbanization Assessment Methodology*. Houston, Texas: University of Houston, 1976.

Kinnison, W.A. "Model for Urban Innovation: Land-Grant System." *Educational Record* 53 (1):45-50, 1972.

Lesslie, P.A. *User's Guide to a Subregional Land Use Allocation Model*. Oak Ridge, Tenn.: Oak Ridge National Laboratory, Energy Research and Development Administration, 1976.

Mausel, P.W., and Johannse, C.J. "Application of Remotely Sensed Data to Agricultural Land Use Distribution Analysis." *Professional Geographer* 25 (3):242-48, 1973.

Meier, P.M. "Land Use Model for Service Area Projection." *Journal of the Environmental Engineering Division-ASCE* 102 (1):71-85, 1976.

Merewitz, L. "Models for Urban Land Use, Housing and Transportation, Public Transportation: Wish Fulfillment and Reality in San Francisco Bay Area." *American Economic Review* 62 (2):78-86, 1972.

Miller, J.R., et al. "Eco-Acres: Land Use Simulation Game." *Journal of Geography* 74 (3):134-43, 1975.

Muth, R.F. "Numerical Solution of Urban Residential Land Use Models." *Journal of Urban Economics* 2 (4):307-32, 1975.

Nichol, J.E. "Photomorphic Mapping for Land Use Planning." *Photogrammetric Engineering and Remote Sensing* 41 (10):1253-57, 1975.

Pearl, L. "Land Use Design Model." *Urban Studies* 11 (3):315-21, 1974.

Perlman, E., and Raney, R.K. *An Experiment in the Application of Remote Sensing to Land Use Planning on the Urban Fringe.* Ann Arbor: Environmental Research Institute of Michigan, 1975.

Schaenman, Philip S., and Muller, Thomas. *Measuring Impacts of Land Development. An Initial Approach.* Washington, D.C.: Urban Institute, 1974.

Wickersham, Kirk, et al. *A Land Use Decision Methodology for Environmental Control.* Denver: Rocky Mountain Center on Environment, 1975.

4. The Environment and Land Use

Alford, Michael, and Hudson, James F. *Local Controls for Environmental Management: Improving Environmental Quality Through Land Use Ordinances.* Boulder, Colo.: Westview Press, 1977.

Amir, S. "Land Resources Assessment Framework: Tool for Environmental Policy Making." *Journal of Environmental Management* 4 (1):1-13, 1976.

Batcheld, R.W. "Land Use Transportation Controls for Air Quality." *Urban Lawyer* 6 (2):235-87, 1974.

Berindan, Cornelia. *Interrelationships Between Air Pollution and Green Spaces as Criteria for Protecting Industrial Cities.* Research Triangle Park, N.C.: U.S. Environmental Protection Agency, Transportation Services Section, 1969.

Berry, Brian J., et al. *Land Use, Urban Form, and Environmental Quality.* Chicago: Ill.: University of Chicago, Department of Geography, Research Papers, 1974.

Blitch, S.G. "Airport Noise and Intergovernmental Conflict. Case Study in Land Use Parochialism." *Ecology Law Quarterly* 5 (4):669-705, 1976.

Chatterji, M., and Rompuy, P. Van, eds. *Energy, Regional Science, and Public Policy.* New York: Springer-Verlag, 1976.

Dare, C.E. "Transportation, Land Use, and Air Quality Programs." *Transportation Engineering Journal* 102 (2):411-25, 1976.

Everett, M.D. "Roadside Air Pollution Hazards in Recreational Land Use Planning." *Journal of the American Institute of Planners* 40 (2):83-89, 1974.

Freeman, A.M. "Estimating Air Pollution Control Benefits from Land Value Studies." *Journal of Environmental Economics and Management* 1 (1):74-83, 1974.

Futrell, J.W. "Environment, Natural Resources and Land Use." *Mercer Law Review* 28 (1):109-22, 1976.

Geertsen, H.R., and Bylund, H.B. "Land Use and Related Environmental Issues in Utah." *Cornell Journal of Social Relations* 10 (1):97-109, 1975.

George, M. "Land Use and Nature Conservation in Broadland." *Geography* 61 (272):137-42, 1976.

Hagevik, George, et al. *The Contribution of Urban Planning to Air Quality.* New Brunswick, N.J.: Center for Urban Policy Research, Rutgers, The State University, 1974.

Haynes, K.E., et al. "Market Consumer Model of Residential Property Values. Airport Noise Land Use Impact Problem." *Environment and Planning* 8 (3):271-87, 1976.

Heckscher, August. *Open Spaces: Tradition and Change in American Cities.* New York: Harper & Row, 1977.

Hendrix, W.G., and Fabos, J.G. "Visual Land Use Compatibility as a Significant Contributor to Visual Resource Quality." *International Journal of Environmental Studies* 8 (1):21-28,1975.

Hussey, Elaine T., et al. *Proceedings of the Conference on Air Quality Impact Analysis for Application in Land Use and Transportation Planning Held in Berkeley California on June 24-26, 1974.* Berkeley, Cal.: University of California, Berkeley. Continuing Education in City, Regional, and Environmental Planning, 1975.

Kaiser, E.J., and Reichert, P.A. "Land Use Guidance System Planning for Environmental Quality." *Natural Resources Journal* 15 (3):529-65, 1975.

Kanemoto, Y. "Optimum, Market and 2nd-Best Land Use Patterns in a Vonthunen City with Congestion." *Regional Science and Urban Economics* 6 (1):23-32, 1976.

Keyes, D.L. *Land Development and the Natural Environment: Estimating Impacts.* Washington, D.C.: Urban Institute, 1976.

Keyes, D.L. "Energy and Land Use: Instrument of United States Conservation Policy." *Energy Policy* 4 (3):225-36, 1976.

Kuklinski, A., ed. *Regional Sociology, Environment, and Regional Planning*. Atlantic Highlands, N.J.: Humanities Press, 1977.

Laroe, Edward T. *Ecological Aspects of Land Use Planning*. Washington, D.C.: Conservation Foundation, 1974.

Leahy, C.F. "Environmental Issues in Local Land Use Regulation." *Real Property Probate and Trust Journal* 11 (3):457-70, 1976.

LeMay, Joseph, and Harrison, Eugene, eds. *Environmental Land Use Problems: A Study in Northern New Jersey*. New York: Marcel Dekker, 1974.

McAllister, Donald M. *Environment: A New Focus for Land Use Planning*. Los Angeles, Cal.: University of California, Los Angeles, School of Architecture and Urban Planning, 1973.

Mandelker, Daniel R. *New Developments in Land Use and Environmental Controls*. Indianapolis: Bobbs-Merrill, 1974.

Myrup, L.O., and Rogers, D.L. "Relationship Between Land-Use and Emission of Automotive Air-Pollution." *International Journal of Environmental Studies* 8 (4):269-75, 1976.

Northrop, Gaylord M. *Study of the Impact of Economic Development and Land Utilization Policies on the Quality of the Environment with Initial Application to New England. Phase 2: Application of a Model to Determine the Economic and Environmental Impacts of Industrialization at Westover Air Force Base*. Hartford, Conn.: Center for the Environment and Man, Inc., 1975.

Oron, Y., and Pines, D. "Effect of Efficient Pricing of Air-Pollution on Intraurban Land Use Patterns." *Environment and Planning* 7 (3):293-99, 1975.

Oron, Y., et al. "Optimum vs. Equilibrium Land Use Pattern and Congestion Toll." *Bell Journal of Economics and Management Science* 4 (2):619-36, 1973.

Oron, Y., et al. "Effect of Nuisances Associated with Urban Traffic on Suburbanization and Land Values." *Journal of Urban Economics* 1 (4):382-94, 1974.

Osborn, Frederick J. *Green-Belt Cities*. New York: Schocken Books, 1971.

Planning Considerations for Statewide Inventories of Critical Environmental Areas: A Reference Guide. Washington, D.C.: Smithsonian Institution, Center for Natural Areas, 1974.

Plater, Z.J.B. "Coal Law from Old World: Perspective on Land Use and Environmental Regulation in Coal Industries of United States, Great Britain, and West Germany." *Kentucky Law Journal* 64 (3):473-506, 1976.

Platt, Rutherford H. *The Open Space Decision Process: Spatial Allocation of Costs and Benefits.* Chicago: University of Chicago, Department of Geography, Research Papers, 1972.

Schwartz, S.I., et al. "Landowner Benefits from Use-Value Assessment Under California Land Conservation Act." *American Journal of Agricultural Economics* 58 (2):170-78, 1976.

Schwind, P.J. "Environmental Impacts of Land Use Change." *Journal of Environmental Systems* 6 (2):125-45, 1976.

Shapiro, M.E. "Energy Development on Public Domain: Federal-State Cooperation and Conflict Regarding Environmental Land Use Control." *Natural Resources Lawyer* 9 (3):397-439, 1976.

Shomon, Joseph James. *Open Land for Urban America: Acquisition, Safekeeping, and Use.* Baltimore: Johns Hopkins University Press, 1971.

Solow, R.M. "Congestion Cost and Use of Land for Streets." *Bell Journal of Economics and Management Science* 4 (2):602-18, 1972.

Tobias, H. "Land Use and Environmental Policy, Litigation of Nuisances as a Land Use Control. Spur Industries Case." *Oklahoma Law Review* 26 (4):583-88, 1973.

Tolley, G.S., and Cohen, A.S. "Air Pollution and Urban Land Use Policy." *Journal of Environmental Economics and Management* 2 (4):247-54, 1976.

Venezia, R.A. "Air Quality Management Through Land Use Measures." *Journal of the Urban Planning and Development Division-ASCE* 102 (1):95-103, 1976.

Wallace, David A., ed. *Metropolitan Open Space and Natural Process.* Philadelphia: University of Pennsylvania Press, 1970.

Weerdenburg, L.J.M. "Changes in Rural Cultural Landscape. Research Into Relation Between Land Use and Landscape." *Sociologia Ruralis* 16 (3):200-20, 1976.

Welch, H.W., and Lewis, G.D. "Assessing Environmental Impacts of Multiple Use Land Management." *Journal of Environmental Management* 4 (3):197-209, 1976.

Werczberger, E. "Urban Land Use Planning and Environmental Pollution." *Environment and Planning* 7 (3):301-13, 1975.

Wood, C., and Lee, N. "Cities and Pollution." *International Journal of Environmental Studies* 8 (4):293-300, 1976.

5. The Law and Land Use

Adams, R.C. "Land Use Policy and Planning Assistance Act of 1973. Legislating a National Land Use Policy." *George Washington Law Review* 41 (3):604-25, 1973.

Anderson, R.M. "Land Use Control." *Syracuse Law Review* 25 (1):457-64, 1974.

Anderson, R.M. "Land Use Control." *Syracuse Law Review* 26 (1):149-59, 1975.

Andrews, Richard N.L. *Environmental Policy and Administrative Change: Implementation of the National Environmental Policy Act.* Lexington, Mass.: Lexington Books, 1976.

Babcock, Richard F., and Bosselman, Fred P. *Exclusionary Zoning: Land Use Regulation and Housing in the 70's.* New York: Praeger, 1973.

Berchin, S.E. "Regulation of Land Use. From Magna Carta to a Just Formulation." *UCLA Law Review* 23 (5):904-35, 1976.

Berger, Curtis J. *Land Ownership and Uses: Cases, Statutes, and Other Materials.* Boston: Little, Brown, 1975.

Beuscher, Jacob H., et al. *Cases and Materials on Land Use.* St. Paul, Minn.: West, 1976.

Bobo, Benjamin F., et al. *No Land is an Island: Individual Rights and Government Control of Land Use.* San Francisco: Institute for Contemporary Studies, 1975.

Booth, R.S. "Adirondack Park Agency Act: Challenge in Regional Land Use Planning." *George Washington Law Review* 43 (2):612-34, 1975.

Bosselman, Fred P. "Statewide Land Use Regulations." *Real Property, Probate and Trust Journal* 8 (3):515-22, 1973.

Bosselman, Fred P., et al. *EPA Authority Affecting Land Use.* Washington, D.C.: U.S. Environmental Protection Agency, Office of Planning and Evaluation, 1974.

Caldwell, Lynton K., et al. *Citizens and the Environment: Case Studies in Popular Actions.* Bloomington: Indiana University Press, 1976.

Coke, J.G., and Brown, S.R. "Public Attitudes About Land Use Policy and Their Impact on State Policy Makers." *Publius—The Journal of Federalism* 6 (1):97-134, 1976.

Davis, M.R. "Land Use Planning and Public Zoning by Initiative." *Montana Law Review* 36 (2):301-09, 1975.

Deal, D.T. "Public Law and Land Use Control. Massanutten Mountain Area—Case in Point." *Natural Resource* 6 (2):189-215, 1973.

Farringt, D. "New Ideas in Land Use Controls." *Current Municipal Problems* 14 (2):197-201, 1972.

Fishman, Richard, ed. *Housing for All Under Law: New Directions in Housing, Land Use and Planning Law.* Philadelphia: Ballinger, 1977.

Floyd, Charles F., and Rowan, Michael J. *Implications of Zoning as an Urban Water Management Measure.* Atlanta: Environmental Resources Center, Georgia Institute of Technology, 1976.

Fox, C.A. "Environmental Protection: Constitutional Limitation on Land Use Control Powers of Pennsylvania Municipalities." *University of Pittsburgh Law Review* 36 (2):255-84, 1974.

Freeman, A.D. "Give and Take. Distributing Local Environmental Control Through Land Use Regulation." *Minnesota Law Review* 60 (5):883-970, 1976.

Gifford, K.D. "Islands Trust. Leading Edges in Land Use Laws." *Harvard Journal on Legislation* 11 (3):417-61, 1974.

Grant, Malcolm. "The Community Land Act: An Overview." *Journal of Planning and Environmental Law* 675:90, November 1976.

Haldsworth, Michael. "Why the Land Act Must be Scrapped: The Community Land Act is Incapable of Operating Effectively . . ." *Municipal and Public Services Journal* 85:17-18, January 1977.

Heyman, I.M. "Legal Assaults on Municipal Land Use Regulation." *Urban Lawyer* 5 (1):1-24, 1973.

Krooth, D.L. "Control of Land Use in United States. Statutory Developments and Case of New Communities." *Urban Lawyer* 4 (3):519-32, 1972.

Kushner, J.A., and Werner, F.E. "Metropolitan Desegregation After Milliken v. Bradley. Case for Land Use Litigation Strategies." *Catholic University of American Law Review* 24 (2):187-216, 1975.

"Land Use, Planning and Zoning." *Urban Lawyer* 8 (4):747-88, 1976.

Lesser, J. "Recent Developments in Land Use Regulation." *Real Estate Review* 6 (2):22-27, 1976.

Linowes, R. Robert, and Allensworth, Don T. *The States and Land Use Control*. New York: Praeger, 1975.

Linowes, R. Robert, and Allensworth, Don T. *The Politics of Land Use Law: Developers vs. Citizens Groups in the Courts*. New York: Praeger, 1976.

Loewen, R.W. "Nuisance Damages as an Alternative to Compensation of Land Use Restrictions in Eminent Domain." *Southern California Law Review* 47 (3):998-1069, 1974.

Low, J.L. "State Land Use Control. Why Pending Federal Legislation Will Help." *Hastings Law Journal* 25 (5):1165-95, 1974.

Lundberg, W. "Restrictive Covenants and Land Use Control: Private Zoning." *Montana Law Review* 34 (2):199-217, 1973.

Lundberg, W. "Land Use Planning and Montana Legislature: Overview for 1973." *Montana Law Review* 35 (1):38-52, 1974.

Mandelker, Daniel R. "Critical Area Controls: New Dimension in American Land Development Regulation." *Journal of the American Institute of Planners* 41 (1):21-31, 1975.

Miller, W. "New Jersey Land Use Law Revision. Lesson for Other States." *Real Estate Law* 5 (2):138-54, 1976.

Mills, Edwin S., and Oates, Wallace E. *Fiscal Zoning and Land Use Controls*. Lexington, Mass.: Lexington Books, 1975.

Mogulof, Melvin B. *Saving the Coast: California's Experiment in Inter-Government Land Use Regulation*. Lexington, Mass.: Lexington Books, 1975.

Moss, Elaine, ed. *Land Use Controls in the U.S.: A Handbook on the Legal Rights of Citizens*. New York: Natural Resources Defense Council, Dial Press, 1977.

Nelson, Robert H. *Zoning and Property Rights*. Cambridge, Mass.: M.I.T. Press, 1977.

Pearlman, K. "State Environmental Policy Acts. Local Decision Making and Land Use Planning." *Journal of the American Institute of Planners* 43 (1):42-53, 1977.

Peterson, C.A. "Flexibility in Rezonings and Related Governmental Land Use Decisions." *Ohio State Law Journal* 36 (3):499-544, 1975.

Platt, Rutherford H. *Land Use Control: Interface of Law and Geography*. Washington, D.C.: Association of American Geographers, 1976.

Rose, Jerome G. *Legal Foundations of Land Use Planning*. Washington, D.C.: Center for Urban Policies Research, 1974.

Rose, Jerome G., ed. *The Transfer of Development Rights: A New Technique of Land Use Regulation*. New Brunswick, N.J.: Transaction Books, 1975.

Sagalyn, Lynne B., and Sternlieb, George. *Zoning and Housing Costs: The Impact of Land Use Controls on Housing Price*. New Brunswick, N.J.: Transaction Books, 1973.

Schnidman, F. "Evolving Role of Judiciary in Land Use Litigation." *State Government* 49 (1):18-21, 1976.

Sloane, M.E. "Changing Shape of Land Use Litigation: Federal Court Challenges to Exclusionary Land Use Practices." *Notre Dame Lawyer* 51 (1):48-78, 1975.

Urban, M. "Evaluation of Applicability of Zoning Principles to Law of Private Land Use Restrictions." *UCLA Law Review* 21 (6):1655-89, 1974.

Vrooman, D.H. "Regional Land Use Controls in Adirondack Park." *American Journal of Economics and Sociology* 34 (1):95-102, 1975.

6. Taxation and Land Use

Bails, D. "Alternative Land Value Tax Argument for Continued Use of Part of General Property Tax." *American Journal of Economics and Sociology* 32 (3):283-94, 1973.

Beeman, William J. *Property Tax and the Spatial Pattern of Growth Within Urban Areas.* Washington, D.C.: Urban Land Institute, 1969.

Currier, B.A. "Exploring Role of Taxation in Land Use Planning Process." *Indiana Law Journal* 51 (1):28-90, 1975.

Gaffney, M. "Land Rent, Taxation, and Public Policy: Sources, Nature and Functions of Urban Land Rent." *American Journal of Economics and Sociology* 31 (3):241, 1972.

Gaffney, M. "Land Rent, Taxation and Public Policy: Taxation and Functions of Urban Land Rent." *American Journal of Economics and Sociology* 32 (1):17-34, 1973.

Heller, T.C. "Theory of Property Taxation and Land Use Restrictions." *Wisconsin Law Review* 1974 (3):751-800, 1974.

Kelley, W.A. "Multiple Use Land Development: Real Property and Tax Problems." *Real Property, Probate and Trust Journal* 7 (4):585-705, 1972.

Leroy, S.F. "Urban Land Rent and Incidence of Property Taxes." *Journal of Urban Economics* 3 (2):167-79, 1976.

Lyall, K.C. "Tax Base Sharing: Fiscal Aid Towards More Rational Land Use Planning." *Journal of the American Institute of Planners* 41 (2):90-100, 1975.

Peterson, G.E., and Galper, H. "Tax Exempt Financing of Private Industries Pollution Control Investment." *Public Policy* 23 (1):81-103, 1975.

Rahm, Karen. "Tax Base Sharing: A Fiscal Tool for Land Use Planning in Washington State." *Washington Public Policy Notes* 5:1-6, Summer 1977.

Schwartz, S.I., et al. "Preferential Taxation and Control of Urban Sprawl: Analysis of California Land Conservation Act." *Journal of Environmental Economics and Management* 2 (2):120-34, 1975.

Whyte, Robert O. *Land and Land Appraisal.* Atlantic Highlands, N.J.: Humanities Press, 1977.

Zimmerma, E.A. "Tax Planning for Land Use Control." *Urban Lawyer* 5 (4):639-78, 1973.

Zube, E.H., et al. *Landscape Assessment: Values, Perceptions, and Resources.* New York: Dowden, Hutchinson and Ross, 1975.

7. Water Resources and Land Use

Bromley, Daniel W., et al. *Procedures for Evaluation of Water and Related Land Resource Projects: An Analysis of the Water Resources Council's Task Force Report.* University of Wisconsin. Madison: Center for Resource Policy Studies and Programs, 1970.

Cassidy, H.A. "Environmental Protection Agency and Coastal Zone Management. Striking a Federal State Balance of Power in Land Use Management." *Houston Law Review* 11 (5):1152-93, 1974.

Davenport, S., et al. *Issues Related to Interfacing Water Resource Planning and Land Use Planning: Development and Application of Quantitative Procedures.* Menlo Park, Cal.: INTASA, 1976.

Federman, A.B. "1972 Water Pollution Control Act. Unforeseen Implications for Land Use Planning." *Urban Lawyer* 8 (1):140-55, 1976.

Jacobs, J.J., and Timmons, J.F. "Economic Analysis of Agriculture Land Use Practices to Control Water Quality." *American Journal of Agricultural Economics* 56 (4):791-98, 1974.

Jungman, M. "Areawide Planning Under Federal Water Pollution Control Act Amendments of 1972. Intergovernmental and Land Use Implications." *Texas Law Review* 54 (5):1047-80, 1976.

Lewis, W. Cris, et al. *Regional Growth and Water Resources Investment.* Lexington, Mass.: Lexington Books, 1973.

Pereira, H.C. *Land Use and Water Resources.* New York: Cambridge University Press, 1973.

Reid, George W., and Southard, William R. *The Evaluation of Water and Related Land Resource Projects: A Procedural Test.* Norman: University of Oklahoma, 1969.

Rosentraub, Mark S., et al. *Coastal Zone Development and Coastal Policy in Southern California: A Two Year Analysis of the South Coast Regional Commission.* Los Angeles: University of Southern California, Los Angeles, Sea Grant Program, 1975.

Sax, Joseph L. *Water Law, Planning and Policy: Case and Materials.* New York: Bobbs-Merrill, 1968.

Shubinski, Robert P., and Nelson, Steven N. *Effects of Urbanization on Water Quality.* Springfield, Va.: Water Resources Engineers, Inc., 1975.

State Guidelines for Local Planning in the Coastal Area Under the Coastal Area Management Act of 1974. (Adopted by the Coastal Resources Commission on January 27, 1975 and amended by the Coastal Resources Commission October 15, 1975.) Raleigh: North Carolina Coastal Resources Commission, 1975.

Tabors, Richard D., et al. *Land Use and the Pipe: The Effect of Sewer Extension.* Lexington, Mass.: Lexington Books, 1976.

A Test of Proposed Procedures for Evaluation of Water and Related Land Resources Projects. A Special Study of the Detroit River. Trenton Channel Project. Detroit, Mich.: Army Engineer District, 1970.

Unterberg, Walter, et al. *Urban Water Development and Management in Arid Environments. Volume I: Completion Report.* Canoga Park, Cal.: Rocketdyne, 1975.

Walker, W.R., and Cox, W.E. "Water Element of Land Use and Urban
Growth Policies." *Journal of the Urban Planning and Development
Division-ASCE* 102 (1):81-94, 1976.

8. Economic Impact of Land Use

Alsop, S.R. "Land Use Planning and Relocation Assistance." *Urban
Lawyer* 6 (3):665-76, 1974.

Andrews, Richard B. *Urban Land Economics and Public Policy.* New
York: Free Press, 1971.

Averous, C.P., and Lee, D.B. "Land Allocation and Transportation Pricing in a Mixed Urban Economy." *Journal of Regional Science* 13
(2):173-85, 1973.

Barlowe, Raleigh. *Land Resource Economics.* Englewood Cliffs, N.J.:
Prentice-Hall, 1972.

Clawson, Marion. "Economic and Social Conflicts in Land Use Planning."
Natural Resources Journal 15 (3):473-89, 1975.

Conkling, Edgar C., and Yeates, Maurice H. *Man's Economic Environment.* New York: McGraw-Hill, 1976.

Economic Analysis for the Land Use Planning Program. Sacramento, Cal.:
California State Air Resources Board and California State Office of
Planning and Research, 1974.

Ely, Richard T., and Wehrwein, George S. *Land Economics.* Madison:
University of Wisconsin Press, 1964.

Ervin, David, and Stoevener, Herbert H. *Land Use Control: Evaluating
Economic and Political Effects.* Philadelphia: Ballinger, 1977.

Field, R.C., and Convery, F.J. "Estimating Local Economic Impacts in
Land Use Planning." *Journal of Forestry* 74 (3):155-56, 1976.

Hale, C.W. "Impact of Technological Change on Urban Market Areas,
Land Values, and Land Uses." *Land Economics* 49 (3):356-61, 1973.

Harris, Curtis C. *The Urban Economics.* Lexington, Mass.: Lexington
Books, 1973.

Harrison, A.J. *Economics and Land Use Planning.* New York:
St. Martin's Press, 1977.

Isard, Walter. *Ecologic Economic Analysis for Regional Development.*
New York: Free Press, 1972.

Jacobson, S. "Land Use Dispute in Illinois—Nuclear Power vs. Crops."
Atomic Scientists 29 (1):43-45, 1973.

Muller, Thomas. *Economic Impacts of Land Development: Employment,
Housing, and Property Values.* Washington, D.C.: Urban Institute,
1976.

Prescott, James R., and Cris, Lewis W. *Urban Regional Economic Growth and Policy.* Ann Arbor, Mich.: Ann Arbor Science, 1975.

Scott, A.J. "Land Use and Commodity Production." *Regional Science and Urban Economics* 6 (2):147-60, 1976.

Soot, S. "Transportation Costs and Urban Land Rent Theory: Milwaukee Example, 1949-1969." *Land Economics* 50 (2):193-96, 1974.

Stull, W.J. "Land Use and Zoning in an Urban Economy." *American Economic Review* 64 (3):337-47, 1974.

Sullivan, John J., ed. *Explorations in Urban Land Economics.* Cambridge, Mass.: Lincoln Institute Land Policy, 1970.

United States Council on Environmental Quality. *The Growth Shapers: The Land Use Impacts Infrastructure Investments.* Washington, D.C.: Superintendent of Documents, 1976.

Waldo, R.D. "Urban Land—Values and Accessibility." *Land Economics* 50 (2):196-201, 1974.

9.Transportation Systems and Land Use

Babcock, W.F. *An Analysis of the Impact of Freeways on Urban Land Developments in North Carolina. (Including Guidelines for Highway Planning and Design.)* Raleigh: Highway Research Program, North Carolina State University, June 1974.

Berechman, J. "Interfacing Urban Land Use Activity System and Transportation System." *Journal of Regional Science* 16 (2):183-94, 1976.

Capozza, D.R. "Subways and Land Use." *Environment and Planning* 5 (5):555-76, 1973.

Capozza, D.R. "Land Use in a City with 2 Modes of Transportation." *Southern Economic Journal* 42 (3):442-50, 1976.

DeSalvo, Joseph J. *Regional Transportation Planning.* Lexington, Mass.: Lexington Books, 1973.

Floyd, C.F. "Projecting Employment in a Transportation-Planning Land Use Model." *Annals of Regional Science* 10 (3):91-105, 1976.

Garrison, William L., et al. *Studies in Highway Development and Geographic Change.* Westport, Conn.: Greenwood Press, 1959.

Gessaman, P.H., and Sisler, D.G. "Highways, Changing Land Use, and Impacts on Rural Life." *Growth and Change* 7 (2):3-8, 1976.

Goldberg, M.A. "Evaluation of Interaction Between Urban Transport and Land Use Systems." *Land Economics* 48 (4):338-46, 1972.

Lee, D.B., and Averous, C.P. "Land Use and Transportation—Basic Theory." *Environment and Planning* 5 (4):491-502, 1973.

Pushkarev, Boris S., and Zupan, Jeffrey M. *Public Transportation and Land Use Policy.* Bloomington: Indiana University Press, 1977.

Robson, A.J. "Cost Benefit Analysis and Use of Urban Land for Trans-
portation." *Journal of Urban Economics* 3 (2):180-91, 1976.
Solow, R.M. "Congestion, Density and Use of Land in Transportation."
Swedish Journal of Economics 74 (1):161-73, 1972.
Trygg, Lisa, and Sgourakis, Alice. *Land Use Impacts of Rapid Transit.*
Monticello, Ill.: Council of Planning Librarians. (Exchange
bibliography no. 13770)
Turner, C.G. "Design of Urban Growth Models for Strategic Land Use
Transportation Studies." *Regional Studies* 9 (3):251-64, 1975.
Wendt, P.F., ed. *Forecasting Transportation Impacts Upon Land Use.* At-
lantic Highlands, N.J.: Humanities Press, 1977.

10. Recreational Uses of Land

Boley, Robert E., ed. *Land: Recreation and Leisure.* Washington, D.C.:
Urban Land Institute, 1970.
Brockman, C. Frank, and Merriam, Lawrence C. *Recreational Use of Wild
Lands.* New York: McGraw-Hill, 1973.
Buschman, C.G. "Preserving Scenic Areas—Adirondack Land Use Pro-
gram." *Yale Law Journal* 84 (8):1705-21, 1975.
Cheek, Neil H., et al. *Leisure and Recreation Places.* Ann Arbor, Mich.:
Ann Arbor Science, 1976.
Committee on Agricultural Land Use and Wildlife Resources. *Land Use
and Wildlife Resources.* Washington, D.C.: National Academy of
Sciences, 1970.
Fischer, David W., and Lewis, John E. *Land and Leisure: Concepts and
Methods in Outdoor Recreation.* Chicago: Maaroufa Press, 1974.
Gold, Seymour M. *Urban Recreation Planning.* Philadelphia: Lea and
Febiger, 1973.
Horn, A.F. "Questions Concerning Proposed Private Land Use and De-
velopment Plan for Adirondack Park." *Syracuse Law Review* 24
(3):989-1016, 1973.
Johnson, Julia, and Dunning, Glenna, eds. *Land Planning in National
Parks and Forests: A Selective Bibliography.* Monticello, Ill.: Council
of Planning Librarians, 1977.
Knopp, T.B., and Tyger, J.D. "Study of Conflict in Recreational Land
Use: Snowmobiling vs. Ski-Touring." *Journal of Leisure Research* 5
(3): 6-17, 1973.
McKeener, J. Ross, ed. *Business Parks, Office Parks, Plazas and Centers.*
Urban Land Institute, 1970.
Moses, R.J. "Water as a Tool for Recreational Land Use Planning."
Syracuse Law Review 24 (3):1047-56, 1973.

Oleary, J.T. "Land Use Redefinition and Rural Community: Disruption of Community Leisure Space." *Journal of Leisure Research* 8 (4):263-74, 1976.

Robson, Arthur J., and Scheffman, David T. "The Crunch, the Boom, and the Recreational Land Market." *Canadian Journal of Economics* 11:38-55, February 1978.

Shivers, Jay S., and Hjelte, George. *Planning Recreational Places.* Rutherford, N.J.: Fairleigh Dickinson University Press, 1971.

About the Contributors

Richard F. Babcock is an attorney in the Chicago firm Ross, Hardies, O'Keefe, Babcock, and Parsons.

*Fred P. Bosselman is an attorney in the Chicago firm Ross, Hardies, O'Keefe, Babcock, and Parsons and is a coauthor of three monographs on land policy issues: *The Quiet Revolution in Land Use Controls* (1972), *Exclusionary Zoning* (1973), and *The Taking Issue* (1973).

*Lynton K. Caldwell is Bentley Professor of Political Science and Professor of Public and Environmental Affairs at Indiana University, author of numerous books and articles on environmental policy, and advisor to governments at all levels including international as well as state and federal. His books include *Environment: A Challenge to Modern Society* (1970), *Man and His Environment: Policy and Administration* (1975), and *Citizens and the Environment: Case Studies in Popular Action* (with L.R. Hayes and I.M. MacWhirter, 1976).

David Callies is an attorney in the Chicago firm Ross, Hardies, O'Keefe, Babcock, and Parsons and a coauthor with Fred P. Bosselman of several studies on land policy issues.

Donald R. Denman is professor of land economy at Cambridge University; author of many articles and books on land ownership, economics, and use; and advisor to many governments. His books include *Land Use and the Constitution of Property* (1969), *Land Use: An Introduction to Proprietary Land Use Analysis* (1971), and *Landownership and Resources* (1960).

Duane A. Feurer is an attorney in the Chicago firm Ross, Hardies, O'Keefe, Babcock, and Parsons.

*Daniel R. Fusfeld is professor of economics, The University of Michigan.

*Wesley H. Gould is professor of political science, Wayne State University.

Samuel P. Hays is professor of history, The University of Pittsburgh. He is author of *Conservation and the Gospel of Efficiency: The Progressive Conservation Movement, 1890-1920* (1959) and *The Response to Industrialism, 1885-1915* (1957).

Robert G. Healy is a senior associate of the Conservation Foundation. His books include *Land Use and the States* (1975) and *The Lands Nobody Wanted: Policy for National Forests in the Eastern United States* (with W.E. Shands, 1977).

Peggy Ann Kusnerz is head of the Library Extension Service, The University of Michigan.

Charles E. Little is a Washington-based writer and consultant on land use policy.

*Janet D. Lynn is executive vice-president of the Citizen's Council for Land Use Research and Education (CLURE) and was project director of the Symposium "The Face of America: This Land in the Year 2000" for which many of these papers were originally prepared.

Stewart D. Marquis, Jr. is associate professor of natural resource policy and regional planning, The University of Michigan. He has combined work in engineering and urban planning with teaching in natural resource and environmental policy, planning, and management.

*Frank J. Popper is a Chicago planning consultant and coauthor of *Urban Nongrowth* (1976). He is currently completing a book sponsored by the Twentieth Century Fund entitled *The Politics of Land Use Reform*.

*John G. Sobetzer is an attorney and executive director of the East Michigan Environmental Action Council.

*William H. Whyte since 1970 has directed a foundation-sponsored study of how people use the streets and open spaces of the center city. The work of his group, The Street Life Project, led to the adoption by New York City of a new open space zoning code in 1975. He is currently completing a film and a book on the lessons learned from the study; previous books include *The Organization Man* (1956) and *The Last Landscape* (1968).

---

*Indicates participants in the 1977 Symposium for which many of these papers were originally prepared.

About the Editor

Richard N.L. Andrews is associate professor and chairman of the Natural Resource Policy and Management Program, The University of Michigan, and associate professor of urban and regional planning. He has written extensively on subjects related to environmental policy and planning. His publications include *Environmental Policy and Administrative Change* (1976) and *Environmental Values in Public Decisions* (1978).